TOP SECRET
TOURISM

TOP SECRET
TOURISM

HARRY HELMS

FERAL HOUSE

Feral House
P.O. Box 39910
Los Angeles, CA 90039

www.feralhouse.com

info@feralhouse.com

10 9 8 7 6 5 4 3 2 1

I want to thank my family and longtime friends—particularly Cindy Ballard, Jon Erickson, Kelly Johnson, Carol and Jack Lewis, Hugh McCallum, Forrest Mims, Tina Otis, and Alan Rose—for their support and encouragement during my recent bout with cancer. Special thanks also go to Matthew Deans and Rachel Roumeliotis for their assistance. Above all, I want to thank my wife Dianna for her patience, courage, and love during my illness. It is no exaggeration to say that without her I wouldn't still be alive to write these words.

Contents

Introduction

There is another America out there, an America of top secret programs, facilities, and installations protected by a wall of secrecy, deception, and misinformation. It includes huge isolated areas (some larger than the states of Connecticut and Rhode Island) along with innocuous-looking office buildings located in urban areas like Las Vegas. This "other America" has an enormous impact on your life, but you probably have no idea of its extent, scope, and power. In fact, it's doubtful that anyone—even the President—has an accurate idea of the true extent, power, and activities going on in what I call "Top Secret America."

I want you to visit that Top Secret America.

Top Secret Tourism is your travel guide to germ warfare laboratories, government VIP relocation centers, electronic eavesdropping locations, espionage agent training sites, and other places in the United States that you're not supposed to know about. In addition, private facilities and companies that provide support services to Top Secret America are also included. Listings are organized in alphabetical order by state, and each facility/site entry gives its history, discusses the activities carried on there, explores various rumors about the site, and gives directions to the location. I've also added commentary, trivia, and sarcastic remarks to many of the listings.

Am I serious when I say I want you to visit the facilities and locations that make up Top Secret America? Yes I am. Even though plenty of people try to keep Top Secret America secret, it is still your country, not only theirs. Even if you didn't realize it, ordinary Americans like you paid for Top Secret America—sometimes through your taxes, sometimes through curtailment of your liberties and privacy—and you have the right to know about it. As you will discover in this book, "national security" is often just a convenient shield for hiding incompetence, failure, waste, and corruption in Top Secret America programs and activities. In those cases, secrecy is more "necessary" to deceive the American people and Congress rather than potential enemies and terrorists.

You might be wondering how I found out all this stuff. I started researching this topic in 1999, and a surprising amount of this information was available on government websites prior to the September 11, 2001 attacks. Since the attacks, however, much of that information has been removed from public dissemination. Government documents (particularly environmental impact statements) and maps often inadvertently provided key details. (For example, aeronautical maps for a region that indicated all overflights, civilian and military, were forbidden 24/7 were always a strong clue that something top secret was going on in those areas.) Congressional hearings and budgets were another important source, and I was able to personally visit several of the sites in this book. None of the information in here was obtained from classified sources; everything was on the public record and obtained by patient digging. And for those who think a book like this discloses vital government secrets... get real. If I can find this stuff out, the Russians, Chinese, and various terrorist groups also found it out a long time before I did.

How Top Secret America Was Born

It's difficult today to comprehend how transparent the United States government was prior to World War II. The amount of government secrecy was minimal, and then restricted almost exclusively to military matters such as capabilities of weapons, codes and ciphers, etc. There were no classified programs and items in the federal budget, no secret government agencies, and no secret locations where clandestine activities were carried out. But all that changed after the attack on Pearl Harbor, especially when development of atomic weapons got underway with the Manhattan Project. Because of its extreme importance to the war effort and the dangers if atomic secrets fell into the hands of Nazi Germany and Japan, unprecedented security steps were taken. Massive new facilities—like those at Oak Ridge, TN, Los Alamos, NM, and Hanford, WA—were built in almost total secrecy. Elaborate systems of information classification were created, and extensive background checking systems for persons needing access to classified information were put into place. The basic forms of those methods and systems are still used today.

Most of these programs and activities were not created by Congressional legislation, but instead by President Franklin Roosevelt using something called an executive order. An executive order is like an order from your boss: it tells an agency or department of the U.S. government to do something and carries the full force of law. Presidential executive orders derive their authority from the president's constitutional authority as chief executive or commander in chief; the president may also receive authority to order certain actions via Congressional legislation or court decisions. In the case of President Roosevelt, he broadly interpreted his authority as commander in chief to create the Manhattan Project without the knowledge of Congress. To conceal it, his budgets hid the expense of the Manhattan Project under various broad categories (such as "munitions," "research," and the ever-popular "miscellaneous"). This practice continues today, except that some secret projects are referenced in the federal budget by cryptic code names or even alphanumeric codes. The net result is that Congress has largely kept in the dark about almost all secret projects for over 60 years. (Senior Congressional leaders do receive briefings on classified projects, but these briefings are cursory and lack detail; many are also after-the-fact briefings about projects that have been underway for some time.)

After World War II, the National Security Act of 1947 and the Internal Security Act of 1950 granted the president wide latitude in classifying government programs and activities, and presidents have not been reluctant to use the powers granted to them under such legislation. Much of Top Secret America has been created under the authority of those two pieces of legislation. For example, the National

Security Agency (NSA) was created not by an act of Congress but instead by an executive order issued by President Truman in 1952. The very existence of the NSA was classified for over two decades, even though it spent hundreds of millions of dollars over that span; its funding was hidden in the federal budget under various "cover" names and in the funding for non-secret agencies such as the Central Intelligence Agency. Likewise, the National Reconnaissance Office (NRO) was created by President Eisenhower in 1960 with another executive order. The NRO coordinated the operations of America's spy satellites and the processing of intelligence gathered by them, yet its existence remained classified until 1994 (even the term "National Reconnaissance Office" was classified until then). A congressional audit after the existence of NRO was disclosed revealed that NRO had spent over $4 billion since its founding that could not be accounted for. Congressional investigators did not feel this was the result of sloppy management, bad accounting, or fraud; instead, it was believed that money had been diverted to—as difficult as it may be to imagine—even more highly classified programs and agencies.

It is highly likely there are other agencies of the scope and power of the NSA and NRO operating today that are just as highly classified as those two once were.

Several "overt" government agencies had classified components during the 1950s and 1960s. For example, the Office of Civil Defense ran many public programs encouraging people to build fallout shelters, stockpile emergency supplies, and coordinated state and local plans for dealing with nuclear war. But at the same time it also developed and administered a plan known as "Continuity of Government," whose aim was to protect as many high federal officials as possible in the event of a nuclear attack. In great secrecy, underground shelters capable of housing thousands of government officials (including the entire U.S. Congress) were built near Washington, DC. A variation of the Continuity of Government is carried on today by the Federal Emergency Management Agency, and some senior government officials (such as Vice President Dick Cheney) were taken to those underground shelters in the first hours after the September 11, 2001 attacks. It is likely that similar classified activities go on today in publicly-known government departments and agencies.

Caveats and Warnings

While the tone of this book is often flippant and irreverent, please do take the following warnings seriously.

It can't be emphasized strongly enough that you must avoid trespassing into any restricted area and obey all posted warning signs. Every year, people are arrested for accidentally trespassing into restricted areas such as Nevada's Area 51. The boundary line in isolated areas may be poorly marked—such as orange posts located over 100 feet apart—and it's easy to wander across unless you're paying attention. And ignorance of where the boundary is will not prevent you from being arrested. In other words, don't try to set a record for getting as close to a site's boundary before crossing over. Play it safe and make certain you're on public land at all times. And avoid any deliberately provocative actions, like any threatening gestures or actions toward security personnel. Those "use of deadly force authorized" warning signs are not mere symbols; they're for real.

You may be stopped, questioned, and even harassed by police and security services at certain locations, even when you're on public roads or land. You might even be ordered to surrender any film, digital camera cards, video tapes, etc., to security personnel. While the legality of such actions might be dubious, any resistance on your part could result in your arrest. You might win your case at trial or on appeal, but it will be an expensive, time-consuming process (especially if you are arrested out of state). My advice is not to engage in arguments or confrontations with security or law enforcement personnel (even if you believe you're in the right), comply with their orders, and to pursue any legal action you feel like after you're safely home and have had the opportunity to discuss what happened with a lawyer.

Several of the listings in this book for isolated sites in the West include warnings about making sure your car is in good mechanical condition, having a spare tire, keeping your gas tank as full as possible, etc. If you haven't previously traveled much in the hinterlands of the American West, it can be difficult to comprehend how distant gasoline, food, and emergency services can be; it's not at all unusual to be over 100 miles from the nearest gas station or doctor, and mobile phone service is often spotty or unavailable. In other words, if you suffer a car breakdown, get stuck in sand or mud, or experience a medical emergency (like, say, a rattlesnake bite), you're likely to be on your own for quite a while until help arrives (or you can reach help). I don't want to frighten you away from visiting places such as Tonopah Test Range in Nevada or Dugway Proving Grounds in Utah, but I do want you to be prepared before leaving and to be smart when you arrive at such sites.

While every effort has been made to ensure the accuracy of the information in this book, things change quickly and without notice in Top Secret America. You might find access roads have been closed, boundary perimeters have changed, certain buildings may no longer be visible from the road, etc. On the other hand, some interesting new things might be going on at a location that weren't happening when this book was written.

Top Secret America is waiting out there for you. Enjoy visiting it!

Harry Helms

ALABAMA

1. Anniston Army Depot, Anniston

Anniston Army Depot, Anniston

Large quantities of nerve gases and mustard gas are stored at this facility deep in the piney woods of east-central Alabama. You don't want to be downwind from this place in case of a leak, okay?

Anniston Army Depot is located about 50 miles west of Birmingham and is named for the nearby city of Anniston. It was opened in 1941 as a repair and storage depot for tanks, other combat vehicles, and artillery equipment. In 1963, it became a storage facility for chemical weapons and is now transitioning to a chemical weapons disposal facility. Original plans called for it to be out of the chemical weapons storage business by 2006. However, this deadline has been extended.

What's There: Chemical weapons are stored here in the form of cartridges, shells, small rockets, and land mines filled with various chemical agents. The inventory included over 40,000 land mines loaded with VX nerve gas and over 100 one-ton containers of mustard gas.

Key Facilities: Chemical weapons are stored in the northeastern corner of the depot in an area occupying approximately 760 acres (the entire depot covers over 18,000 acres). The chemical weapons are stored in over 150 "igloo" structures designed to contain the gases in case of a leak.

Getting a Look Inside: No public tours are currently offered and the chemical storage facilities are not visible from roads or other public property.

Getting There: The main entrance is located west of Anniston along Highway 78.

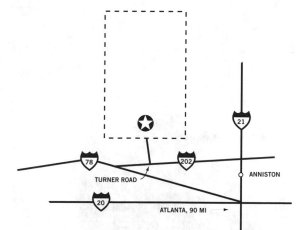

Roads to Anniston Army Depot, Anniston

ALASKA

1. HAARP Radio Transmission Facility

High Frequency Active Auroral Research Program (HAARP), Gakona

In the wilds of Alaska, the Air Force and Navy are building the world's most powerful radio transmitting station so they can blow holes in the Earth's ionosphere.

The ionosphere is a region of the Earth's atmosphere that stretches from approximately 40 miles to over 300 miles above the Earth's surface. Ultraviolet radiation from the sun "ionizes" the atoms of gas (causes them to gain an extra electron) in the ionosphere. When that happens, the ionosphere can reflect radio signals back to Earth like a giant mirror in the sky. The ionosphere is why you can hear distant AM band stations at night and why shortwave stations can communicate around the world. When the ionosphere is especially ionized, such as after a solar flare, there are brilliant auroral displays and radio communications are disrupted.

HAARP is a joint effort of the Air Force (through its Air Force Research Laboratory) and the Navy (Office of Naval Research). They have built the world's most powerful radio transmitting facility so they can screw around with the ionosphere, because all sorts of interesting things happen when you do. As HAARP's official website notes, "There are indications that ground-based HF (high frequency) transmitters, including radars and strong radio stations, also modify the ionosphere and influence the performance of systems whose radio paths traverse the modified region. Perhaps the most famous example of the latter is the 'Luxembourg' effect, first observed in 1933. In this case a weak Swiss radio station appeared to be modulated with signals from the powerful Luxembourg station, which was transmitting on a completely different frequency. Music from the Luxembourg station was picked up at the frequency of the Swiss station."

HAARP was first conceived back in the heady days of Reagan's "Star Wars" initiative and Gakona was selected for its location in 1990. Initial testing began in 1994 and the site went fully operational in 1998. From the beginning, HAARP was described as a scientific research project with no military applications.

However, there is plenty to suggest HAARP is being used for far more than just research. When radio waves strike a metallic object, they set up tiny electrical currents. That's how a radio or TV antenna works; those tiny currents are amplified and then converted to sound or pictures. So what happens when you pump out as much power as HAARP will? According to the environmental impact statement filed for construction of the HAARP facilities, HAARP could ignite road flares stored in the trunks of nearby cars, detonate explosives that use electronic fuses, and scramble the communications, navigation, and flight control systems of aircraft. If you're made of flesh and blood instead of metal, you're still not safe. The same environmental impact statement also mentions that HAARP could raise the internal body temperatures of persons near the transmitter site.

HAARP's location suggests its potential as a defensive weapon. At the time HAARP was conceived, the main threat to the United States came from Soviet nuclear missiles. The flight path of these missiles from the USSR to the United States would take them over Alaska, where a powerful directed radio beam, such as HAARP, could disrupt their electronics and navigation systems by the currents induced by the beam. Redirecting the beam could produce similar results against missiles from China or North Korea. Because of their lower altitudes, manned bombers would receive stronger signals from HAARP and be even more vulnerable to having their systems disrupted.

The Air Force and Navy are well aware of HAARP's potential to interfere with aircraft operation—there is an "aircraft alert" radar system at the HAARP site. According to the HAARP website, "The radar will be used to disable HAARP transmissions when aircraft are detected in air space close to the array."

Another possible military application of HAARP is to locate hidden underground installations and facilities. When the HAARP signal is reflected off the ionosphere and back to ground at a distant point, the signal would then be reflected back off the ground and back to the HAARP transmitter site. A signal of HAARP's power would be able to penetrate below the ground at the distant point, and the reflected signal would be altered by underground facilities.

The scary thing about HAARP, however, is no one knows exactly what happens when you beam that much power to a relatively small section of the ionosphere. Some speculate that the energy could disperse throughout the ionosphere and disrupt radio communications worldwide, much like a solar storm. Others worry that HAARP could create a temporary hole in the ionosphere or alter the weather, since there is evidence for a connection between levels of solar activity and weather patterns. Since migrating birds depend on the Earth's magnetic field for direction-finding, there is even speculation that HAARP could cause changes in the Earth's magnetic field to alter migration patterns.

All we know for sure is this: the military never funds research projects like HAARP unless they hope there is a potential military application for anything discovered, and something damn strange is going on near Gakona.

What's There: HAARP consists of a mammoth antenna system and transmitters. HAARP has 180 antenna towers, each 72 feet high, spaced over 33 acres. It uses 360 ten-kilowatt transmitters, for a total transmitter power of 3,6000,000 watts. The signal gain from the antennas means HAARP can radiate a signal with an effective radiated power of over one gigawatt, meaning it would be over a thousand times more powerful than any other radio transmitting facility in the world. Six 2500-kilowatt electric generators supply the power.

Key Facilities: The heart of HAARP is the ionospheric research instrument (IRI). This uses the antenna and transmitters to create narrow beams of radio energy on frequencies from 2.8 to 10 MHz in the shortwave range. The beams can be projected in any direction, including directly overhead. There is also an incoherent scatter radar (ISR), which operates in the 430 to 450 MHz range and an "ionosonde" (a sort of radio-based "sonar" device) that operates from 1 to 30 MHz (or roughly from the middle of the AM broadcasting band to the end of the shortwave range). These two devices are supposedly used to measure the effect HAARP is having on the ionosphere. There are also magnetometers and other passive measuring devices. An operations center controls all of these items.

Secret Stuff: If you suspect you're being heated up by HAARP, or just want to complain about radio interference it's causing, the phone number of the transmitter site is (907) 822-5497.

Getting a Look Inside: HAARP currently offers no public tours. However, the antenna installations are other facilities are easily visible from the Tok Highway.

Getting There: Gakona is about 200 miles southeast of Fairbanks near Wrangell-St. Elias National Park. HAARP is located eight miles northeast of Gakona at milepost 11.3 on Highway 1, also known as Tok Highway.

Unusual Fact: Despite its clear links to the military and the obvious military applications of its research, HAARP insists that it is a completely unclassified project.

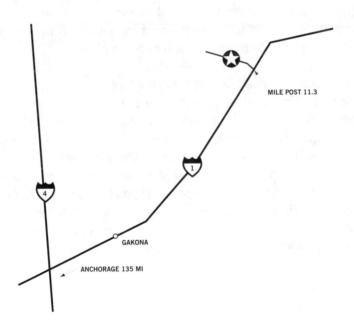

Roads to HAARP

ARIZONA

1. Fort Huachuca, Huachuca City 2. Marana Northwest Regional Airport, Marana
3. Yuma Proving Ground, Yuma

Fort Huachuca, Huachuca City

What do you do with a frontier Army post when you're finished exterminating those annoying Native Americans? Train military spooks, of course!

A now-declassified 1997 "white paper" described Fort Huachuca's mission as "to derive information collected from and provided by human sources that penetrate an adversary's decision-making architecture for data regarding capabilities (strength and weaknesses), vulnerabilities, dispositions, plans and intentions." The same paper described the goals of these activities as being "to conduct non-lethal strikes at decisive points to deter hostile action, impose order, protect the force, or compel an adversary or ally to do our will." In plain English, Fort Huachuca is where the Army trains its spooks, tests eavesdropping and surveillance equipment, and conducts information and electronics warfare exercises.

Fort Huachuca was established in 1877 as part of the wars against Native Americans and in 1886 was the base of operations for the campaign against Geronimo. In 1913, it became home to the 10th Cavalry "Buffalo Soldiers." Its current mission began in 1954, when control passed to the U.S. Army Signal Corps. In 1971, the U.S. Army Intelligence Center was relocated to Fort Huachuca and its transformation into an intelligence and electronic warfare facility began in earnest.

Fort Huachuca is one of those places you don't drive by; you have to work to get there. Located at the foot of the Huachuca Mountains, it's located approximately 70 miles southeast of Tucson and 16 miles north of the Mexican border. Fort Huachuca covers more than 70,000 acres and more than 17,000 personnel and their families live on or near the base. Much of the airspace above the facility is restricted.

What's There: If it has anything to do with signals intelligence, eavesdropping and surveillance, electronic warfare, or military communications, it's here. The U.S. Army's Intelligence Center, Signal Command, Information Systems Engineering Command, the 11th Signal Brigade, the Electronic Proving Ground, and the Military Affiliate Radio System are all based here. In addition, intelligence operations for the U.S. Army Reserve and National Guard are also at Fort Huachuca. There's even an Army Intelligence Museum on the "Old Post" section that's open to the public.

Key Facilities: The U.S. Army Electronic Proving Ground for electronic warfare occupies a large portion of Fort Huachuca's total area. According to official Fort Huachuca literature, "eye-hazard lasers," GPS "exploitation, deception, and denial" systems, and artificial intelligence systems based on neural computer networks are all tested here.

Secret Stuff: While the signals intelligence, eavesdropping, and surveillance activities here are supposed to be deployed only against hostile military forces, they can be easily used to monitor civilian communications and activities. Since any sort of military activity in a foreign nation would require keeping track of civilian as well as military communications, it's not too far-fetched to assume some monitoring of civilian communications, at least for practice, might be going on already at Fort Huachuca. In other words, be careful what you say on your cell phone around here.

The GPS "exploitation, deception, and denial" technology developed here has all sorts of interesting future implications as GPS technology becomes increasingly common in cars, trucks, and other civilian transportation systems. If GPS signals were subject to "deception," then hordes of commuters and UPS drivers could be confused and re-routed, creating massive traffic jams and disruptions. If you have a portable GPS receiver or system in your car, you might want to check it in this area for erratic or inaccurate operation.

The potential of military electronic warfare capabilities to disrupt civilian communications such as cell phones and wireless computer networks (including wireless Internet access) cannot be underestimated. As such, you may encounter unusual noises, static, and interference on your car's AM and FM radios as well as cell phones.

Scanner radios will likely receive numerous unusual signals, including data, signaling, tones, and encrypted voice communications.

Military aircraft will be active in this area. There is a possibility prototype and still-secret aircraft will be tested against the electronic warfare systems here. However, most of these tests will probably be conducted at night and the mountains will restrict your viewing of the test ranges.

Getting a Look Inside: The "Old Post" area of Fort Huachuca is open to the public and has several historic buildings along with two museums. The Fort Huachuca Museum covers the history of the U.S. Army in the Southwest, and is worth visiting just for the exhibits about the all-black "Buffalo Soldiers." The Army Intelligence Museum was, perhaps prophetically, built as a morgue in 1887. Its exhibits mainly deal with military intelligence activities in the safely distant past (World War II, etc.); if you're looking for more contemporary stuff, you'll be disappointed. The Army Intelligence Museum is open Monday, Wednesday, and Thursday from 10 a.m. to 2 p.m. Admission is free, although a $2.00 donation is suggested.

The Old Post area is far removed from the areas of Fort Huachuca where training, testing, and development activities are conducted. Unfortunately, most test and development activity takes place in areas shielded from public view by mountains.

Unusual Fact: The key training facility here is Nicholson Hall, a modern 76,000-square-foot training facility for courses in electronic warfare. It is named for the late Lieutenant Colonel Arthur Nicholson. Quoting from official Fort Huachuca literature, "on 24 March 1985, LTC Nicholson was killed in the former GDR performing a daring and sensitive mission." What daring and sensitive mission was Col. Nicholson performing and why was he in the former East Germany? Sorry; that's classified information.

Getting There: The easiest way to reach Fort Huachuca is from Interstate 10. Take Exit 302 and head south on State Route 90. When you reach Fort Huachuca, follow the signs to the Old Post area and museums. Do not attempt to enter the facility except through the indicated gates!

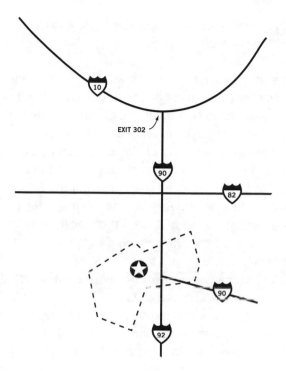

Roads to Fort Huachuca, Huachuca City

Marana Northwest Regional Airport, Marana

When the CIA needs to run a clandestine flight into Central America, this has been one of their favorite airports.

Marana is a small town located northeast of Tucson along Interstate 10. Marana Northwest Regional Airport is due east of Marana, and at first glance appears to be an ordinary freight and maintenance airport. Cargo jets operated by such companies as Federal Express and United Parcel Service are the main users of Marana; the only passenger flights involve small private jets. Marana is also used as a storage facility for mothballed commercial jets, and they glisten in the Arizona sun.

To look at it, you'd never guess Marana has long been popular with the CIA for espionage against Cuba, covert operations in Asia and Africa, and, more recently, clandestine drug and weapons flights to Latin America. In fact, only the Mena airport (see ARKANSAS) can top Marana for sheer amount of covert weirdness associated with it.

What's There: Even for a cargo airport, Marana looks dull. In fact, it doesn't even have an operational control tower. Its ordinariness was undoubtedly one of its big attractions for the CIA, along with its proximity to Mexico. It has four runways, hangars, and repair and fueling facilities. While the airport is not open to the public, there are no extraordinary security measures in place; the flight instruction, aircraft rental, and repair facilities are open to anyone with business there. The odds are very good that a typical user of Marana has never heard of the airport's CIA connections.

Adjacent to the Marana airport is the Pinal Aviation Park, which has a facility housing the local operations of Evergreen Aviation (see below). This building does have tight security, including prohibitions against photography on their premises. Trespassers on this property have been detained and arrested, so respect any warning signs that may be posted.

Secret Stuff: Marana first became a location for CIA projects in 1961 when it was a center for Skyhook balloon launches intended for reconnaissance of Cuba. Skyhook was a classified CIA project to launch high-altitude camera-equipped balloons to drift over foreign nations, take photos, and then release the camera via parachute when it drifted back over a friendly or neutral (like the ocean) territory. Because of their high-altitude (behind the range of surface to air missiles until the mid-1960s) and silvery color, Skyhook balloons were responsible for many UFO reports in the 1950s and early 1960s.

Skyhook operations at Marana were conducted through Intermountain Aviation, a CIA-created and owned company. A specially equipped B-17 bomber would depart from Marana and launch the balloons at night while in flight. Later Intermountain greatly expanded its fleet of aircraft and became global in its support of CIA operations. Intermountain Aviation was identified as a CIA front company during Senator Frank Church's Senate hearings in the mid-1970s. One consequence of these hearings was that the CIA was forced to sell its front companies, and Intermountain Aviation was purchased in 1979 by Evergreen Aviation of Oregon. For most of the 1980s, the Evergreen operations at Marana were outwardly normal. Evergreen leased airplanes to, and provided support services for, government agencies such as the U.S. Forest Service and the U.S. Postal Service. However, Evergreen's cover began to unravel in 1989 when it hired Gary Eitel, a pilot for the CIA in Angola in 1976, as a pilot for its DC-9 and 727 fleet.

Soon after Eitel was hired, he noticed that card-carrying CIA employees were at Marana's Evergreen facilities and that CIA contracts made up a substantial portion of Evergreen's revenues at Marana. He also discovered that Evergreen was overbilling some government clients, such as a $52 million overcharge for the U.S. Postal Service during a two-year span, and using the overbilling to provide additional services to the CIA above those specified in their contracts. Eitel also discovered that Evergreen was paying several pilots less than the compensation provided for in the government contracts, and this revelation resulted in angry pilots telling Eitel what they knew about CIA operations at Marana.

Eitel learned that numerous C-130 transport craft leased to the U.S. Forest Service for firefighting support were actually being flown out of Marana by the CIA for missions to Latin America. 727 jets supposedly leased to the U.S. Postal Service were being packed with electronic surveillance gear and flown out of Marana on intelligencez missions. He further learned that most of the C-130 flights to Latin America were transporting weapons to Nicaragua, El Salvador, and Colombia; many of the return flights carried cocaine and other drugs to finance the arms shipments. But Eitel also learned that an Evergreen pilot named Dean Moss, who had been embroiled in a labor dispute, had been murdered when he threatened to go public with similar revelations about illegal activities at Marana. Moss had been murdered in an especially gruesome way: chlorine bleach had been injected directly into his stomach.

Eitel didn't wait to see if he would be next. He left Evergreen in the summer of 1989 and filed a "whistleblower" complaint against Evergreen for the overcharges of the U.S. Postal Service and the use of U.S. Forest Service planes by the CIA. He also filed suit against Evergreen, and testified before Congress in 1993 about Evergreen's activities. In 1996, the U.S. Attorney for Arizona indicted two former Evergreen employees for fraud in connection with the overbillings. Eitel received several death threats after he went public, but his high public profile apparently protected him. Eitel now leaves quietly in Washington state.

The use of Marana for CIA operations dropped precipitously after Eitel went public with his accusations and the Clinton administration de-emphasized clandestine operations. However, Marana is still ideally located for clandestine flights to Latin America and the continued large Evergreen presence indicates they expect a heavy need for their services sometime in the future at Marana.

Getting a Look Inside: There are several businesses open to the public at Marana, although they don't want the curious just dropping in. As previously noted, the Evergreen Aviation operations have high security and most definitely do not want uninvited visitors. However, it has a large sign in front that makes it easy to identify.

Unusual Fact: The promotional materials for Evergreen's facilities at Marana boast of a "24-hour gated entrance along with armed roving security officers in marked and unmarked vehicles. Basewide Overt & Covert CCTV and Intrusion Detection Systems insures [sic] safety and security for our customers. In order to track and maintain the strictess [sic] confidence all employees and visitors are required to wear identification badges at all times."

Getting There: Marana is about 20 miles northwest of Tucson on Interstate 10. The airport is due east of downtown Marana on Avra Valley Road.

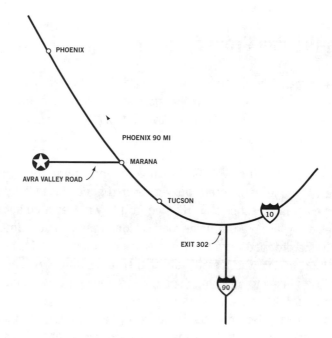

Roads to Marana Northwest Regional Airport, Marana

Yuma Proving Ground, Yuma

It's bigger than Rhode Island—this is site #1 of several locations in Top Secret America sharing that honor—and miles from anything of significance. That's why this is the Army's favorite place to test things they don't want you to know about.

Quoting from official Yuma Proving Ground literature: "On a recent day, Apache helicopters buzzed over rugged desert landscape where the actual Apaches once roamed, artillery pieces fired at targets 40 miles away, armored vehicles roared along road courses, dozens of parachutists dropped from the air, and a new technique for clearing buried land mines was tested—all at the same time." At any given time, there's likely to be a small-scale war going on inside Yuma Proving Ground's 1300 square miles.

Yuma Proving Ground was first used in 1942, where it was a test and training center for desert warfare troops and weaponry. After World War II, it became a multi-purpose facility for anything and everything that needed to be tested in isolation. In addition to the Army, other branches of the U.S. military use this facility as well as the military forces of friendly nations. The airspace above the facility is off-limits to all but authorized traffic, and mountains keep most of the area from public view.

What's There: The testing ranges are loaded with all kinds of instrumentation and communications installations, photographic equipment, data loggers, and computers. In addition, much of the land is used for training exercises. Troops and equipment were trained here just before the Persian Gulf War. The global positioning system (GPS) was developed and tested here during the late 1970s and early 1980s.

Key Facilities: Yuma boasts a 55-mile-long artillery range and an actual minefield to test mine detection and removal techniques. A "smart weapons" test range occupies more than 15,000 acres.

Secret Stuff: In recent years, there have been numerous reports of slowly moving lights in the night sky above this facility. These are believed to be various unmanned aerial vehicles (UAVs) undergoing tests. It is known that the Navy has tested UAVs that can take off and land vertically here; these UAVs would be used in carriers. These UAVs replace human pilots with on-board computers and can perform missions (like low-flying surveillance) too risky for human pilots. All publicly-known UAVs are propeller craft and carry non-lethal payloads (like cameras and instruments), although rumors are that jet-powered UAVs for bombing missions (like reusable cruise missiles) and balloon reconnaissance platforms are being tested at Yuma.

Getting a Look Inside: The only part open to the public is the Yuma Proving Ground Heritage Center, located in the main post building (S-2). If you've always wanted to visit a museum loaded with displays of artillery shells, mortars, and bazookas, then a visit to the Heritage Center is a must! It's open from 10 a.m. to 3:30 p.m. Monday through Thursday and admission is free.

Unusual Fact: The desert scenes in the Sylvester Stallone movie *Rambo III* were filmed near here; some actual helicopters from Yuma Proving Ground appeared in the film.

Getting There: Yuma Proving Ground is located north of Yuma along Highway 95. Highway 95 can be reached from either Interstate 8 or Interstate 10.

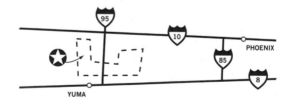

Roads to Yuma Proving Ground, Yuma

ARKANSAS

1. Mena Intermountain Municipal Airport, Mena 2. Pine Bluff Chemical Activity, Pine Bluff

Mena Intermountain Municipal Airport, Mena

Oh dear God, it sounds too good to be true—a conspiracy theorist's wet dream! Bill Clinton, drug smuggling, the CIA, Oliver North, money laundering, the Contras, gun smuggling, assassinations by Colombian drug lords, Area 51, the original President George Bush, all tied together by this airport deep in the Arkansas backwoods...

There's nothing much going on around Mena Intermountain Municipal Airport these days. It attracted too much attention and too many reporters during the Clinton years, and even the slightest hint of something funny going on today would quickly be fodder for Rush Limbaugh. But, just for historical reasons alone, Mena is still an essential stop on any tour of Top Secret America. Maybe one day the Top Secret Government will make Mena its first national park.

Shady doings around Mena began long before Bill Clinton and Oliver North entered the picture. Rural Arkansas, like much of the rural South, has a long and rich tradition of local law enforcement officials turning a blind eye to illegal activities, such as moonshine production, in return for cash. In the late 1960s, rural areas with airports, like Mena, became importation and distribution centers for the drug trade. The sum of money offered to ignore a single airplane full of cocaine could easily be more than a local sheriff's annual salary, and soon drug smugglers like Adler Berriman "Barry" Seal were finding the Ouachita Mountains of western Arkansas an ideal base of operations.

Seal's activities prior to 1981 are a murky web of half-truths, omissions, and outright lies. He said he had been a member of the U.S. Army Special Forces; he also claimed to have ties to the Central Intelligence Agency. In 1981, he arrived in Mena and bought an interest in Rich Mountain Aviation, one of the aircraft maintenance and operations businesses at the Mena airport. Arriving soon after Seal were enormous quantities of cash; secretaries at Mena and local bank employees later told investigators of Seal purchasing numerous cashiers checks just under the $10,000 limit that would require a filing of a federal currency transaction report. One teller told a federal grand jury that in 1982 Seal walked into a local bank with a suitcase with over $70,000 in cash and bought cashiers checks; similar transactions of $50,000 were not uncommon.

In the early 1980s, the area around Mena was filled at night with scores of low-flying planes. Rumors swirled around Mena that loads of drugs and money were being dropped from these planes. There were also reports of Spanish-speaking men in camouflage moving through the woods around Mena at night, along with what sounded like automatic weapons fire. Witnesses to such things decided, wisely, to keep quiet.

You would expect these events would have soon attracted the attention of local and federal authorities. But, with only a few notable exceptions, the official reaction was indifference. The exceptions were Russell Welch, an Arkansas State Police investigator, and William Duncan, an Internal Revenue Service investigator. However, their efforts were stymied by indifference of local law enforcement officials in Arkansas (in fact, Welch was ordered by his superiors to drop his investigation into possible drug smuggling in Mena) and a puzzling lack of support from other agencies of the federal government. It wasn't until 1983 that the Drug Enforcement Administration finally caught up to Barry Seal. However, instead of being arrested, Seal became an informant for DEA. While an informant, Seal continued his massive drug smuggling activities out of Mena.

Seal's informant role was a risky one, involving several flights to Colombia and meetings with leaders of the Medellin cartel, including Carlos Lehder. Seal later would testify in several high-profile drug cases. As a reward, Seal received sentencing to a "halfway house" in Baton Rouge instead of prison for his drug crimes. It was a soft way to do time; Seal was often seen driving around Baton Rouge in his white Cadillac. Seal's "turning over" to the DEA may have kept him out of prison, but it didn't keep him safe from some very angry Colombians after he testified in court. At twilight on February 19, 1986, Seal was stepping out of his Cadillac in Baton Rouge when suddenly four Colombians, armed with silencer-equipped automatic weapons, opened fire on him. Seconds later, Seal was slumped over the steering wheel—dead.

Barry Seal would have remained a footnote in history had it not been for the unraveling of the Iran-Contra conspiracy a few months after his death. In a neat bit of irony, Seal was, in death, indirectly responsible for blowing the lid off the entire Iran-Contra mess.

On October 5, 1986, a C-123K cargo plane was shot down over Nicaragua with a load of arms destined for the Contras. The lone surviving crew member, Eugene Hasenfus, was captured and began the public unraveling of the Iran-Contra affair.

The flight that Hasenfus was aboard had originated in Mena. The C-123K had previously been owned by Barry Seal. As more about the Iran-Contra affair became public, it was learned that the same C-123K had been used in a 1984 sting operation in which the CIA had installed hidden cameras before a flight to Nicaragua, and several photos were taken of various Sandinista representatives loading cocaine aboard the aircraft when it landed in Managua. Checks of Federal Aviation Administration records after Seal's death revealed that a number of the aircraft he used in his Mena operation had been previously owned by Air America, the CIA proprietary company active in southeast Asia during the Vietnam War.

Of course, the Iran-Contra investigations eventually sputtered to a halt with many unanswered questions. Oliver North has steadfastly denied any knowledge of drug running at Mena, as has Bill Clinton. Congressional hearings and investigations were largely fruitless. However, a December 1988 report by the Senate Subcommittee on Narcotics and Terrorism, then chaired by Sen. John Kerry (D-Massachusetts), concluded "It is clear that individuals who provided support for the Contras were involved in drug trafficking. The supply network of the Contras was used by drug trafficking organizations, and elements of the Contras themselves received financial and material assistance from drug traffickers." Speaking of criminal investigations related to Mena, the report continued, "cases were dropped. The apparent reason was that the prosecution might have revealed national security information, even though all of the crimes which were the focus of the investigation occurred before Seal became a federal informant."

There was hope that the true story of Mena would be told once the Republicans were out of the White House. In the 1992 campaign, Clinton said he learned officially about the activities at Mena only in April 1988. In his only public statement on the matter, in September 1991, Clinton said investigations by the Arkansas State Police had found "linkages to the federal government" and "all kinds of questions about whether he (Seal) had any links to the CIA, and if that backed into the Iran-Contra deal." But once inaugurated, Clinton was strangely reluctant to open investigations into a case that, on the surface, seemed to have great potential to embarrass Republicans. Part of the reluctance may have been because several of Clinton's Arkansas associates reportedly had dealings with Seal, especially involving Seal's efforts to launder large amounts of cash through Arkansas banks.

The mainstream press, with the exception of *The Wall Street Journal*, largely ridiculed the notion of CIA involvement in drug smuggling at Mena. In 1996, the *San Jose Mercury-News* ran a series by Gary Webb titled "Dark Alliance," in which Webb developed a compelling case that the CIA's involvement in drug running to support the Contras was responsible for the dramatic rise in crack cocaine use. After the series was published, the paper seized upon some relatively minor inaccuracies to repudiate the entire series and fire Webb.

Oh yes, when Eugene Hasenfus and Barry Seal's C-123K were shot down in October 1986, the Sandinistas recovered several flight logs indicating the C-123K had recently made flights out to places in Nevada, including Groom Lake. At the time, Groom Lake meant nothing except to a handful of Americans. It wasn't until the 1990s that it became well-known under another name: Area 51.

What's There: For all of the mystery surrounding it, the Mena airport is a pretty dull place. There are two landing strips and numerous aircraft maintenance, refurbishment, and servicing companies on the airport property. Those other businesses were supposedly one of the main reasons Mena was selected; the level of activity was very high for such an isolated airport.

Getting a Look Inside: Since it's a public facility, you're welcome anywhere the public can go, although the private businesses there would likely not appreciate having to deal with non-customers.

Unusual Fact: Mena likes to boast that it is midway between Fort Smith and Texarkana. Go check a map... by God, they're right!

Getting There: Mena is in west-central Arkansas near the Oklahoma border. Highways 8, 59, 71, and 88 all intersect there.

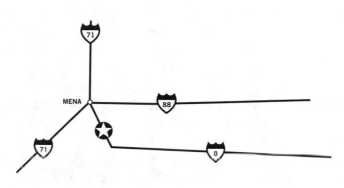

Roads to Mena Intermountain Municipal Airport, Mena

Pine Bluff Chemical Activity, Pine Bluff

The lush, green countryside northwest of Pine Bluff is home to about 12% of America's stockpile of chemical weapons, including blister and nerve gases. But it's also where the Army produces and maintains protective clothing and protective masks for soldiers.

Pine Bluff Army Arsenal was established in 1941 and from its beginning was a storage and production facility for chemical weapons. Storage of biological weapons was added in 1953, although this was discontinued in 1969. The arsenal is currently used to manufacture and store incendiary and non-lethal riot control weapons (such as tear gas) in addition to chemical weapons. The chemical weapons are stored in the Pine Bluff Chemical Activity section located on 430 acres in the northwest section of the almost 15,000-acre arsenal.

What's There: Over 3,500 tons of mustard gas in one-ton containers, over 100,000 small rockets with nerve gas, over 200 rocket warheads with nerve gas, and over 9,000 mines with nerve gas. Chemical/biological suits, masks, and filters are also stored here.

Key Facilities: Several hundred "igloo" structures designed to contain the gases in case of a leak dot this facility. In addition, a chemical weapons disposal site is currently under construction.

Getting a Look Inside: No public tours are offered, but several buildings can be seen from Highway 365, which parallels Pine Bluff Chemical Activity for several miles.

Unusual Fact: Pine Bluff was the birthplace of former heavyweight champion Sonny Liston.

Getting There: Pine Bluff Chemical Activity is located approximately eight miles northwest on Highway 365, or about 35 miles south of Little Rock.

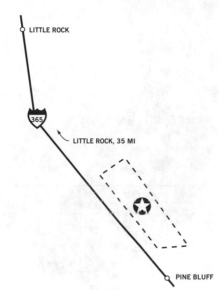

Roads to Pine Bluff Chemical Activity, Pine Bluff

CALIFORNIA

1. Beale Air Force Base, Marysville 2. Bechtel Corporation, San Francisco
3. China Lake Naval Weapons Center, China Lake 4. Continuity of Government Facility,
Oakville Grade 5. Edwards Air Force Base, Rosamond 6. Lawrence Livermore National Laboratory, Livermore 7. Manzanar Relocation Center, Manzanar 8. Onizuka Air Force Station,
Sunnyvale 9. Plant 42, Palmdale 10. Vandenberg Air Force Base, Lompoc

Beale Air Force Base, Marysville

Just north of Sacramento, Beale is home to America's fleet of U-2 spy planes and was the last operational site for the SR-71 Blackbird. It is also the home to the unmanned successors to spy planes, such as the RQ-4 Global Hawk drone. In other words, this is where Top Secret America keeps an eye on things from high above. As Beale's own public relations material boasts, "At any given moment, day or night, 24 hours a day, 365 days a year, there is probably a U-2 flying an operational mission somewhere in the world."

Beale Air Force base is spread over 23,000 acres and is home to the 9th Reconnaissance Wing, the U.S. Air Force group responsible for high-altitude reconnaissance flights. All remaining operational U-2 spy planes are based here (even though such planes may be temporarily based outside the United States for various missions). It was also the last operational base for the U-2's successor, the SR-71 Blackbird, until the SR-71 was retired in the mid-1990s due to cost and the fact that many SR-71 missions could be handled by unmanned drone aircraft, such as the RQ-4 Global Hawk. Drones have the advantage of being able to hover over an area for days at a time (manned craft such as the U-2 merely overfly an area once on a mission) and there is no risk of a pilot being killed or captured if the drone is shot down or suffers mechanical failure.

Beale was opened in 1942 as an Army infantry training base. It was also used to house German prisoners of war, and a block of prison cells, complete with German graffiti on cell walls, is maintained there for historic purposes. After creation of the Air Force in 1947, Beale was transferred to it and as a B-52 base for many years. The 9th Reconnaissance Wing arrived in 1983, and Beale's mission gradually evolved to reconnaissance and high-altitude intelligence-gathering. Today about 4000 people are stationed or employed at Beale.

What's There: Unfortunately, Beale just doesn't look that exciting from the outside. There is a control tower, several aircraft hangars, numerous other support buildings, and other structures normally associated with an Air Force base. There is a long runway, and maybe your best chance to see something secret in progress is when a U-2 takes off on a reconnaissance mission.

Key Facilities: Inside a large pyramidal structure is a phased array warning systems radar known as PAVE-PAWS. This system keeps track of airborne and space-borne objects approaching North America from the Pacific Ocean.

Getting a Look Inside: Group tours may be arranged on weekdays through the base public affairs office; individual visitors are discouraged. Information on each member of the tour group must be furnished and all visitors are subject to background checks.

Unusual Fact: Beale is named for the founder of the U.S. Army's Camel Corps, Lieutenant Edward Beale.

Getting There: Beale is located approximately 40 miles north of Sacramento. From Interstate 5, take Highway 70/99 north until it splits and then continue on Highway 70 toward Marysville until you see the exit for Beale Air Force base.

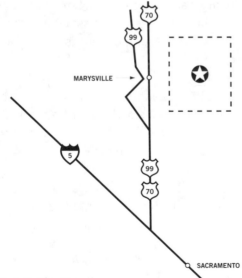

Roads to Beale Air Force Base

Bechtel Corporation, San Francisco

When the Top Secret Government needs a major construction project or management of a large installation, it frequently turns to this privately held, family-run company.

In Bechtel's promotional literature, they point with pride to some of the projects they have built: Hoover Dam, the San Francisco-Oakland Bay Bridge, the "Chunnel" between England and France, and the Bay Area Rapid Transit (BART) System. For some reason, they downplay the fact they manage installations such as the Nevada Test Site (see NEVADA section), have offices in areas (like Oak Ridge, Tennessee) where the Top Secret Government is the only game in town, and have built some of the most highly classified facilities in America.

Bechtel was founded in 1898 and today has over 41,000 employees worldwide, with revenues in recent years topping $14 billion. It is a private company mainly owned and managed by the Bechtel family, although some prominent outsiders with government connections (like former Secretary of State George Shultz) have served as CEO and on their board.

Bechtel has special expertise in the construction of large underground facilities, as demonstrated by their participation in the "Chunnel" project. In fact, the company authored a report entitled "Research Report for Tomorrow's Needs in Tunneling and Excavation" for the National Science Foundation. Besides the usual tunneling methods (water jets, various types of drills, borers, and hammers, etc.), the report also discussed such methods as lasers, plasmas, microwaves, electron beam guns, and "electrical disintegration." Since Bechtel is a private company, it does not have to detail its income sources and projects as a publicly traded company must. But it's virtually certain that Bechtel has been involved in some major "black" construction projects.

Secret Stuff: Perhaps the most interesting part of Bechtel's operations is Bechtel Nevada. Bechtel Nevada is responsible for the Nevada Test

Site operations and management and also has, despite its name, operations outside of Nevada. As Bechtel's publicity materials explain, "Bechtel Nevada partners with the Lawrence Livermore National Laboratory, Los Alamos National Laboratory, and Sandia National Laboratories on many projects. Bechtel Nevada also works on projects for other federal agencies such as the Defense Threat Reduction Agency, NASA, the Nuclear Regulatory Commission, and the U.S. Air Force, Army, and Navy." Bechtel Nevada's operations are assisted by Lockheed Martin and Johnson Controls, Inc.

Two of Bechtel Nevada's other activities include, in their words, "stockpile stewardship" and "national security response." To quote Bechtel Nevada's descriptions, stockpile stewardship involves "experimental capabilities necessary to maintain confidence in the safety and performance of weapons in the United States nuclear weapons stockpile" while national security response is described cryptically as "timely, worldwide support throughout the Emergency Response stages of pre-crisis, crisis, and consequence management."

Bechtel Nevada also maintains a special technologies laboratory in Santa Barbara, California. Quoting from their description, "Scientists at the STL design and develop compact, rugged sensor systems for numerous projects including ground penetrating radar, thermo graphic phosphor techniques, associated particle imaging and laser-induced florescence imaging. Other activities include sensors for ultra-high magnetic fields, very high bandwidth optical data recording and radiation sensors." From this description, it seems likely that Bechtel Nevada is heavily involved with development of systems for the detection of clandestine nuclear facilities and stockpiles.

Other Bechtel subsidiaries or joint ventures that manage facilities discussed in this book include Bechtel BWXT Idaho (Idaho National Engineering and Environmental Laboratory) and Bechtel Jacobs (Paducah, Kentucky Gaseous Diffusion Plant).

Getting a Look Inside: There are no scheduled tours of the Bechtel headquarters building. You'll have to be content with strolling through the lobby.

Getting There: Bechtel's world headquarters is at 50 Beale Street in San Francisco.

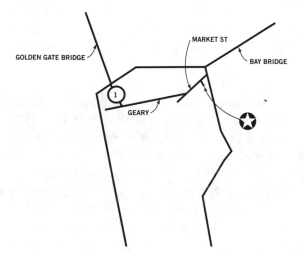

Roads to Bechtel Corporation

China Lake Naval Weapons Center, China Lake

Covering over 1700 square miles—yes, Top Secret America site #2 is larger than Rhode Island!—this is where the Navy tests and develops secret airborne weapons systems.

In 1943, the Navy needed lots of land to test its new carrier-based airplanes and the bombs they carry. They found it about 120 miles northeast of Los Angeles, in a section of the Mojave Desert sandwiched between the Sierra Nevada mountains and Death Valley. The facility gets its name from the dry bed of China Lake, and encompasses most of the Coso Range, a group of volcanic mountains and cinder cones that are still geothermally active. Numerous lava flows, hot springs, steam vents, and boiling mud pots dot China Lake, and the most recent volcanic activity took place only a few hundred years ago. Minor earthquakes are common, and geologists consider future volcanic eruptions to be inevitable.

China Lake is located adjacent to Ridgecrest, a town of about 30,000. Most of the engineers and scientists who work at China Lake live in Ridgecrest, giving the town one of the highest average levels of adult education in the country. The China Lake facility is split into two parts, with Highway 178 from Ridgecrest to Death Valley National Park serving as the dividing line between the parts.

Much of China Lake is hidden behind mountains and the area around the base is lightly populated. Because of this, China Lake is seeing an increasing amount of activity, especially since the area around Edwards Air Force Base is getting heavily populated. All of the airspace above China Lake is restricted and off limits to all civilian and military traffic without advance permission.

What's There: If it can take off from an aircraft carrier or be launched from a Navy ship, they're working on it here. Cruise missiles, air-to-ground missiles, air-to-air missiles, sea-to-sea missiles, anti-radar missiles, and electronics weapons systems are still being tested at China Lake. It is also used by the military of friendly nations, such as Britain's Royal Air Force, for training missions as well as testing. Daytime operations are limited to known weapons systems, with testing of classified projects generally done at night. Sonic booms and distant, unexplained columns of smoke from the base are common occurrences in Ridgecrest.

Key Facilities: China Lake is fully equipped to handle all types of military aircraft. The area has numerous radar domes and instrumentation facilities, many of which are easily visible on the base and atop mountains on the base area. A recent addition is a "live fire" range, where aircraft can be subjected to actual anti-aircraft fire, missiles, and other defensive weapons. The military's newest radar cross-section (RCS) range is located here, which strongly indicates that stealth-related development and testing is taking place. This is the Randsburg Wash Test Range, which was described as "a highly classified, sensitive, electronic warfare facility" by the Navy in 1994 when they filed to withdraw the area from the Bureau of Land Management and add it to China Lake. This area is located southeast of Ridgecrest, south of Highway 178.

Secret Stuff: Silent, slow-moving, and low-flying black triangular aircraft have been reported over China Lake airspace east of Highway 395 north of Ridgecrest; this highway runs parallel to China Lake for several miles. A few have reported being "buzzed" by these mystery craft as they drove in their cars. These aircraft are believed to be a new generation of unmanned surveillance/reconnaissance platforms, and are most commonly reported in the early hours of the morning during mid-week.

Because of its location between Edwards Air Force Base and Nevada facilities such as the Nevada Test Site and Area 51, China Lake is believed to be a prime facility for operations involving such facilities, such as test flights from Edwards to Area 51. China Lake could also serve as an emergency landing facility for flights out of such locations. Most such operations take place between local midnight and dawn on weekdays, when most potential onlookers would be sound asleep.

Getting a Look Inside: Thanks to the centuries-old efforts of Native American shamans, you can venture further inside China Lake than almost any other comparably secure facility.

China Lake is home to the largest collection of petroglyphs—Native American rock art—in North America. Over 13,000 are found in canyons located at an elevation of over 5000 feet in the base's interior mountains. All tours are escorted and scheduled for weekends in the fall and spring, and are conducted under the auspices of the Maturango Museum in Ridgecrest. Advance registration is required and you will have to submit such personal data as your social security number; you may be denied permission to take the tour if you are believed to be a "security risk" of some sort. Tours begin at the Maturango Museum and you will travel in a car convoy through the base to the petroglyph site, and will not be allowed to use any photographic or recording device until you get to the petroglyph site.

The drive to the petroglyph site takes almost an hour and climbs from the valley floor into the volcanic mountains that shield much of the base from public view. While nothing top secret can be seen along the route, you will notice several even more secure areas (high fences, warning signs, guarded entrances, etc.) within the confines of China Lake, indicating several parts of the facility are off-limits even to many who work there. The petroglyph site itself is very isolated with nothing visible for miles. However, the petroglyphs are spectacular and well worth the trip for their own sake.

The U.S. Naval Museum of Armament and Technology is near the entrance to China Lake; it has displays of weapons developed at China Lake, including the Polaris submarine-launched missile, the Tomakawk cruise missile, and the Sidewinder air-launched missile (unfortunately, none of their current projects are on exhibit). The museum is open 10 a.m. to 4 p.m. Monday through Thursday.

Unusual Fact: Highway 178 from Ridgecrest to Death Valley is a playground for jet fighters; it's not unusual for cars along this isolated road to be buzzed by jets flying only a couple of hundred feet overhead.

Getting There: Ridgecrest is located along Highway 395, the main north-south route along the eastern face of the Sierra Nevada mountains. The exit for Highway 395 is just west of Victorville along Interstate 15; Ridgecrest can also be reached by taking Highway 395 south from Reno, NV. An alternate route to Ridgecrest is to take Highway 178 east from Bakersfield; this crosses the southern end of the Sierra Nevada. The entrance is at the end of China Lake Boulevard, the main thoroughfare in Ridgecrest.

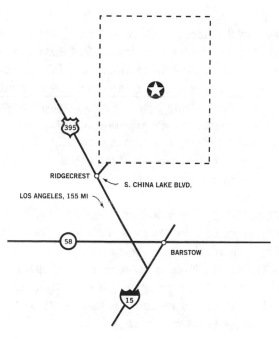

Roads to China Lake Naval Weapons Center, China Lake

Continuity of Government Facility, Oakville Grade

Up in the wine country of Napa County, there is a mysterious installation deep in the woods that may be a Continuity of Government facility. Since this facility was constructed in the mid-1990s, there have been numerous reports of black helicopters flying in and out of the area.

In 1992, the Napa Sentinel reported that something very strange was going on in the woods of Oakville Grade, a steep, twisting road north of the town of Napa off Highway 29. Citizens were witnessing unmarked black helicopters flying in and out of Bureau of Land Management land off Oakville Grade; some flights were reported as late as 3 a.m. Private aircraft flying over the area discovered large concrete bunkers under construction, excavations indicating some sort of large underground construction, and numerous satellite and microwave antennas being erected. However, the facility did not (and still doesn't) appear on any military, Bureau of Land Management, or Federal Aviation Administration maps.

The *Napa Sentinel* was able in 1995 to have a spokesman for Hamilton Air Force Base in nearby Novato admit the helicopter traffic was originating there. However, the spokesman maintained, "the helicopter traffic over the Napa Hills is a classified operation." No comment was offered as to the purpose of the facility or even that such a site existed. However, subsequent civilian flights over the area confirmed that the facility is still there.

Key Facilities: Aerial photographs show several completed concrete bunkers with large concrete doors, a freshly graded road from Oakville Grade, and several large satellite and microwave towers. From the air, it is impossible to know whether any underground facilities are at this site. However, this site very similar to other known Continuity of Government facilities, and it is highly likely that there are extensive underground living and support facilities at this site. The site occupies 87 acres.

Secret Stuff: Previously known Continuity of Government sites at Benicia and Ukiah, California were closed at around the time the Oakville Grade facility was being constructed, giving credence to speculation this is a replacement for them. In the event of an atomic attack or other major national emergency, this facility could be used by the president, vice president, or other senior government officials if they were on the west coast at the start of the emergency.

Getting a Look Inside: One could presumably hike to the facility, although to do so would require trespassing on private land. The facility itself is fenced and, it must be assumed, likely protected by a variety of security devices and personnel.

Unusual Fact: Prevailing wind patterns would keep most fallout from a nuclear strike on the San Francisco/Oakland area from reaching the Napa area.

Getting There: The exit for Oakville Grade is just south of the town of Oakville on Highway 29; Oakville Grade is the first exit south of Oakville Cross Road and runs in a westerly direction. While the facility can't be accessed by the public from Oakville Grade, it is located northwest of a fire station near Dry Creek Road.

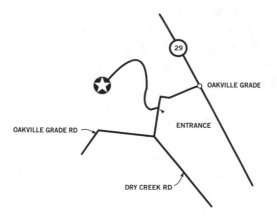

Roads to Continuity of Government Facility, Oakville Grade

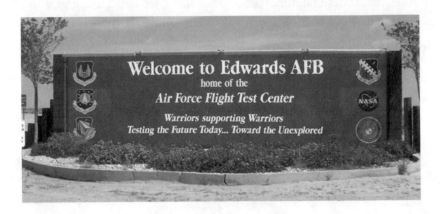

Edwards Air Force Base, Rosamond

This is the original home of top secret aircraft tests, like the first supersonic flight by Chuck Yeager. Now they're testing airborne laser weapons here.

Edwards Air Force Base drips history. It was here that Chuck Yeager first broke the sound barrier in October 1947 (an achievement that was kept classified for several months), followed by a series of speed and altitude records set in experimental aircraft ranging from the X-2 to the X-15. The first aircraft to reach 100,000, 200,000, and 300,000 feet altitude all flew out of Edwards. The exploits of its early test pilots were immortalized in the book and film *The Right Stuff*. It was later the site of the first Space Shuttle landings. And it's still home to a variety of classified programs.

Edwards was first chosen as a site for aircraft tests because of two dry lake beds, Rogers Lake and Rosamond Lake, that make superb natural landing strips. Originally known as Muroc Field, it was renamed for Capt. Glen Edwards, a test pilot killed there in 1948. In addition to the dry lake beds, most days at Edwards are clear with excellent visibility. Edwards occupies over 301,000 acres.

What's There: Edwards is home to the Air Force Flight Test Center, which is responsible for all aircraft flight testing for the Air Force. The Air Force Research Laboratory Propulsion Directorate, NASA's Dryden Flight Research Center, the Air Force Test Pilot School, and the Marine Aircraft Group 46 all have operations here. In addition, it can be safely assumed that many black projects are located here.

Key Facilities: The key facilities here are natural—the two dry lakes. There are also conventional runways, a control tower, repair and maintenance facilities, and base support operations. Unconfirmed rumors say that some underground installations are also here.

Secret Stuff: Edwards is located in the Antelope Valley area of southern California. This area is east and west of Highway 14, and includes the cities of Rosamond, Palmdale, Lancaster, Mojave, and California City. Late on moonless nights, many people report seeing exotic, unknown aircraft that are presumably being tested.

One of the more puzzling sightings has been of irregular, cloud-like objects being paced by conventional aircraft. Speculation has it these objects may be tests of new daytime stealth "cloaking" technology that could be used in overcast or cloudy skies.

There have also been frequent reports of diamond-shaped or arrowhead-shaped craft in the night skies over the Antelope Valley. However, there is no way to know whether these are reports of new stealth designs or just existing stealth aircraft, like the F-117A, seen from various angles. Some of these reports may be of the rumored TR-3A "Black Manta" stealth reconnaissance airplane.

In addition to such relatively "normal" sightings of unknown aircraft, there continue to be scattered reports of slow-moving lights in and around Edwards, especially over the mountains to the west. These lights are often described as being gold in color, completely silent, and appear to be football-shaped when viewed through binoculars. Brightness can vary over the period they are visible. These lights often abruptly appear in an otherwise dark sky and vanish just as abruptly. Sometimes several of these lights will be seen at once and will move in alignment with each other.

The areas over which these lights are seen have three radar cross-section (RCS) ranges designed to test how visible objects are on radar. This is a strong clue these objects are involved in some way with de-

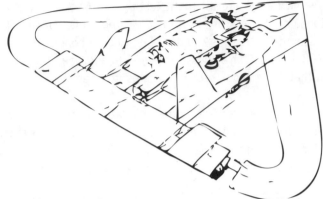

Sketch of the TR-3A "Black Manta"

veloping and testing of new stealth technologies. Their shape and "glow" indicate they may also be tests of electroluminescent surfaces that would be used in daytime stealth; the electroluminescent surfaces would change color to match the background color of the sky. Since the objects producing these lights appear to be small, they are likely models or unmanned aerial vehicles (UAVs) instead of manned aircraft.

There are some people who are convinced these lights are actually UFOs being tested at Edwards. I disagree, but who knows?

Getting a Look Inside: Edwards is surprisingly accessible during the daytime.

The Air Force Flight Test Center Museum has on display a replica of the X-1 (the first supersonic airplane), the X-25, the first F-16, an F-111, and a B-52. It also has a gift shop! The museum is open from 9 a.m. to 5 p.m. Tuesday through Saturday and admission is free. However, you must call in advance to request "sponsorship" before entering Edwards. The number for "sponsorship" is (661) 277-8050. Visitors who are not American citizens must apply at least three weeks in advance.

Weekly guided bus tours were scheduled at the time this book was being written each Friday at 10 a.m. The tour is free and photography is permitted at selected locations. Tour reservations can be made by calling (661) 277-3517.

An "open house" is held at Edwards annually, usually on the last weekend of October. At this time, the public is invited on base and can wander freely within limited boundaries. Aircraft are on display, and there are also air shows and flight demonstrations. However, the base is highly "sanitized" during this open house and your chances of seeing anything classified or otherwise secret is nil.

Getting There: Edwards is located 90 miles northeast of Los Angeles and about 20 miles east of Rosamond. From Highway 14, take the Rosamond exit and continue east on Rosamond Boulevard. An alternate route is to take the 120th Street exit from Highway 58.

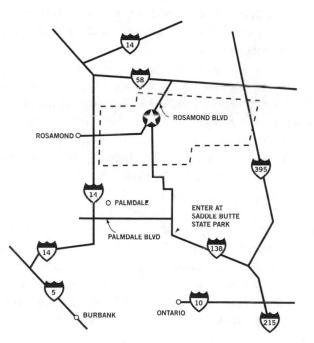

Roads to Edwards Air Force Base

Lawrence Livermore National Laboratory, Livermore

When you think of the University of California-Berkeley, you probably think it's a hotbed of dope-sucking liberals. And you're right. But there is another side to Berkeley. It also operates Lawrence Livermore National Laboratory, one of the most important research facilities for the Top Secret Government. It began as a facility to develop bigger and badder hydrogen bombs, and today is working on high-powered lasers, supercomputers, Mach 10 aircraft—and, of course, bigger and badder atomic weapons.

The Lawrence Livermore National Laboratory was the result of the first Soviet atom bomb test in 1949. Two key members of the Los Alamos team that developed the first atomic bomb, Ernest Lawrence and Edward Teller, believed that a second atomic weapons laboratory, to be operated in competition with Los Alamos, was necessary to spur development of the more powerful hydrogen bomb and other advanced atomic weapons. They proposed establishing such a laboratory to the Atomic Energy Commission, and in 1952 the new laboratory opened on the site of a former naval air station located in the East Bay south of Berkeley. Livermore occupies 7321 acres near Interstate 580.

Since then, Livermore's research areas have been expanded to include almost any area with possible weapons or defense potential. Areas of research currently going on include advanced microchips, genomes, biological weapons detection, biomedicine, radiographic imaging, 3-D simulations, supercomputers, and quantum-level physics. In addition to pure research, Livermore also does work on engineering projects such as "HyperSoar," a hypersonic aircraft capable of traveling Mach 10 and reaching any point on Earth in less than two hours.

Key Facilities: Livermore is home to the National Ignition Facility. While it sounds like some sort of space-age cigarette lighter or spark plug, it is actually the world's largest laser facility. What is it used for? According to Livermore's press releases, it "will provide the means for investigating the thermonuclear physics of weapons in the absence of nuclear testing and for exploring the promise of fusion energy." However, high-powered lasers would be the cornerstone of any space warfare or missile defense system as well.

Another interesting facility is the Advanced Strategic Computing Initiative. As weapons systems become increasingly computer-controlled, powerful computers are as much of an asset as aircraft carriers and missiles—maybe even more so. This program is meant to ensure that the U.S. military and intelligence agencies have the fastest and most powerful computers in the world.

Secret Stuff: The San Francisco Bay Area is perhaps the most anti-nuclear, environmentally activist region of the country. That's why it's ironic that Livermore keeps supplies of plutonium-239 and uranium-235—two highly fissionable isotopes used in the fabrication of atomic bombs—on its premises. Plutonium-239 is also one of the most toxic substances known. It is normally stored in powder form, but inhalation of a grain the size of a dust mote would usually bring about a swift death due to massive bleeding in the lungs. Let's say the Bay Area has a major earthquake, the "plute-239" escapes its containment vessels, and the wind is blowing... well, you connect the dots.

Getting a Look Inside: There is a visitor's center on Greenville Road, near the east gate to the laboratory, and it is open Monday through Friday from 1:30 to 4:30 p.m. Displays at the center cover Livermore's programs in national security, lasers, energy, etc., as well as the history of the laboratory. Livermore also offers monthly guided tours of the laboratory; the tour is open only to U.S. citizens and advance registration (including your social security number and driver's license number) is required; admission may be denied to those deemed security risks. Details on these tours can be obtained at the visitor's center.

Getting There: From Interstate 580, take the Greenville Avenue exit. Turn left at the stop sign, and then turn right onto Greenville. Follow Greenville to the intersection with Lupin Way, and turn right. The visitor's center and parking lot will be on your left, just before the guard gate.

Manzanar Relocation Center, Manzanar

Although it was closed in 1945, Manzanar is an essential stop on any tour of the Top Secret Government. It was here that thousands of Japanese Americans citizens, including children, were forcibly interned for the duration of World War II under an executive order issued by President Roosevelt. While never charged with any crimes—indeed, most had never been to Japan and couldn't even speak Japanese—they were kept behind barbed wire and guarded by machine guns because they had the wrong skin color. Supreme Court decisions during and after the war upheld the legality of Roosevelt's executive order and laid the legal foundations for more sweeping executive orders now in effect for future mass detention and relocation of American citizens. Anyone who says "it can't happen here" needs to visit Manzanar—not only can it happen here, it already has.

Manzanar is America's answer to the "Hanoi Hilton," except the POWs held here were law-abiding American citizens who made the bad decision to be of Japanese descent.

Manzanar's origins were in the rabid anti-Japanese hysteria that followed Pearl Harbor. In the first few days following the attack, General John L. DeWitt, commander of the Western Defense Command, sent a report to President Franklin Roosevelt accusing Japanese Americans of engaging in espionage and disloyal conduct. His suspicion of Japanese Americans was based strictly on racism and his report is the work of a very bewildered mind; he believed that the total lack of evidence that Japanese Americans were disloyal and engaging in sabotage must be proof that his fears were true. In DeWitt's own convoluted words: "[t]he Japanese race is an enemy race and while many second and third generation Japanese born on United States soil, possessed of United States citizenship, have become 'Americanized,' the racial strains are undiluted... The very fact that no sabotage has taken place to date is a disturbing and confirming indication that such action will be taken." Newspapers also did their part to feed racist hysteria among the public. *The Los Angeles Times* editorialized, "[a] viper is nonetheless a viper wherever the egg is hatched, so a Japanese American—born of Japanese parents—grows up to be a Japanese, not an American."

President Roosevelt responded by issuing executive order 9066 on February 19, 1942. Its scope was breathtaking, giving the military unprecedented powers over the civilian population. It permitted "the Secretary of War and the Military Commanders whom he may from time to time designate, whenever he or any designated Commander deems such action necessary or desirable, to prescribe military areas in such places and of such extent as he or the appropriate Military Commander may determine, from which any or all persons may be excluded, and with respect to which, the right of any person to enter, remain in, or leave shall be subject to whatever restrictions the Secretary of War or the appropriate Military Commander may impose in his discretion."

The implementation of executive order 9066 was draconian. Posters headlined "INSTRUCTIONS TO ALL PERSONS OF JAPANESE ANCESTRY" appeared in Los Angeles and other cities with significant Japanese American populations ordering Japanese Americans to report to "control stations." They were instructed to report carrying no more than two suitcases per person, and permitted items were restricted to necessities such as clothing, toiletries, and food. After arriving at the control centers, Japanese Americans were then relocated to various internment camps. In addition to Manzanar, there were nine other camps scattered through the western United States. Over 120,000 Japanese Americans were eventually interned at various camps, and most did not have time to close their businesses, store their property, or otherwise settle their affairs. As a result, most internees incurred significant financial losses.

While executive order 9066 did not single out Japanese Americans as its target, it was only applied against Japanese Americans. Some German and Italian nationals were interned during World War II, but never any German-American or Italian-American citizens (one can't help but wonder how postwar American popular culture would've been different if, say, Frank Sinatra and Dean Martin had been packed off to a place like Manzanar). It is difficult to understand why people like General DeWitt thought German Americans and Italian Americans were less prone to disloyalty than Japanese Americans... oh hell, we all know the reason! Let's just say it! Their skin was white!

Manzanar was a particularly brutal place to be interned. It is located along the eastern range of the Sierra Nevada mountains, almost directly underneath 14,375-foot Mount Williamson. The area is in the "rain shadow" of the Sierras and as a result quite arid, making it difficult to grow most crops or other plants. Summer temperatures often top 100, while snow and freezing temperatures are common in winter; violent storms and high winds can sweep down from the Sierras any time of year with little warning. It is little wonder that pneumonia was common in Manzanar and was the cause of several internee deaths. Most internees were housed in one-room barracks measuring 20 x 25 feet, with four people sharing each one. When possible, families were housed in a single barracks.

Manzanar was closed in September 1945, and most of the wooden structures were disassembled and removed. In a symbolic gesture, executive order 9066 was withdrawn by President Ford in 1976.

What's There: For many years, the camp auditorium and the two pagoda-shaped guardhouses at the entrance were the only buildings standing at Manzanar, although there were many foundations left of the wooden buildings and tents that were used to house internees. However, the National Park Service now administers Manzanar as a national historic site. It has announced plans to construct replicas of a typical barracks used to house internees and a guard tower; the camp auditorium is being converted into a visitor center/museum that will contain interpretive exhibits.

Presently there is a driving tour road through the site, and you are free to walk around the 500-acre site on foot. (Be careful, however, as this is rattlesnake country; the stone and rock foundations are their favorite hiding places.) The Park Service has added signs indicating the locations of various buildings and what different areas were used for. For example, you can see the locations of the schoolhouses, medical clinic, housing for the staff, and even the site of the camp's Catholic church.

If you walk around the area on foot, you may still find various relics, such as bottles or chunks of stone with Japanese characters on them. Please leave these where and as you find them so future visitors may enjoy them.

On the last Saturday in April of each year, a day of remembrance is held at Manzanar. Surviving internees and families of deceased internees return.

Key Facilities: It's not a facility, but the cemetery is the most moving part of Manzanar. A stone obelisk was added years ago in its middle, and the area is fenced off and well maintained.

Most of the graves are unmarked, and several are obviously those of children. Couldn't the money have been found somewhere in the budget to buy headstones for their graves?

Secret Stuff: The legitimacy of executive order 9066 was challenged in four separate cases reaching the U.S. Supreme Court and it was upheld each time.

In the most famous case, *Hirabayashi v. United States*, 320 U.S. 81 (1943), the Court upheld "differentiating citizens of Japanese ancestry from other groups in the United States." The Court further wrote, "[t]he adoption by Government, in the crisis of war and threatened invasion, of measures for the public safety, based upon the recognition of facts and circumstances which indicate that a group of one national extraction may menace that safety more than others, is not wholly beyond the limits of the Constitution and is not to be condemned merely because in other and in most circumstances racial distinctions are irrelevant."

In another case, *Korematsu v. United States*, 323 U.S. 214 (1944), the Court ruled that "we are not unmindful of the hardships imposed by [the exclusion order] upon a large group of American citizens. But hardships are part of war, and war is an aggregation of hardships. All citizens alike, both in and out of uniform, feel the impact of war in greater or lesser measure. Citizenship has its responsibilities as well as its privileges, and in time of war the burden is always heavier."

These largely forgotten Supreme Court decisions still serve as the legal underpinning for the standby executive orders allowing detention and relocation of American citizens if the president (not Congress) declares a national emergency. And who decides what constitutes a "national emergency"? The president in his sole judgment.

Getting a Look Inside: The Manzanar site is open during daylight hours, with the exact hours varying with the season. There is currently no admission fee and the site is staffed by Park Service rangers.

Unusual Fact: The number of possible Japanese American internees was only a fraction of what it could have been because it was restricted almost exclusively to those of 100% Japanese descent. DeWitt's racial paranoia was so high that he originally envisioned interning American citizens with as little as one-sixteenth Japanese blood (he actually imposed such restrictions on workers in some defense-related industries).

Getting There: Manzanar is located Highway 395 midway between Lone Pine and Independence. The site is located on the eastern side of the highway; look for the two pagoda-shaped buildings and a sign recently added by the National Park Service.

Roads to Manzanar Relocation Center, Manzanar

Onizuka Air Force Station, Sunnyvale

In the heart of Silicon Valley is a facility operated by the National Reconnaissance Office (NRO) to process data obtained by American spy satellites. This facility is also rumored to be used to eavesdrop on civilian communications satellites.

Onizuka Air Station is named after Ellison Onizuka, an astronaut killed in the *Challenger* disaster. It's easily recognizable by the "Blue Cube," a square glass-sided building that is readily visible from Highway 101, Silicon Valley's main drag (actually, the Blue Cube is more turquoise than blue). It looks like just another high-tech building in Silicon Valley, and indeed it is high-tech—it is where the super-secret National Reconnaissance Office downloads transmissions from orbiting spy satellites and interprets the data. However, the days of this facility are numbered, as its functions are expected to be relocated to Schriever Air Force Base in Colorado by 2008.

What's There: Inside the Blue Cube are supposedly powerful supercomputer systems to collect, process, and analyze process downloaded image data and intercepted communications. Onizuka is home to the Air Force's 750th Space Group and 21st Space Operations Squadron, and is also responsible for managing and networking spy satellites and military communications satellites.

Key Facilities: The Blue Cube is the main facility at Onizuka, along with several large dish antennas used to receive signals from satellites. The facilities occupy 128 acres.

Secret Stuff: The photographic resolution of American spy satellites is reportedly capable of reading the license plates of parked cars on the ground. And, by law, American spy satellites are not supposed to be used to spy on American civilians. Yet a Reuters report on March 13, 1999 noted that American spy satellites were being used to monitor civilian boat traffic in the Florida Keys. According to the report, this was done for environmental impact studies, not to detect drug running. But of course!

Rumors abound that some American spy satellites are capable of intercepting transmissions from civilian communications satellites. Since it would be illegal for the military to eavesdrop on civilian communications, this rumor is undoubtedly false. (Yes, that's sarcasm.)

Getting a Look Inside: No way in hell; forget it.

Getting There: Onizuka is located approximately 37 miles south of San Francisco and 11 miles north of San Jose on Highway 101 at the Mathilda Avenue exit; the Blue Cube is clearly visible from Highway 101.

Roads to Onizuka Air Force Station, Sunnyvale

Plant 42, Palmdale

This is the secret aircraft capital of the universe. The U-2 and SR-71 were built here, as were the B-2 and F-117 stealth aircraft, and it's almost a certainty that other, still-secret prototypes and aircraft are currently being designed and built here. The airport adjacent to Plant 42 has daily flights out to Area 51. In other words, here's where they build the stuff flown at Area 51. And, as mentioned in the previous listing for Edwards Air Force Base, a lot of weird things are seen in the late night skies above this area.

If it's an American top secret aircraft developed in the last four decades, odds are that it was developed at Plant 42. This sprawling facility near Edwards Air Force base was the birthplace of stealth and likely several other technologies, and aircraft, that we still don't know about.

Plant 42's origins date to 1940, when the Army Air Force converted the Palmdale airport into a base. In 1950, the Air Force converted it to an assembly facility for jet aircraft, and in 1953 officially became Plant 42. According to an Air Force press release, "Air Force Plant 42's production flight test installation is specifically tailored to the production, flight testing, modification and depot maintenance of the nation's most advanced aerospace systems built under government contract." Plant 42 employs approximately 8500 people.

Not everything at Plant 42 is military-related, however. The Space Shuttles were built at Plant 42, and undergo periodic refurbishing there. Other advanced NASA research vehicles, like the X-33, were also built here.

What's There: Plant 42 is not a single "plant," but instead several different facilities inside a common restricted area encompassing 5800-acres. While most of the facilities are privately owned, they are operated under the control and direction of the Air Force. Lockheed-Martin, Boeing, and Northup-Grumman have facilities at Plant 42; EG&G also operates inside Plant 42 and is believed to be the supplier of security guards and other support services. EG&G also operates "Janet Airlines" flights from the adjacent Palmdale airport; these flights are believed to go to Area 51 and the Tonopah Test Range in Nevada. (See the description for EG&G in the MARYLAND section and the entry for Janet Airlines terminal in the NEVADA section for more information on Janet Airlines.)

There are eight main production facilities and numerous smaller buildings. From public roads, the visible facilities are enormous hangars clearly intended for aircraft construction, much like the hangars used for commercial aviation construction (such as the Boeing facilities in the Seattle area).

There are two 12,000-foot runways at Plant 42; according to Air Force press releases, these are capable of handling aircraft weighing over 1,000,000 pounds and surviving a magnitude 8.3 earthquake.

The airspace above Plant 42 is restricted and off-limits to all unauthorized civilian and military traffic. Under an agreement with the Air Force, the adjacent Palmdale Airport can accommodate a certain number of civilian flights each day.

Key Facilities: While the buildings inside Plant 42 have no external signs to identify them, the road signs around Plant 42 point to individual buildings and identify them by plant number. Plant 10 is known to be the current home of Lockheed's famed Skunk Works (responsible for the U-2, SR-71, and F-117 stealth fighter). It is safe to assume they are working on a new generation of similarly amazing aircraft inside Plant 10.

Secret Stuff: As with most other high-security installations, the most interesting things happen late on weekday nights. Air Force C-5 and C-141 transport planes sometimes depart here at such times; these are believed to be carrying disassembled aircraft bound for sites such as Area 51 and White Sands. Also, large covered flatbed trucks leave Plant 42 in the wee hours and travel toward Edwards.

There is a large "Quonset hut" structure and aircraft hangar near the runways that are believed to be operated by EG&G. Twin-engine commuter aircraft have been observed arriving at and leaving from the facility, and control tower radio communications indicate some of these flights are bound for the Nevada Test Site. Since the Nevada Test Site is adjacent to Area 51, it is believed that some of these flights are actually carrying Plant 42 employees to Area 51. Normal engineering practice would call for key design engineers to be present when a new aircraft is undergoing tests, so the presence of Plant 42 engineers when their designs are being tested at Area 51 would be expected.

Getting a Look Inside: No way in hell. In fact, the security here is proactive and highly aggressive even if you are on public property near the facility. If you are parked for any length of time along a public road adjacent to Plant 42, don't be too surprised if you get a visit from a security guard who will remind you of the laws against photographing or sketching the facility. You might even be told to move along by a Los Angeles county deputy sheriff. (Reportedly this is to prevent someone from copying the license plate numbers of cars entering or leaving the plant.) Such a hardassed approach to security is a strong indication that highly classified stuff is indeed going on inside Plant 42.

Getting There: Plant 42 can be accessed by taking either the Avenue M or Avenue N exits off Highway 14 from Los Angeles and traveling east. The roads surrounding the facility are often confusing; be alert for the sometimes abrupt transition from public property to the restricted area around Plant 42, as this can occur several hundred feet before a security checkpoint. Fences along the side of the road and a change in the color of the road pavement indicate you are approaching the Plant 42 boundary. Even if you cross the border by accident, you could be arrested for trespassing even if you turn around and leave before reaching a security checkpoint.

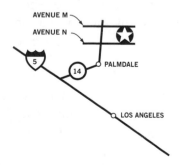

Roads to Plant 42, Palmdale

Vandenberg Air Force Base, Lompoc

When a satellite is in polar orbit, it will eventually pass over every inch of the Earth's surface. That's why almost all spy satellites are placed in polar orbit, and also why Vandenberg is the launching spot for almost all U.S. spy satellites.

Vandenberg is home to the 30th Space Wing, the Air Force command responsible for all missile and space launch activities on the West Coast. Because a launch to the south travels over open water until orbit is reached, Vandenberg is an ideal site for launching satellites for polar orbit—in fact, the world's first polar orbiting satellite was launched from here in 1959. Since spy satellites travel in polar orbits, all U.S. spy satellites are launched from here.

Vandenberg is also used for launches by NASA and private contractors. Many launches use heavy boosters, such as the Titan IV and the latest version of the Atlas. Vandenberg is also where operational tests of American intercontinental ballistic missiles are conducted, with regular test flights of the Minuteman III and Peacekeeper (MX) missiles.

Civilian and non-classified military launches are publicized in advance and are great fun to watch. Even more fun to watch, however, are classified launches. These are not announced in advance and are timed for periods when another nation's spy satellites are not overhead. Often these take place in the middle of the night or otherwise odd times.

What's There: Vandenberg juts out into the Pacific Ocean, giving clear, no-land paths to the west and south for rocket launches. The base covers over 98,500 acres amid rolling hills.

Key Facilities: The main launch facilities at Vandenberg include space launch complex 2 (SLC-2), SLC-3, SLC-4, SLC-5, and SLC-6. SLC-2 consists of two launch pads and is used for the Delta rocket. SLC-3 has two pads and is used for Atlas rockets. SLC-4 has two pads and is used strictly for military launches. SLC-5 has one pad and is used for Scout research rockets. SLC-6 was originally intended to be the site for polar launches of the Space Shuttle, but that idea was abandoned (see Unusual Fact below). However, a slightly smaller version of the Vehicle Assembly Building at Cape Canaveral was completed here, and the facility is now used for much smaller rockets. SLC-10 can be visited on the public tour; it is not an active launch site any longer and instead has Thor, Thor-Agena, and Bomarc missiles on display.

Secret Stuff: The National Reconnaissance Office (NRO) is the biggest single reason why Vandenberg exists today. Vandenberg came into being in 1957, after the first studies were being made into the possibility of military reconnaissance satellites. It was determined early that polar orbiting satellites were necessary to give photo coverage of the entire planet, and Vandenberg was the only place in the continental United States where polar launches would be feasible. The hilly terrain at Vandenberg also afforded protection from prying eyes aboard ships and submarines. Almost all launches from SLC-4 are spy satellites launches.

Getting a Look Inside: Currently, the Public Affairs Office at Vandenberg offers free tours on Wednesday at 10 a.m. The tour lasts about two hours and includes the various launch complexes and the Heritage Center that details the history of the rockets launched from Vandenberg. Advance registration is required, along with social security numbers, and persons deemed to be security risks may be refused admission. For more information and registration, call the Public Affairs Office at (805) 606-3595.

Unusual Fact: So why was Vandenberg abandoned as a Space Shuttle launch site after the facilities for it were almost 100% complete? The reason is a problem not discovered until the *Challenger* disaster in 1986. When it was determined that cold temperatures at launch time were responsible for the failure of the solid fuel booster rocket seals on the *Challenger,* the entire Vandenberg Shuttle launch facility had to be abandoned—even in summer, cold winds off the Pacific here would routinely cool the booster rocket seals below their failure temperatures.

Getting There: Vandenberg is about 55 miles north of Santa Barbara along Highway 1 (the Pacific Coast Highway). In the town of Lompoc, follow the signs for Vandenberg/Highway 1. Take the Vandenberg exit off Highway 1 and follow it for about 12 miles to the main gate and visitor center.

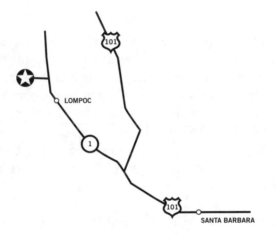

Roads to Vandenberg Air Force Base, Lompoc

COLORADO

1. Buckley Air Force Base, Aurora 2. Cheyenne Mountain Operations Center, Colorado Springs
3. Peterson Air Force Base, Colorado Springs 4. Project Rulison Test Site, Garfield County
5. Pueblo Chemical Depot, Pueblo 6. Rio Blanco Test Site, Rio Blanco County
7. Rocky Flats Environmental Test Site, between Golden and Boulder
8. Schriever Air Force Base, Colorado Springs

Buckley Air Force Base, Aurora

In the suburbs of Denver, our newest Air Force base is the home of Detachment 45, responsible for detecting and reporting hostile missile launches and nuclear explosions in the atmosphere. They also have the capability of keeping track of a lot of other stuff that can be seen from space.

Colorado is the space warfare capital of the United States. The newest addition to the Air Force's facilities is Buckley Air Force Base (formerly Buckley Air National Guard Base), which became an Air Force base in October 2000. Detachment 45 is responsible for receiving, collecting, and analyzing data from spy satellites to detect nuclear explosions as well as missile launches and other events. With the increased emphasis on space warfare, it's likely this facility and the activities there will grow in the years ahead.

What's There: Until recently, Buckley was just an Air National Guard base, so it's missing most of the amenities found on other Air Force bases, like housing, recreation facilities, and even (at the time this was written) a chapel. It has the usual nondescript buildings, aircraft hangars, a control tower, and a runway. The only indication that something unusual is going on inside is the abundant satellite dishes. Detachment 45 is located in a secure building near the East Sixth Avenue side of the base.

Key Facilities: In the Detachment 45 building, two operators are constantly on duty monitoring for missile launch and nuclear explosion data. The data is downloaded from orbiting satellites and processed by supercomputers. According to an official Air Force press release, Detachment 45 also performs "special data collections" for other government agencies, including "nuclear event notification" (what's the difference between a "nuclear event" and an "explosion"?), fuel air explosions, and "natural phenomena" (how about UFOs?). And the press release says that any "anomalies" are reported to "the appropriate authorities."

Secret Stuff: The frequencies used for downlinking data from spy satellites are also used for civilian industrial and scientific applications in most of the country. However, the Federal Communications Commission will create a "special exclusion zone" banning all civilian terrestrial use of those frequencies used to download spy satellite data. The FCC has created such a zone extending out to 150 kilometers, centered on the geographic coordinates for Buckley.

Getting a Look Inside: Buckley Air Force Base offers no public tours.

Getting There: Buckley is located east of Aurora on Highway 30; take the exit for that highway from Interstate 225.

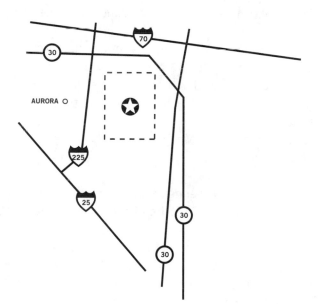

Buckley Air Force Base, Aurora

Cheyenne Mountain Operations Center, Colorado Springs

This place is something out of a 1960s James Bond movie. Inside a hollowed-out mountain designed to withstand a direct strike from an atomic bomb are 15 buildings—11 of which are three stories tall— keeping track of everything in outer space and all planes flying in North American airspace. Large, backlit maps of the world display information received from orbiting spy satellites; a large video screen constantly shows the location of the president and vice-president. In case of a nuclear war, over 800 personnel could survive in here for more than 30 days completely cut off from the outside world. They once offered guided tours, but—alas!—had stopped doing so at the time this book was being written.

Where does one start when discussing Cheyenne Mountain?

How about the 1,319 springs, each weighing over 1000 pounds, that the buildings rest upon so they can absorb the impact of a nuclear strike? How about the 25-ton blast doors that can close in 15 seconds when a nuclear attack is detected? How about the 1,700 feet of granite that covers it?

It's no use. Cheyenne Mountain is off the scale no matter how you try to describe it.

Construction of Cheyenne Mountain began in 1961 and finally became operational in 1966. Its elevation is 7,100 feet above sea level. The interior of the mountain was hollowed by a series of excavating explosions that delayed construction of the interior until 1963. The 15 buildings inside total over 250,000 square feet and are connected by 2.8 miles of tunnels through granite. Over 1,200 personnel work there (although not all are present at once). It has its own supplies of water and fuel plus six generators to supply electricity; it also has battery systems capable of running the facility for a half-hour. It operates without air conditioning or heaters; the natural temperature of this artificial cave is 57 degrees and recovered heat from the computer systems is used to provide additional warmth. The construction cost when it was built was $142 million. In today's dollars, that's over $18 billion.

Several activities are based inside Cheyenne Mountain. Perhaps the best known is the North American Aerospace Defense Command (NORAD), a joint American/Canadian effort to defend North America from attack by missiles or aircraft. (Since NORAD is a joint effort, several members of the Canadian military work inside Cheyenne Mountain.) The Air Operations Center ties together military and civilian radar systems to track aircraft over North America; it logs over 2,500,000 flights annually. (Some of the lingering questions from the September 11, 2001 attacks concern how well Cheyenne Mountain was able to track the hijacked jets and feed any data to appropriate civilian and military authorities.) The U.S. Space Command controls all military satellites, including spy communications, and navigation satellites. The main purpose of this command is to provide warning of enemy missiles; it detects all missile launches around the world and then has to decide, in no more than two to three minutes, whether the missile is hostile. Finally, the Air Force Space Command tracks and catalogues all objects in orbit, ranging from the Space Shuttle to debris the size of a large bolt (a piece of space junk that size, orbiting the Earth at a speed of 17,500 miles per hour, could do serious damage to a satellite or the Space Shuttle if there was a collision). It also operates the global positioning satellite (GPS) network.

What's There: Back when the Air Force conducted guided tours of Cheyenne Mountain, visitors entered via a 5,000-foot-long tunnel drilled through the mountain. The tunnel has no doors at either end, and the doors leading into the facility are parallel to the tunnel. The theory behind this design is that the force of a nuclear blast would "blow through" the tunnel and minimize stresses on the doors.

The interior buildings are constructed of steel and laid out in a grid pattern. They remind many visitors of what it feels like to be below deck of a large Navy ship, such as an aircraft carrier or destroyer. Besides strength, steel has the added advantage of being able to absorb much of the electromagnetic pulse that would be produced by a nearby nuclear explosion. Some openings in the wall allowed visitors to view the huge springs the buildings are mounted on and the tunnels that connect the buildings. There are no barracks or other living quarters for personnel; cots and other temporary bedding are stored in the facility in case the Big One lands.

Most visitors were surprised by how small the various rooms are, especially the various command centers. Movies like *War Games* have long depicted these areas as huge, auditorium-sized facilities with high ceilings, much like mission control at NASA. Those inside Cheyenne Mountain, however, aren't much larger than the control room of a television station. There are several monitors on the walls, but workers sit close together and the ceiling is about as high as that in most houses. Instead of awe, most visitors felt claustrophobia. However, some of the command center furnishings are like a movie; generals with two or three stars are often in command, and they do have a red telephone that connects them directly to the president. Duty officers responsible for monitoring various activities (such as missile launches or aircraft intruding from south of the United States) have a beige phone at their duty station. If an officer detects something unusual, he or she picks up their phone, all other beige phones ring, and the officers at those stations respond as necessary.

Key Facilities: The main command center for Cheyenne Mountain has several large, backlit maps of North America and other areas of the world. One shows the current location of the president, vice president, the Canadian prime minister, and other senior government and military leaders. Other maps and monitors track moving aircraft (especially those approaching the airspace of North America) and display data received from spy satellites and ground-based space radars.

Secret Stuff: According to a 1999 CNN report, Cheyenne Mountain detected over 670 "unknowns" in North American airspace in 1997 and turned that information over to other government agencies, such as the Drug Enforcement Administration. To augment these efforts, balloon-carried radar systems are being deployed along the border with Mexico. It is not known which other agencies receive information from Cheyenne Mountain or the exact degree of cooperation between this facility and civilian law enforcement organizations.

Getting a Look Inside: Until recently, the Air Force conducted guided tours inside Cheyenne Mountain. These tours began soon after the facility was opened in 1967, were discontinued in 1980, resumed in 1985, and were again discontinued after the September 11 attacks. It is not known whether public tours will be resumed in the future. When public tours were offered, reservations had to be made well in advance and potential visitors were subject to rigorous security checks. Two forms of photo identification (including verification of social security number) were required and visitors could not bring cameras, recorders, cell phones, pagers, etc., into the facility; visitors had to walk through a metal detector and all handbags, etc., were searched.

Unusual Fact: Cheyenne Mountain really isn't nuclear bomb-proof anymore. While it can withstand a nearby blast, the Air Force admits that a direct hit from today's more accurate missiles would likely take out Cheyenne Mountain.

Getting There: Cheyenne Mountain is southwest of Colorado Springs but can't be accessed via any public roads; the area is highly guarded and any attempt to hike into the facility will likely result in arrest. Moreover, private landowners in the area around Cheyenne Mountain have been known to call police to arrest hikers attempting to cross their land on the way to the facility. While there are no longer guided tours of Cheyenne Mountain, there is a multimedia "General Public Presentation" about the facility offered at the adjacent Cheyenne Mountain Air Station. The presentation does include a look at the inside of the facility (or at least how they looked when public tours were discontinued; it is likely some changes have been made since then). Information about viewing the presentation can be obtained by calling (719) 474-2238. The Cheyenne Mountain Air Station is about as close as you can get these days; take Highway 115 south from Colorado Springs and take the Cheyenne Mountain Air Station exit. Merge onto NORAD Road and continue toward the west until you reach the visitor center.

Peterson Air Force Base, Colorado Springs

Peterson is the "host" base for NORAD and the Cheyenne Mountain facility. It is also the home of the 76th Space Control Squadron, whose mission is to test offensive and defensive space weapons systems, and the United States Space Command, which oversees all U.S. military operations in space. In other words, this is where the United States is planning to fight a war in outer space.

If the Colorado Springs area has become the de facto center of American military space efforts, then Peterson is the "Pentagon" for those efforts. If there is eventually a war in outer space or one involving space-based weapons, it will be directed from Peterson.

What's There: If it has anything to do with military uses of space, it is directed, administered, planned, compiled, or analyzed here. The United States Space Command is the umbrella organization for all military space operations, including the Air Force, Navy, and Army. Military surveillance (including missile launch and atomic explosion detection), communications, and navigation (including GPS) satellite operations are also based here. Space training activities—such as how to download and interpret data from satellites or maneuver satellites—are conducted here. Activities at other space-related Air Force bases such as Onizuka Air Force Station in California or Buckley Air Force Base in Colorado are commanded from Peterson.

Key Facilities: Peterson Air Force Base occupies 1,277 acres and from the outside looks much like any other Air Force base, with runways, control tower, aircraft hangars, and several government-issue office and housing facilities. The good stuff—the supercomputers, command and control facilities, communications facilities, etc.—are safely hidden from public view.

Secret Stuff: Perhaps no secrets in the U.S. military are more tightly guarded than those involving offensive space weapons. However, it is widely reported that small, highly maneuverable "killer microsatellites" are being developed and tested at Peterson. These are designed to take out another country's satellite systems through such methods as high-energy lasers, directed-energy beams (such as a "rain" of neutrons), or electrostatic discharges (to destroy the integrated circuits inside enemy satellites). It is also believed that other killer microsatellites under development will be able to jam communications and navigation satellites with false signals. For example, this would mean that cruise missiles or other weapons systems that depend upon satellite signals to find their targets could be redirected back toward targets within the enemy country that launched them.

Getting a Look Inside: Peterson does not currently offer public tours. However, the Peterson Air and Space Museum, located just inside the north gate of the base, is open to the public and features exhibits about NORAD and many types of aircraft. The museum is at 150 East Ent Avenue. For current hours of operations and admission procedures, call (719) 556-4915.

Unusual Fact: In January 2001, the Air Force announced that it was investigating reports that some of its personnel at Peterson were using Ecstasy and LSD. 15 persons were eventually relieved of their duties while being investigated. Imagine having a laser-armed killer microsatellite under your control while tripping on X or Purple Haze!

Getting There: Peterson Air Force Base is on the east side of Colorado Springs, south of Platte Avenue near Highways 24 and 94. It is just north of the Colorado Springs airport.

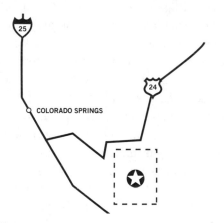

Roads to Peterson Air Force Base, Colorado Springs

Project Rulison Test Site, Garfield County

On September 10, 1969, the Atomic Energy Commission conducted a 43-kiloton underground atomic bomb test in western Garfield County to see if atomic blasts could be used to increase production of natural gas by ripping apart the subterranean sandstone formations in which gas was trapped. It worked, except the gas was too radioactive to use.

Ever wonder why the term "rocket scientist" instead of "nuclear scientist" is used to describe somebody who is highly intelligent? Perhaps the saga of Project Rulison offers some clues to that mystery.

In the mid-1960s, "Operation Plowshare" was launched to find peaceful uses of atomic weapons. Amazing as it now seems, there were serious proposals to use atomic weapons to excavate large amounts of land for mammoth civilian construction projects such as artificial harbors, irrigation of the Sahara Desert, and a larger replacement for the Panama Canal that would cut across Nicaragua. Only slightly less preposterous was the notion to use underground atomic blasts to free reserves of oil and gas trapped in rock formations.

The test site was approximately 14 miles south of Rifle, Colorado, in Garfield County. There are abundant natural gas reserves trapped in the underground sandstone and shale formations of the county, but most reserves are so tightly "locked" in the formations that commercial exploitation of the reserves is not economically feasible. The theory behind Project Rulison was that an underground atomic explosion could shatter the formations, releasing huge quantities of natural gas that could be recovered at little cost. The test was essentially underwritten by the Austral Oil Company of Houston, TX, which paid the Atomic Energy Commission $6,500,000 to conduct it.

Project Rulison was one of the first atomic tests to attract widespread opposition. Even though the bomb was located over 8,400 feet underground, there were major concerns over radiation leakage and the projected thousand-plus underground explosions in Colorado alone that could follow a successful test. One of the leaders of opposition to the test was Dick Lamm, a future governor of Colorado. Several lawsuits were filed to stop the test and succeeded in delaying it for several months. When the test was finally conducted on September 10, 1969, the nearby town of Rifle was subjected to a shock equivalent to a 5.5 earthquake.

The test was both a success and a failure. It did produce an artificial cavern measuring 350 feet high and 75 feet across and resulted in the release of large quantities of natural gas from the sandstone and shale formations. However, the gas contained so much radioactive material that the necessary decontamination and safety precautions against accidental release of radiation made the extraction of the gas prohibitively expensive. It was instead burned away at the test site.

What's There: Not much. At the time this book was written, the big attractions are a few warning signs, a fenced-off pond, and a couple of sealed "pits" that mark the locations of the tunnels drilled down to the location of the test.

Getting a Look Inside: Despite the abundant federal land in the area, the test was actually conducted on private land leased from the Hayward family, who had a potato farm on the site in 1969. As a result, you might find access to this site blocked at any time; be sure to respect any "no trespassing" signs or closed roads you might encounter.

Unusual Fact: The Project Rulison site is still administered by the Nevada Test Site and Bechtel Nevada (see NEVADA). They offer for sale a ten-minute VHS tape showing (quoting from their sales literature) "the explosion, underground rock fracturing, gas release, and underground well operations in schematic operation."

Getting There: The site is located approximately three miles south of the town of Parachute and may be reached from an exit off Interstate 70.

Roads to Project Rulison Test Site, Garfield County

Pueblo Chemical Depot, Pueblo

The Pueblo Chemical Depot is located approximately 15 miles east of Pueblo, two miles north of the Arkansas River. It was first used as a chemical weapons depot in the 1950s and currently is used to store over 2,500 tons of mustard gas contained in various weapons. The total area occupied by the depot is over 23,000 acres.

What's There: There are hundreds of thousands of 105mm cartridges and 155mm projectiles loaded with mustard gas here, along with smaller quantities of 4.2-inch cartridges. As the name implies, mustard gas produces burn-line "blistering" injuries when inhaled or when it makes contact with exposed skin.

Key Facilities: There are over 900 storage "igloos" at the depot. The chemical weapons are currently stored in a little over 100 igloos located away from public view on the north side of the depot.

Getting a Look Inside: No public tours are currently offered of the depot itself. However, the Pueblo Chemical Depot Community Outreach Office is located at 301 North Main Street, Suite 306B, in downtown Pueblo and has information and documents about the depot and the chemicals stored there.

Getting There: The main entrance is located at 45825 East State Highway 96, east of downtown Pueblo.

Roads to Pueblo Chemical Depot, Pueblo

Rio Blanco Test Site, Rio Blanco County

After the failure of the Project Rulison test (see previous), you figured the Atomic Energy Commission would've learned its lesson. No way, compadre! Instead, they came up with a bright new idea: if one atomic explosion didn't work, how about setting off three simultaneously???

Undeterred by the failure of the Project Rulison test to free commercially exploitable quantities of natural gas, another test was conducted on May 17, 1973, at a location approximately 35 miles to the northwest in Rio Blanco county. The underground sandstone and shale formations were similar to those at Rulison, and the Rio Blanco site had the advantage of being more remote.

Exactly why the gas freed by the Rio Blanco test was supposed to be less radioactive and thus more commercially recoverable than the gas produced by the Rulison test isn't clear. In retrospect, Rio Blanco seems to have been based more on a hope the Rulison test outcome was a fluke than scientific data. As with Rulison, the Rio Blanco test was underwritten by two private companies, CER Geonuclear and Equity Oil Company.

The Rio Blanco test used three 30-kiloton bombs placed at a depth over a mile. The bombs were detonated simultaneously and did succeed in releasing large quantities of natural gas. But, as was the case in Project Rulison, the gas was too radioactive for commercial use. The gas was burned away at the site.

What's There: A concrete marker and plaque explaining the Rio Blanco test is at the site. The mile-deep shaft in which the bombs were placed has been sealed shut with concrete, and scattered pipes and other metal objects can be found amid the grasses and scrub at the site.

Getting a Look Inside: The Rio Blanco site is on public land, so look all you want. But this is very isolated country. You should fill up with gas in Rio Blanco and your car should be in good mechanical condition and have a full spare; extra food, water, and warm clothing should also be taken in case of a problem since you are a long way from help out here.

Getting There: The site is about 52 miles northeast of Grand Junction, and can be reached by traveling about 21 miles west of the town of Rio Blanco along Black Sulphur Creek road. At that point, a road bears left toward the southwest; the Rio Blanco test site is located a little over four miles down that road.

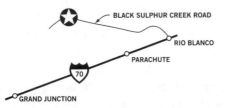

Roads to Rio Blanco Test Site, Rio Blanco County

Rocky Flats Environmental Test Site, between Golden and Boulder

This innocuously-named facility located 21 miles northwest of Denver is a former nuclear weapons fabrication site and a storage facility for over 12 tons of Plutonium-239, over 6.5 tons of uranium-235, and over 160 tons of depleted uranium. It is also the site of numerous cases of unauthorized dumping of radioactive materials that eventually resulted in a FBI raid. In other words, this was Uncle Sam's atomic landfill site. But at least efforts are now being made to clean up the mess.

Rocky Flats was opened in 1952 to manufacture the hollow plutonium spheres used as "triggers" for hydrogen bombs. It originally duplicated work done at Oak Ridge, TN, but soon added other tasks such as recycling nuclear material from older atomic bombs and storing atomic material. Employment at the site peaked at over 18,000 but sharply declined at the end of the Cold War and was under 10,000 today. Original plans called for the site to be free of all nuclear materials, decontaminated, and converted to a national wildlife refuge by the end of 2006, but that deadline has been extended into the indefinite future. Most operations are concentrated on roughly 380 acres within the 6,262-acre site; the remainder of the acreage serves as a safety/buffer zone.

The environmental problems at Rocky Flats first came to national attention in 1989, when reports surfaced that safety and environmental guidelines were being widely ignored. These reports from current and former workers at Rocky Flats resulted in the FBI raid to gather records and documents. The seized materials revealed a pattern of delayed or ignored maintenance, inadequate staff training, non-working safety equipment in some buildings, dangerous levels of explosive hydrogen gas in storage drums, and unreported cases of leaks of radioactive materials (including cases where the radioactive materials had seeped into ground water). Nuclear production activities ended soon after the 1989 FBI raid.

In 1995, the Department of Energy began cleanup and environmental restoration activities at Rocky Flats, and those continue as this book is being written. However, problems with radiation monitoring, access control to radiological areas, and personnel management came to light in 1996. These have supposedly been remedied as of this writing.

What's There: Buildings 371 and 374 were the main facilities for treatment and reprocessing of plutonium and associated waste. Buildings 771 and 774 were used for the recovery of plutonium from waste materials, including liquids. Analysis of materials containing plutonium was done in building 559. There are numerous other buildings at Rocky Flats that were used for weapons assembly. All of these buildings have been removed or are in the process of being torn down.

Getting a Look Inside: According to the Rocky Flats Tours & Visits Department (yes, there is such a thing), public tours are occasionally scheduled to "enhance community relations, increase public awareness of site closure activities, and meet public informational needs." All visitors must be screened and approved in advance, and being part of a tour group is by far your best chance of getting a look inside. Cameras, recording devices, cell phones, and computers (including PDAs) are some of the prohibited items on tours.

Unusual Fact: Several former Rocky Flats workers now suffer from a variety of ills, including chronic pains in their joints, severe episodes of fatigue, immune system deficiencies, and degenerative bone disorders. Tests have determined that most of these workers have small amounts of radioactive materials in their systems. However, the Department of Energy maintains there is no connection between worker exposure to radioactive materials at Rocky Flats and any medical conditions they may be suffering.

Getting There: The Rocky Flats visitor center is located at 10808 Highway 93 in Golden. Rocky Flats itself occupies an area of ten square miles.

Schriever Air Force Base, Colorado Springs

Part of the Colorado Springs space warfare infrastructure, Schriever is home to the rather innocuous-sounding Joint National Test Facility, which is actually the war-gaming center where Air Force brass are planning how to fight and win battles in outer space.

In April 2001, NBC reported that senior Air Force officers gathered for several days of war games pitting the United States against a fictitious country that strongly resembled China. However, the officers weren't planning bomber attacks or missile strikes against their adversary; instead, they were planning battles fought entirely in outer space using those "killer microsatellites" being tested nearby at Peterson Air Force Base.

Those war games took place at the Joint National Test Facility at Schriever. This is where America is training real-life Jedi Knights.

What's There: Schriever occupies 3,840 acres and the visible buildings and facilities look like they belong to a Silicon Valley company except for the satellite dishes and communications domes. In addition to the Joint National Test Facility, you'll also find the Jack Swigert Space Operations Facility here (Swigert was command pilot on Apollo 13). Its functions are to manage military satellite operations, remote tracking stations, and other space warfare facilities. The Space Warfare Center and Ballistic Missile Defense Organization are also at Schriever.

Secret Stuff: The big secret here is what space warfare scenarios are being planned at the Joint National Test Facility. From public statements, it is clear that both Air Force officers and civilian Pentagon analysts fear the equivalent of a Pearl Harbor in space, namely a surprise attack on American satellites that could destroy much of the military's communications and navigation capabilities. Such an attack would render many land-based weapons systems (such as missiles) inoperable. Thus, most of the publicly released information about the Joint National Test Facility stresses its role in planning defensive measures. However, a similar attack by the United States against an adversary's military satellites in the event of war would inevitably be as routine as strikes against the adversary's radar installations or military supply lines.

Getting a Look Inside: Schriever does not currently offer public tours.

Getting There: Schriever is located east of the Colorado Springs airport; take the exit for Enoch Road off Highway 94.

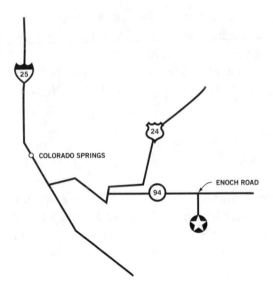

Roads to Schriever Air Force Base, Colorado Springs

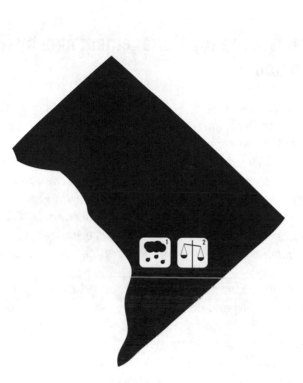

DISTRICT OF COLUMBIA

1. Federal Emergency Management Agency (FEMA), Washington
2. Foreign Intelligence Surveillance Act (FISA) Court, Washington

Federal Emergency Management Agency (FEMA), Washington

When most people think of FEMA, they think of its criminally inept handling of the Hurricane Katrina disaster in 2005. But that was because FEMA is really intended to handle different sorts of "emergencies" in very different ways. In the 1998 film The X-Files: Fight The Future, *the character of scientist Dr. Al Kurtzweil says to David Duchovny's Agent Mulder: "Are you familiar with FEMA? What the Federal Emergency Management Agency's real power is? FEMA allows the White House to suspend constitutional government upon declaration of a national emergency. Think about that, Agent Mulder!"*

The *X-Files* movie got it a little bit wrong: FEMA doesn't allow the White House to suspend constitutional government upon declaration of a national emergency; the President already has the ability to declare a state of national emergency and greatly restrict civil liberties and constitutional government under the provisions National Security Act of 1947. But if the President does declare such a national emergency, it will be FEMA that will be largely responsible for carrying out the President's order.

The Federal Emergency Management Agency is arguably the scariest agency in the whole federal government. Its public face is that of a relief agency for natural disasters such as earthquakes, floods, and hurricanes. However, the bulk of its budget is devoted to national security programs and it operates several programs that are highly classified. Because of its emphasis on classified national security matters, FEMA is largely unprepared to respond to natural disasters. For example, the *Washington Post* reported that the city manager of Homestead, Florida requested that FEMA send 100 handheld radios to assist in communications in the aftermath of 1992's Hurricane Andrew. Instead, FEMA sent several high-tech vans capable of encrypted communications with military aircraft on the other side of the world.

This situation is not really surprising, because FEMA is an outgrowth of the 1950s Civil Defense programs against nuclear attack. FEMA was not created by an act of Congress, but instead by executive order 12148 issued on July 20, 1979 by President Carter. His order consolidated the various provisions of the Federal Civil Defense Act of 1950, the National Security Act of 1947, the Defense Production Act of 1950, the Disaster Relief Act of 1970, the Strategic and Critical Materials Stockpiling Act, and several other emergency acts into a single umbrella agency, FEMA.

The relatively benign names of most of the acts consolidated under FEMA hide their truly radical nature when the president proclaims a national emergency. For example, the Act of August 29, 1916, empowers the president to take possession of any transportation system (including privately owned vehicles) during a national emergency. The Defense Production Act of 1950 allows the president to take control of virtually the entire U.S. economic system in a national emergency and convert it to a highly regulated command economy. Under this act, wages and prices could be fixed and various products rationed to the public (as happened in World War II). And the National Security Act of 1947, among many other things, created the National Security Agency and its massive eavesdropping and surveillance capabilities. Carter's executive order also incorporates various executive orders into FEMA, such as those allowing, if a national emergency is declared by the president, for control of all communication media, relocation of segments of the population, and control of economic and financial activity.

And just who decides what constitutes a "national emergency"? The answer is the President, who has almost unlimited discretion in deciding what constitutes a national emergency. (For example, President Richard Nixon declared a national emergency in 1971 and imposed wage and price controls because he felt the U.S. balance of payments deficit was too high). Once the President has declared a national emergency, Congress can not vote to override the declaration until six months have passed.

A major function of FEMA is administration of the Continuity of Government (COG) program. It operates the various COG centers and facilities around the country, including the now legendary Mount Weather facility in Virginia. One of FEMA's acknowledged tasks is the operation of various COG centers that would house the president and other government officials in the event of a catastrophic event, such as an atomic or biological attack against the United States, a major natural disaster, or a civil insurrection or disturbance so widespread that it would be impossible to carry on government functions from Washington. As a report in the November 18, 1991 *New York Times* stated, "Acting outside the Constitution in the early 1980s, a secret federal agency [FEMA] established a line of succession to the presidency to assure continued government in the event of a devastating nuclear attack, current and former United States officials said today. The program was called 'Continuity of Government.' In the words of a recent report by the Fund for Constitutional Government, 'succession or succession-by-designation would be implemented by unknown and perhaps unelected persons who would pick three potential successor presidents in advance of an emergency. These potential successors to the Oval Office may not be elected, and they are not confirmed by Congress.'"

The COG program had its roots in a nuclear-age possibility that could not have been anticipated when the Constitution was drafted— what would happen if the entire leadership of the federal government was wiped out at once? Suppose a nuclear device is exploded in Washington during the President's annual State of the Union address and the President, Vice President, various Cabinet secretaries, both houses of Congress, and the Supreme Court are all instantly vaporized. Who would be in charge if everyone in the entire line of presidential succession specified in the Constitution got killed?

That is a problem the U.S. has had to consider ever since the development of atomic missiles in the 1950s made that a real possibility. The September 11 attacks actually forced FEMA to implement some of those plans. While the exact contingency plans are still tightly guarded secrets, several sources indicate that FEMA maintains "government in waiting" groups at COG facilities in California, Maryland, and Virginia (see listings for those states). The members of these groups, secretly appointed by the president, would have the rank and perform the duties of various Cabinet officers if a national emergency were declared and those Cabinet officers were killed or otherwise unable to perform their duties. For example, there is a "standby" Secretary of State in these groups; if the actual Secretary of State were killed or incapacitated during a national emergency, this person would assume the duties of that office when so directed by the President.

And that takes us back to our original question: what happens if the President and all Constitutional successors were killed in a sudden attack or other disaster? Various sources indicate that FEMA maintains an "Office of the Presidency" at Mount Weather and possibly other FEMA facilities. If the executive branch of government were suddenly and catastrophically eliminated, a person (or persons) on a list of "standby presidents" would be transported to the nearest FEMA COG facility and act as the chief executive of the United States until such time as normal Constitutional government could be restored.

Who are these "standby presidents"? A 1992 CNN report on FEMA said Howard Baker, Richard Helms, Jeanne Kirkpatrick, James Schlesinger, Richard Thornberg, Ed Meese, Tip O'Neill, and Dick Cheney (who would eventually become Vice President) all served in that role at different times.

Of course, none of this can be definitely confirmed. Any executive orders or presidential directives covering such events would be classified at the highest levels. All we can be certain of, however, is that plans must be in place for such catastrophic events and have probably been in place since the late 1940s.

When attention was focused on FEMA's budget in the wake of its hapless performance in the aftermath of Hurricane Andrew, it was discovered that it was spending 12 times more on "black" national security programs than it was on disaster relief. In the 1982–1992 period, FEMA budgeted $243 million for disaster relief but budgeted $2.9 billion for "black" and classified operations. While that spending ratio dropped during the Clinton years, FEMA still spends the bulk of its budget on classified programs and the proportion has increased since the September 11 attacks.

FEMA and Rex84: During the 1987 Iran-Contra hearings, the following exchange took place between Representative Jack Brooks of Texas, Senator Daniel Inouye of Hawaii, and Brendan Sullivan, attorney for Oliver North, during North's testimony before Congress:

REPRESENTATIVE BROOKS: Colonel North, in your work at the NSC, were you not assigned, at one time, to work on plans for continuity of government in the event of a major disaster?

BRENDAN SULLIVAN: Mister Chairman?

SENATOR INOUYE: I believe that question touches upon a highly sensitive and classified area so I request that you not touch on that.

REPRESENTATIVE BROOKS: I was particularly concerned, Mister Chairman, because I read in Miami papers, and several others, that there had been a plan developed by that same agency, a contingency plan in the event of emergency, that would suspend the American constitution. And I was deeply concerned about it and wondered if that was the area in which he had worked. I believe that it was and I wanted to get his confirmation.

SENATOR INOUYE: May I most respectfully request that this matter not be touched upon at this stage. If we wish to get into this, I'm certain arrangements can be made for an executive session.

Brooks, a crusty, no-nonsense Democrat from Texas, had touched upon what may have been the most incredible, but least discussed, aspects of the entire Iran-Contra investigations: the expansion of FEMA's mandate during the Reagan administration to include capabilities to detain large number of American citizens, similar to the internment of Japanese American citizens in World War II. This was planned during a military planning exercise known as Readiness Exercise 1984, or "Rex84."

Rex84 came about in April 1984, when President Reagan signed Presidential Directive 54. This authorized FEMA to conduct a simulation of a "state of domestic national emergency" that would be declared, under the rules of the simulation, as a result of a U.S. military operation in Central America. Rex84 was conducted on the fifth floor of the FEMA building in Washington under conditions of especially heavy security; new metal security doors were installed on that floor and special identification badges were required of all participants.

The first reports about Rex84 appeared in the *Miami Herald* on July 5, 1987 (this is the report referred to by Representative Brooks). According to the *Herald*, the plan the Rex84 group came up with called for the detention of up to 400,000 undocumented immigrants in internment centers at military bases around the country. (These would eventually become known as the "Rex84 camps.) U.S. military forces, including the National Guard, would be deployed for domestic law enforcement, and state and local military commanders would be appointed to assume control of state and local governments. Rex84 also provided for suspension of the Bill of Rights of the U.S. Constitution for the duration of the national emergency.

Oliver North was responsible for drawing up the Rex84 plan but a faction within the Rex84 group, led by Attorney General William French Smith, vehemently opposed him. As Smith wrote in August 1984 to National Security Council chairman Robert McFarlane, "I believe the role assigned to the Federal Emergency Management Agency in the revised Executive Order exceeds its proper function as a coordinating agency for emergency preparedness. . . This department [Department of Justice] and others have repeatedly raised serious policy and legal objections to the creation of an 'emergency czar' role for FEMA." It is believed that Smith's opposition was instrumental in convincing President Reagan not to issue new executive orders that would have made it possible to implement a scenario like that described in Rex84.

However, it was also reported that 22 new executive orders were drafted that would create the framework for making Rex84 a reality, and these orders are kept in readiness for a future President's signature in case of a national emergency.

One task of the Rex84 exercise was to determine what types of "national emergency" would be of sufficient severity to cause the majority of American people to accept even a temporary suspension of normal Constitutional government. Among the situations identified by the Rex84 group as meeting that criterion would be a nuclear attack, imminent threat of nuclear war, massive terrorist attacks in the United States, simultaneous rioting in major American cities, a widespread natural or environmental disaster, and, interestingly, a severe economic depression that would leave millions unemployed and without adequate financial resources.

Of course, Rex84 was just a planning exercise. Relax.

Key Facilities: FEMA owns 300 Mobile Emergency Response Support (MERS) vehicles. These specially equipped, nuclear-hardened vans are located throughout the United States and are designed to shuttle the president and other high government officials around the country in the event of an emergency and deliver them to COG facilities. These are the same vehicles that so bewildered and exasperated the city manager of Homestead, Florida.

FEMA is also reported to maintain databases of individuals to be detained in the event of a national emergency. The databases are believed to vary according to the cause and nature of the emergency. For example, numerous prominent black leaders and black sympathizers could be interned if urban rioting by blacks triggered a declaration of national emergency. (I suppose the names of wiseass authors of books spilling the beans about FEMA could be in some of those databases as well, but I prefer not to think about that possibility.)

Secret Stuff: Has there ever been a time when a president was ready to declare a national emergency and unleash FEMA? It appears there have been three such cases where that was a serious possibility.

One was in 1990 during the Gulf War. There have been numerous reports that FEMA was in "standby mode" in case there were incidents of domestic terrorism; unconfirmed rumors say plans were in place to intern nationals of various Arab nations and members of groups deemed sympathetic to Iraqi causes. The second was in 1992 during the Los Angeles riots following the Rodney King trial verdict. As the rioting entered its third day and began to spill out of the predominantly black areas of Los Angeles, reports claim there was pressure on President Bush to declare martial law in Los Angeles and to send federal troops into Los Angeles. These reports also say that FEMA would have been activated if the rioting had broken out in other cities and had reached the scope and intensity of the Los Angeles riots.

It is now widely known FEMA was very active in the wake of the September 11, 2001 terrorist attacks, including the movement of numerous high-ranking government officials to COG facilities. It is reasonable to assume the scope of FEMA's mission and capabilities have been greatly increased in the aftermath of the attacks and that it could be activated in the event of future terrorist acts on the scale of September 11.

Getting a Look Inside: FEMA's sites currently offer no public tours. When they want you to see the inside of any of their facilities, they'll know where to find you.

Listening In: If you have a shortwave radio capable of receiving upp[er] sideband (USB) transmissions, try listening to 10493 kHz during the daytime and to 5211 kHz at night. These are the common shortwave frequencies used by FEMA facilities across the country for their "national emergency coordination network," and they often have on-the-air drills and exercises. Listen for the call sign WGY912—that's the FEMA headquarters station.

Getting There: FEMA's headquarters is at 500 C Street SW in Washington.

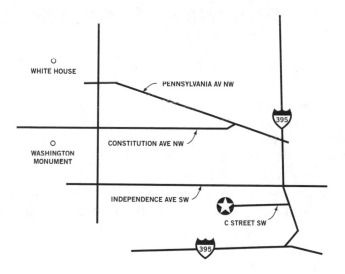

Roads to Federal Emergency Management Agency (FEMA), Washington

Foreign Intelligence Surveillance Act (FISA) Court, Washington

It is a court whose actions may result in criminal charges against Americans. However, this court meets in secret, its rulings are kept secret even from those who are accused of crimes, it authorizes more wiretaps and surreptitious physical searches than the rest of the entire federal judiciary, and you can be its target even if you are not suspected of any criminal activity yourself—for example, you may be targeted if you happen to work for the same office as a suspected spy or if you belong to any organization suspected of being linked to "terrorists." The vast majority of persons whose phones and homes are bugged as a result of its actions, or whose homes are broken into and searched, are unaware of what happened. This is, in effect, the Top Secret Government's Supreme Court.

The Foreign Intelligence Surveillance Act (FISA) of 1978 was partly a response to widespread revelations that the federal government, especially the FBI and CIA, had for years been engaged in widespread domestic surveillance, including wiretaps and physical entries (remember Watergate?). Civil rights and antiwar organizations, and their leaders, had been frequent targets of such surveillance. FISA was an attempt to curb such abuses and restrict surveillance activities to legitimate cases involving foreign espionage; all such surveillance activities would require a warrant and be subject to approval by a panel of judges serving on a "FISA Court." Originally, the FISA Court could only authorize electronic surveillance for the purpose of information gathering. Its powers have now been expanded to include surreptitious physical entry and searches, and evidence gathered can now be used in criminal prosecutions—neither was contemplated when FISA was passed into law.

A warrant request to the FISA Court does not require the government to state a probable cause for the surveillance or search. The subjects of the warrant are not notified. Any evidence produced against someone as a result of a FISA warrant is classified and cannot be reviewed or challenged by the subject or defense attorneys. The very fact that one is the target of surveillance under FISA is likewise a secret unless the individual is eventually indicted or called to testify. You may be caught in a FISA sweep even if you are not suspected of any crime yourself. For example, in 1988 Vernon Bellecourt, Bill Means, and Bob Brown were called before a grand jury investigating a group called the Peoples Committee for Libyan Students; it turned out that the subpoenas issued to them were the result of them having each made a phone call to a person who was a member of that group, and those phone calls were intercepted under a FISA warrant.

History: The original Foreign Intelligence Surveillance Act was introduced in Congress in 1976. It was sponsored by Senator Ted Kennedy and endorsed by President Gerald Ford. After several modifications, President Jimmy Carter eventually signed the bill into law in 1978. For the first time, FISA required agencies like the National Security Agency (NSA) to obtain a warrant through judicial review before conducting any electronic surveillance related to espionage in the United States. However, FISA made significant concessions to the NSA, CIA, and FBI. Traditional applications for warrants to conduct electronic eavesdropping (such as those targeting organized crime figures) require presenting evidence to establish probable cause that a crime is being committed. Under FISA, that test is thrown out the window when the surveillance is needed on the grounds of "national security interests." However, the term "national security interests" is nebulously defined in FISA; it was written that way so judges could have wide latitude in interpreting it.

The FISA Court was not part of the original FISA legislation. It was created in 1979 when President Carter issued executive order 12139. In his order, Carter declared the court was to consist of seven federal judges, each serving a single, non-renewable seven-year term. Membership is staggered so that one member is replaced each year. Members are chosen from the different federal judicial districts, although one member must come from the Washington, DC federal district court. The executive order also established a separate FISA appeals court to hear any appeals of warrant requests denied by the seven-member court.

The Attorney General must approve each application to the FISA Court for a warrant. Approved warrants authorize surveillance of U.S.

citizens for 90 days and one year for foreign nationals; all requests to date for extensions of these time periods have been granted.

Expansion of FISA Powers: In 1995, Congress passed the Intelligence Authorization Act that greatly expanded the scope of FISA. The original act did not authorize physical entries to conduct physical searches, but the new legislation did. Further, the 1995 legislation also allowed FISA surveillance and searches to be used to gather information for criminal prosecutions instead of just for information. However, all information gathered under FISA surveillance or search would be classified and kept from the court record and defendant(s). This meant, for example, that U.S. citizens charged with crimes based upon evidence gathered under FISA, and their attorneys, could not review the evidence against them or see the warrant authorizing the search and surveillance. The evidence is also kept from the jurors—but it can be used against the defendant at trial.

An example of such a Kafkaesque scenario took place during the trial of Richard Johnson, a Boston-area radar engineer convicted of "possession of contraband in aid of foreign insurgents." Johnson was accused of helping to design a fuse to be used in anti-helicopter missiles by the Irish Republican Army. Johnson had been the target of a FISA wiretap prior to his arrest. At Johnson's trial, the presiding judge told the jury that evidence against Johnson existed but could not be presented to them because of national security reasons, and that the jury would have to rely upon the judge's "testimony" that such evidence indeed existed! Not only were Johnson's attorneys unable to examine this evidence for themselves, they could not even challenge the judge's assertion that it existed.

Getting a Look Inside: Dream on!

Unusual Fact: The FISA Court can issue search warrants based upon "national security interests" instead of requiring the agency requesting the warrant to state a "probable cause" for the search. But doesn't that explicitly violate the Fourth Amendment to the U.S. Constitution, which says:

"The right of the people to be secure in their persons, houses, papers, and effects, against unreasonable searches and seizures, shall not be violated and no Warrants shall issue, but upon probable cause, supported by Oath or affirmation, and particularly describing the place to be searched, and the persons or things to be seized."

Guess what—it sure as hell does violate the Fourth Amendment! But don't bother complaining to the Supreme Court. The Chief Justice appoints the members of the FISA Court, so the Supreme Court is already well aware of this shitcanning of the Constitution—and, apparently, they don't care.

Getting There: The FISA Court meets in a secure room on the top floor of the Department of Justice building, 950 Pennsylvania Avenue, in Washington. The room is windowless and secured from unauthorized access.

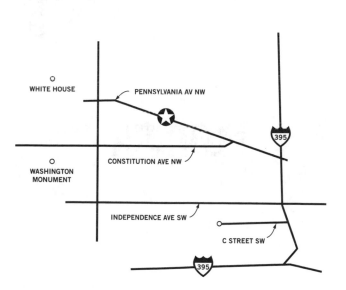

Roads to Foreign Intelligence Surveillance Act (FISA) Court, Washington

FLORIDA

1. Wackenhut Corporation, Palm Beach Gardens

Wackenhut Corporation, Palm Beach Gardens

Whether it's guarding missile silos or Area 51, Wackenhut is one of those companies the Top Secret Government calls when it needs someone else to do its dirty work.

Wackenhut Corporation was formed in 1954 by George Wackenhut, a former FBI agent who was a close friend of Florida politicians, including Senator George Smathers (himself a close friend of President Kennedy) and Governor Claude Kirk. Wackenhut was able to use those connections to obtain a contract for his company to provide security services at Cape Canaveral. Another contract quickly followed to provide security for Titan missile silos around the country. Before long, Wackenhut was the largest supplier of security services to the federal government. It protected embassies in 13 countries, including Chile, Greece, and El Salvador. It also protected the Alaskan oil pipeline, the Savannah River Plant and Hanford nuclear weapons facilities, the Strategic Petroleum Reserve, the Nevada Test Site, and an isolated facility in Nevada that would later become famous as Area 51.

Throughout its history, Wackenhut's board of directors has been a who's who of the military-industrial complex. Among its members have been Captain Eddie Rickenbacker, General Mark Clark, former FBI director Clarence Kelley, former Secretary of Defense Frank Carlucci, former Secret Service director James Rowley, and former CIA director Bobby Ray Inman. Needless to say, such board members have been a major part of Wackenhut's success in securing lucrative government contracts.

George Wackenhut liked to collect data on Americans suspected of being Communist sympathizers or just leaning to the left. In 1965, the Wackenhut Corporation went public, and in its initial public offering documents filed with the Securities and Exchange Commission, the company boasted of maintaining files on 2.5 million Americans—that is, a file on one out of 46 Americans over the age of 18 then living. After Congress held hearings in 1975 on companies holding snoop files on Americans, Wackenhut donated its files to the Church

League of America, a now-defunct anti-Communist group based in Wheaton, Illinois.

In 1976, Congressional hearings chaired by Senator Frank Church of Idaho forced the CIA to abandon its practice of setting up dummy "front" companies in the United States to carry out various activities. In response, the CIA began to contract with companies like Wackenhut to perform tasks done by CIA fronts. Wackenhut soon gained a reputation as one of the companies the CIA called when it wanted something done. "I don't have the slightest doubt that the CIA and Wackenhut overlap," said Philip Agee, a former CIA agent turned author. William Hinshaw, a retired FBI special agent, said, "It is known throughout the industry that if you want a dirty job done, you call Wackenhut."

For much of the Reagan administration, those "dirty jobs" were in Central America. In 1981, Wackenhut formed a new Special Projects Division headed by George Berckmans, a former CIA agent assigned to the Mexico City CIA station. Wackenhut's expansion into Central America was rapid and large; in 1985, Wackenhut had over 1500 employees in El Salvador alone. And Wackenhut employees were seen in the company of people like Eden Pastora, the military leader of the Nicaraguan Contras.

Wackenhut was also involved in some very curious activities in the United States. The September 1992 issue of *Spy* magazine carried a report of some strange goings-on involving Wackenhut in the winter of 1990. David Ramirez, a member of the company's special investigations division, was sent, along with three other members of the division, to San Antonio from their headquarters in Miami. in San Antonio, they rented two Ford Tauruses and drove four hours to the Mexican border town of Eagle Pass. After night fell, they met two truck drivers and then went to a warehouse where an 18-wheel tractor-trailer was waiting. Ramirez's instructions were simple: do not look inside the trailer, secure it, and make sure it got to Chicago. Armed with shotguns, the Wackenhut personnel escorted the truck north. They drove for 30 consecutive hours, stopping only for food and fuel. They eventually drove the truck to an empty warehouse near Chicago, where others took possession of it and told the Wackenhut personnel to fly home to Miami. Ramirez's superiors told him the truck contained $40 million in food stamps; other special investigations division employees told him they had made similar runs from the Mexican border.

However, Ramirez found the "food stamps" story unbelievable due to the secrecy and high-level of security, and he eventually talked to reporters after leaving Wackenhut. In its report, *Spy* magazine queried the Department of Agriculture, who emphatically denied that any food stamps were ever shipped in such a way nor was there any food stamp printing, distribution, or storage facility in Eagle Pass (moreover, food stamps are shipped from metropolitan areas to rural areas, not vice versa). *Spy* theorized the shipments were components used in the manufacture of chemical weapons, and that the components were destined for Iraq. Whatever the shipments were, they were clearly something of a clandestine or contraband nature.

After the election of President Clinton, Wackenhut began scaling back its government security operations and, it must be assumed, its other government services. They did not renew their contracts to provide security to the Nevada Test Site and Area 51, for example (these were taken over by EG&G). Instead, Wackenhut began expanding its "corrections" business, and now is the largest operator of privately-run prisons in the United States. Reportedly, this is a more lucrative business than providing security services, although some believe Wackenhut realized those contracts would be coming to an end because of the company's close ties to previous Republican administrations. But Wackenhut was back in the government security business in a big way after the September 11 attacks. Wackenhut landed several new contracts for security at various government installations and assumed several high-profile civilian security duties, such as stops and inspections of vehicles (especially large ones such as trucks and recreational vehicles) crossing Hoover Dam south of Las Vegas. Wackenhut employees worked on both the Nevada and Arizona sides of the dam, manning roadblocks and selecting vehicles for more intensive secondary inspections. The Wackenhut employees wore official-looking uniforms resembling those worn by state troopers, complete with impressive arm patches reading "Wackenhut."

You didn't know private security employees could stop people on public highways and inspect their vehicles? Hey, they can when they're working for Wackenhut!

Secret Stuff: On March 30, 1999, Wackenhut and Raytheon Aerospace entered into a consent judgment totaling $8 million to settle a lawsuit brought against them by AGES, an aircraft servicing business that was competing against Raytheon Aerospace for a U.S. military aircraft maintenance contract valued at $450 million. AGES claimed Raytheon Aerospace hired Wackenhut to spy on AGES to determine what was in the sealed, confidential bid that was submitted to the military. While the settlement was reached before the case went to trial, depositions from six eyewitnesses stated that Wackenhut investigators were staking out the AGES offices in parked cars and were observed wearing headphones and taking notes. The witnesses reported seeing tape recorders, parabolic and "shotgun" microphones, and various electronic equipment in the car. One of the eyewitnesses reported what appeared to be a flat, oval-shaped antenna mounted behind a sun visor in one of the cars; expert witnesses for AGES identified these as antennas often used to receive signals from short-range bugging devices. Two witnesses reported seeing a woman walk out of the AGES offices with papers in her hand, meet with the Wackenhut investigators at their car, and then drive away in her car, with the Wackenhut investigators following her. Shortly after this happened, AGES discovered that documents were missing from their offices.

In settling the suit, Wackenhut admitted no guilt, but paid several million dollars to AGES.

Getting a Look Inside: There are no tours of the Wackenhut headquarters building. However, you can order genuine Wackenhut caps and tee shirts from their website!

Unusual Fact: George Wackenhut once called the first President Bush "pink," proving that, no matter what else you may say about him, Mr. Wackenhut was a discerning judge of character.

Getting There: Wackenhut's corporate headquarters is located at 4200 Wackenhut Drive in Palm Beach Gardens. The building is along Interstate 95, just south of the intersection with PGA Boulevard, and is easily visible from the highway.

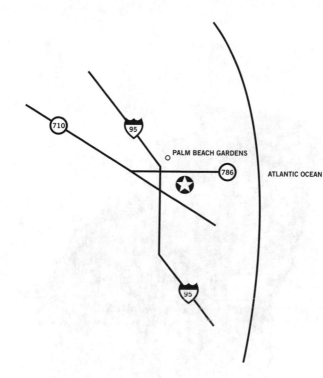

PALM BEACH GARDENS

ATLANTIC OCEAN

Roads to Wackenhut Corporation, Palm Beach Gardens

GEORGIA

1. Regional Security Operations Center, Fort Gordon
2. Western Hemisphere Institute for Security Cooperation/School of the Americas, Fort Benning

Regional Security Operations Center, Fort Gordon

Don't let the bland name fool you. The Regional Security Operations Center (RSOC) at Fort Gordon is a facility shared by the various armed services to perform intelligence and cryptological tasks under the direction of the National Security Agency. In other words, this is perhaps the biggest concentration of military spooks and spies in the world.

Fort Gordon is the home of the U.S. Army Signal Corps, making it a logical place to locate a center for signal interceptions and intelligence, code-breaking, and interpretation. The Regional Security Operations Center (RSOC) includes personnel from each branch of the military, civilian Department of Defense employees, and National Security Agency (NSA) personnel. The main purposes of the RSOC are to supply intelligence data to the various armed services and to train military and civilian personnel in intelligence and cryptological techniques. Approximately 1,000 military and civilian personnel are assigned to RSOC. Fort Gordon itself occupies 56,000 acres near Augusta.

What's There: The 513th Military Intelligence Brigade, operated by the Army, is a mobile intelligence service that can be quickly dispatched to any location in the world. In peacetime, about 10% of this brigade is deployed overseas. The Naval Security Group Activity specializes in signals interception and intelligence-gathering from the world's navies. The 201st Military Intelligence Battalion specializes in signal interception analysis, while the 202nd Military Intelligence Battalion specializes in human intelligence, interrogation, and document analysis. The 297th Military Intelligence Battalion performs, in its words, "strategic all-source fusion intelligence support that includes targeting, collection management, and production to war-fighting commanders." The 31st Intelligence Squadron performs signal intercepts and gathers intelligence on the world's air forces. Company D, Marine Support Battalion, trains U.S. Marines in signals intelligence and cryptography. In addition, there are several smaller military intelligence and cryptological units here.

Key Facilities: The good stuff here is kept away from prying eyes (like yours) inside the secured buildings at Fort Gordon.

Secret Stuff: RSOC at Fort Gordon is where the NSA keeps tabs on signal intercepts and electronic surveillance of Latin America. In other words, this is where the NSA tracks Castro's phone calls, faxes sent by Colombian drug lords, and radio traffic from ships sailing the Gulf of Mexico.

Getting a Look Inside: The Signal Corps Museum in Regimental Hall is open to the public. While there is nothing directly pertaining to RSOC on display, it does have the largest collection of communications equipment and material, both American and foreign, in the United States. It is open 7:30 a.m. to 5 p.m. Tuesday through Friday and 10 a.m. to 4 p.m. on Saturday. Admission is free.

Getting There: From Interstate 20 near Augusta, take Exit 194 to Belair Road and Dyess Parkway. Turn onto Dyess Parkway and follow the Fort Gordon signs.

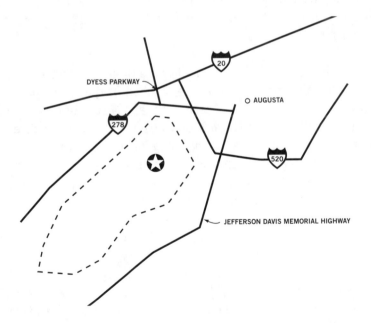

Roads to Regional Security Operations Center, Fort Gordon

Western Hemisphere Institute for Security Cooperation/ School of the Americas, Fort Benning

Headquarters for the renamed School of the Americas, this is where the U.S. Army trains soldiers from Latin American nations in combat, counter-insurgency, and anti-drug trafficking techniques. However, many graduates have put their new skills to use in some of the worst human rights abuses in recent years.

The U.S. Army's School of the Americas (SOA) was established in 1963 to combat the spread of communism in Latin America. To do so, it trained combat soldiers and military officers from Latin American nations in such useful skills as guerrilla combat techniques, counter-insurgency methods, and anti-narcotics operations. Among its more than 60,000 graduates were such distinguished alumni as Manuel Noriega and Omar Torrijos of Panama, Leopoldo Galtieri and Roberto Viola of Argentina, Juan Velasco Alvarado of Peru, Guillermo Rodriguez of Ecuador, and Hugo Banzer Suarez of Bolivia. Perhaps a bit embarrassed to have trained some of the worst dictators in Latin American history, the SOA "closed" on January 17, 2001 and was "replaced" by the Western Hemisphere Institute for Security Cooperation. The Institute is merely the old School of the Americas with a new name; it uses the same facilities and trainers as the School of the Americas and offers the same basic courses, although there have been some new classes on human rights added in response to Congressional pressure. All students at the "new" Institute will be required to have eight hours of classroom instruction in basic human rights.

However, it was more than just famous dictators that gave the School of the Americas such a bad reputation. There have been numerous incidents in which soldiers, fresh from their training at the School, have returned home and committed some of the worst human rights violations in this hemisphere, from El Salvador to Paraguay to Haiti to Mexico. Many of these abuses occurred in counter-insurgency operations and often involved killing of unarmed civilians, torture of suspects, and rape. Numerous SOA graduates have also been linked to the drug trade, where their military skills have been put to use against their competitors. It was for this reason that SOA became known as the "school of the assassins" by its critics.

What's There: The School of the Americas/Western Hemisphere Institute for Security Cooperation is a small part of Fort Benning, which is the headquarters of the U.S. Army infantry and also used for basic training and paratrooper jump school.

Among the classes offered at the Institute are advanced combat arms, psychological operations, intelligence-gathering, and commando tactics.

Key Facilities: The main facility used by the Institute/SOA is Ridgway Hall. This building includes classrooms, office space, and related training facilities. Additional training, such as in commando operations, is conducted elsewhere at Fort Benning.

The John B. Amos Library holds 21,000 volumes, over 90% of which are in Spanish, many on the subjects taught here. While you have to be associated with the Institute to check out materials, everyone was allowed to use the library prior to the September 11 attacks (local high school students studying Spanish often dropped by to read newspapers and magazines from Latin American nations). The library is in room 257 of Ridgway Hall.

Secret Stuff: So what were the textbooks like at the old School of the Americas? Here is an excerpt from one titled *Handling of Sources*. It was used in an intelligence-gathering course, and was originally classified as "SECRET." It was declassified by the Secretary of the Army in 1996.

The following section dealt with the tricky problem of how to "fire" a paid informant who might then, out of anger, compromise the intelligence operation. In particular, note technique 4) below:

c. There are many techniques that could be used to force an employee to accept the separation or to neutralize him to such a degree that he does not constitute a threat to the intelligence effort of the government. Some of the suggested techniques are shown below:

1) Must use the fact that his pay has been exempt of taxes. Depending on the urgency of getting rid of the employee, he could be threatened of being revealed or exposed. Naturally you do not appear as the accuser of taxes. A more subtle means is by means of an anonymous tip to tax authorities that the employee has a source of income that has not been declared. They will investigate the employee and that will achieve his fall. The agent must not meddle in this investigation, even though he must coordinate with them.

2) Another method that could be used, if the employee is receiving illegally goods as compensation, such as foreign cigarettes, liquor or coffee, the agent informs secretly the custom authorities just after the employee receives his goods.

3) In inducing the employee to commit an illegal act for which he could be held responsible could prove effective, especially if the agent can maintain control of the situation in such a way that he could use it as a lever to obtain control of the individual.

4) If the insurrection advances to last phases and the guerrillas dominate certain areas that create borders, there is a series of things that could be done, especially if the main thing is to get rid of him and it is not important if he talks with the guerrillas or not. Changing his identification in a way that he could not pass verifications by the guerrilla security elements, sending him on a especially dangerous mission for which he has been inadequately prepared, or pass information to guerrilla security elements are methods that could be used.

Getting a Look Inside: As part of the Institute's effort to be more open than the old SOA, visitors were actually encouraged prior to the September 11 attacks. Exact hours of admittance varied, but were usually during normal working hours on weekdays. The main entrance to Fort Benning will be able to give more information about current visiting procedures.

Unusual Facts: The new slogan used by the Western Hemisphere Institute for Security Cooperation is "building a better future with our democratic neighbors." They also plan to offer courses via the Internet in the near future.

Getting There: Fort Benning is located ten miles south of Columbus at the end of Interstate I-185. Turn right at the stop light, and then left at the welcome center.

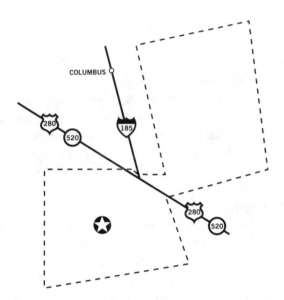

Roads to Western Hemisphere Institute for Security Cooperation/ School of the Americas, Fort Benning

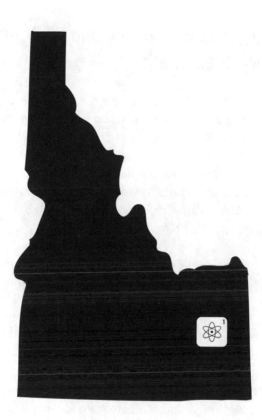

IDAHO

1.Idaho National Engineering and Environmental Laboratory, Idaho Falls

Idaho National Engineering and Environmental Laboratory, Idaho Falls

Since its founding in 1949, 52 nuclear reactors—the largest concentration of nuclear reactors in the world—have been operated here. Currently, there are three reactors in operation and research is being conducted into the next generation of nuclear reactors. Other activities include research into nuclear waste management and cleanup, radiation sensors and monitors, and, since September 11, 2001, "science-based, innovative solutions to the nation's homeland security challenges," as their official literature says.

The Idaho National Engineering and Environmental Laboratory (INEEL) was established because a remote site was needed to test nuclear reactors. Among the tests conducted were intentionally operating reactors past their design limits and pushing them into meltdown; over two dozen reactors suffered that fate. In 1951, the first electricity generated by nuclear power was produced here. The first reactors intended for propulsion of ships and submarines were also designed at INEEL. While only three reactors were in operation when this book was written, a dozen reactors are still capable of operation.

In the 1970s, INEEL's mission was expanded to include nuclear non-proliferation activities such as improved nuclear materials detection and sensing technologies. In the 1990s, research began into methods of detecting the production, storage, and transport of chemical and biological agents. In the wake of the September 11 attacks, several new programs were launched at INEEL for the new Department of Homeland Security. These included ways of protecting critical infrastructure (such as dams, power generation and distribution, water treatment and distribution, etc.), damage mitigation (such as advanced firefighting techniques and cleanup methods in the wake of a chemical or biological attack), and ways to reduce vulnerability of structures to various attacks. However, some of the "counterterrorism" research is in such areas as tracking transfer of large amounts of cash, which—as INEEL's website cheerfully boasts—"will serve as a powerful tool to eliminate drug trafficking."

INEEL is operated for the Department of Energy by Bechtel BWXT Idaho, a division of Bechtel (see listing under CALIFORNIA).

What's There: INEEL sprawls across an 890-square-mile site located 32 miles west of Idaho Falls. In addition to the previously mentioned reactors, there is a supercomputing center, numerous engineering and research buildings, DOE operations facilities, and managerial and administrative office complexes. There's also a lot of really nasty waste materials here, such as over two million gallons of highly radioactive liquids in underground tanks and over 250 tons of highly radioactive heavy metals stored in underground pools. Both of these are stored above the Snake River aquifer, which supplies drinking water to over 250,000 homes in Idaho. The DOE is currently under a court order to remove these materials and is trying to figure out what to do with them.

Getting a Look Inside: While there are no regularly scheduled tours of INEEL, invited visitors and those on official business are processed at the Engineering and Research Operations Building located at 2525 North Fremont Avenue, near the intersection with Science Center Drive. INEEL also occasionally sponsors public events at or near the INEEL site and Idaho Falls.

Unusual Fact: In common with other nuclear-related sites, some long-time employees at INEEL have developed chronic problems with their immune, muscular, and skeletal systems. And of course DOE denies any connection between these mysterious disorders and prolonged exposure to higher-than-normal levels of radiation.

Getting There: INEEL can be reached by taking either Highway 26 or 20 northwest from Interstate 15 south of Idaho Falls; both roads will enter INEEL's territory. The Engineering and Research Operations Building can be accessed by taking Highway 20.

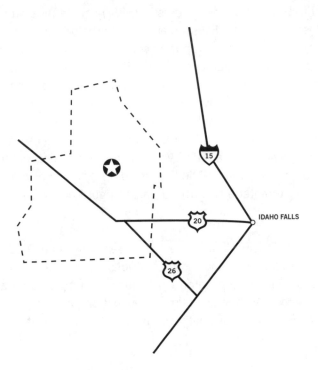

Roads to Idaho National Engineering and Environmental Laboratory, Idaho Falls

KENTUCKY

1. Paducah Gaseous Diffusion Plant, Paducah

Paducah Gaseous Diffusion Plant, Paducah

There's more than just moonshine brewing in the hills of Kentucky. Since 1952, the Paducah Gaseous Diffusion Plant has been cranking out enriched uranium for use in reactors and bombs. It's also been a de facto nuclear landfill over the years, and arguably this is one of the most "nuclear polluted" areas in the United States.

The Paducah Gaseous Diffusion Plant (PGDP) was originally created to produce enriched uranium for nuclear weapons. In the mid-1960s, it began to produce enriched uranium for nuclear power plants and recycling used nuclear reactor fuel rods. Today PGDP employs about 1,400 people and focuses solely on enriched uranium for use in reactors instead of weapons. One of its biggest sources of uranium for processing now comes from former Soviet nuclear warheads.

When PGDP was first opened, local residents welcomed it as a source of well-paying, stable jobs; the historically poor Paducah area had a surge of welcome prosperity as a result of PGDP. The unprocessed uranium arrived in the form of a dusty powder before it was processed into reactor fuel or bomb material. The working conditions were hot and dusty, but workers were told the enriched uranium processed at PGDP was relatively benign for radioactive material. To drive that point home, some supervisors sprinkled green "uranium dust" on sandwiches and ate them. Workers were also told that any ingested uranium dust would quickly be eliminated from the body through the urine.

But something started happening in the 1970s—workers at the plant began developing various cancers and dying at rates far above the national average. And it wasn't until a few years later that workers learned that the dust they worked with and inhaled contained far more dangerous radioactive material: plutonium.

A 1999 investigation by the *Washington Post* revealed that workers exposed to the dust with plutonium were typically "protected" only by cotton gloves and overalls; respiratory protection was optional and usually not used. There were no showers or changing facilities, so workers brought the plutonium-contaminated dust home with them. (According to the *Post*, workers would often find the dust on their bedsheets and furniture.) Unaware of the risks, workers would shovel or wash any spilled powder into the nearest drain or ditch. Other radioactive debris was simply dumped in the woods around the PGDP.

How bad was the plutonium contamination at PGDP? The exact levels, and the extent of the affected areas, have been the subject of numerous lawsuits. It is known that levels as high as 500 picocuries of plutonium were found in certain areas of the plant grounds.

And the Department of Energy has determined that the maximum safe exposure to plutonium without protective clothing, including breathing protection, is just 5 picocuries.

Some of the plutonium dust got into groundwater and several areas, including campgrounds and streams, adjacent to PGDP are still considered unsafe. In the wake of this revelation, massive cleanup efforts were begun and most areas at or near PGDP are now within safety limits. But that is of little consolation to those who lost family members to cancers during the 1970s and 1980s.

What's There: PGDP consists of over 160 separate buildings, including four "process buildings" that are over 1,000 feet long, 900 feet wide, and 90 feet high; it's inside these buildings that uranium enrichment operations are performed. Over 400 miles of piping is contained inside the four main process buildings. The PGDP buildings occupy 750 acres and the entire site (including contaminated areas) totals over 3,400 acres.

Getting a Look Inside: PGDP offers no tours of the site itself, but you can visit their Environmental Information Center at 115 Memorial Drive in Paducah; take exit 7 from Interstate 24.

Unusual Fact: Beginning in the early 1980s, workers at PGDP began reporting a blue glow or "fire" from a burial pit used for radioactive discarded reactor and weapons parts. The glow was seen most often after heavy rains, and the pit was covered by earth. In its October 25, 2000 issue, the *Louisville Courier-Journal* reported that it had obtained a memo written by Ray Carroll, a health physicist employed at Paducah. In his memo, Carroll said the blue glow could be caused by a spontaneous, low-level nuclear fission reaction. "If the cause is a fission source," Carroll added, "personnel entering the area could potentially receive a lethal dose of radiation." Don Seaborg, the DOE manager at Paducah, discounted the possibility of a fission event being the cause of the blue glow and instead said spontaneously igniting metals in the pit, such as uranium or aluminum, were a more likely cause.

Just spontaneously igniting uranium—well, that's a relief!

Getting There: PGDP is located approximately ten miles west of Paducah. Take Exit 3 from Interstate 24 onto Highway 358 and continue approximately eight miles to the intersection with Highway 996.

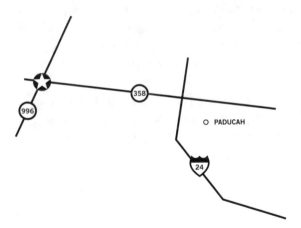

Roads to Paducah Gaseous Diffusion Plant, Paducah

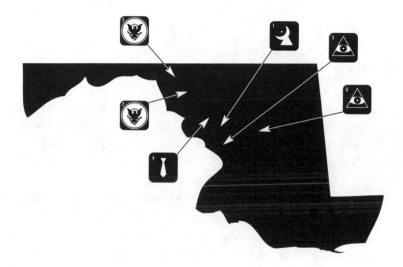

MARYLAND

1. Alternate National Warning Facility, Olney 2. Continuity of Government Facility, Boonsboro 3. Continuity of Government Facility, Hagerstown 4. EG&G, Gaithersburg 5. National Geospatial Intelligence Agency, Bethesda   6. National Security Agency, Fort George Meade

Alternate National Warning Facility, Olney

Manned 24 hours a day, this is FEMA's backup facility to Mt. Weather. In the event of a national emergency, this facility could be used to issue warnings and official announcements. It is also FEMA's main radio communications facility.

The National Warning System (NWS) was created in the 1950s to alert the nation in the event of a nuclear attack. With the establishment of FEMA, NWS's responsibilities were expanded to include all emergency situations, such as natural disasters. Nonetheless, the charter of NWS says its functions are "to support the military effort; to ensure continuity of Federal authority at national and regional levels; and to ensure survival as a free and independent nation under all emergency conditions, including a national emergency caused by threatened or actual attack on the United States." In short, this facility is a part of various Continuity of Government (COG) programs. It backs up the main COG operations at Mt. Weather and also serves as the hub of FEMA's national radio communications network.

What's There: It is known that much of this installation is located underground; rumors say it has anywhere from two to 20 levels underground. Numerous antenna towers and satellite dishes are visible from the air, indicating there is transmitting and receiving equipment at the site. It can also be assumed there must be backup generating systems and other power supplies. Persons who worked on upgrading the facility in the mid-1980s reported there were also offices and barracks inside. While the facility appears a bit neglected from the road, it is actually a high-security installation; trespassers will be stopped and run the risk of arrest.

Getting a Look Inside: Dream on!

Listening In: The call sign of the station here is WGY903, and it is the network control station for FEMA's "national emergency coordination network." If you have a shortwave radio capable of receiving upper sideband (USB) transmissions, try listening to 10493 kHz during the daytime and to 5211 kHz at night. These are the common shortwave frequencies used by FEMA facilities across the country for their on-the-air drills and exercises. As network control, WGY903 will determine which stations will transmit and what messages, if any, they can transmit to other stations.

Unusual Fact: This was a Nike missile site before it became a FEMA facility, so there must be at least two levels underground here because all Nike sites had a minimum of two underground levels.

Getting There: The entrance is at 5321 Riggs Road, off of Route 108, between Olney and Laytonsville.

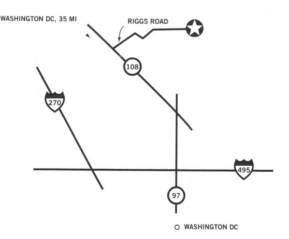

Roads to Alternate National Warning Facility, Olney

Continuity of Government Facility, Boonsboro

Clearly visible from several roads in the Boonsboro area is a FEMA Continuity of Government (COG) facility. This facility is located atop Lambs Knoll and is believed to be intended for housing civilian second-tier government officials (such as cabinet department undersecretaries) instead of senior-level officials.

The Continuity of Government program built a "ring" of fallout shelters around Washington for the use of government personnel in case of a nuclear war. These shelters were intended to house essential government officials and necessary support staff. Unlike the legendary Mount Weather in Virginia, none of these "secondary" shelters were designed to withstand a direct nuclear hit but instead were meant to provide protection against radioactive fallout.

What's There: From aerial observations, we know that the road from the gate proceeds to what appears to be a large farm silo. (On U.S. Geological Survey maps of the area, this is indicated to be a fire lookout, although it is clearly not that.) There are also several collapsible antenna masts. No additional aboveground structures are visible, so the bulk of this facility must be underground. There is a concrete helicopter landing pad a few hundred yards away from the "silo." From the air, people wearing what appear to be blue jumpsuits have been observed; it is not clear what duties (security, maintenance, etc.) these people perform.

This interior of this facility is believed to be very similar to the Mount Pony COG facility that was decommissioned in 1992. That would include shared bedrooms for high-ranking officials and shared "hot bunks" for the rank and file; the maximum number of people that can be accommodated here is believed to be in the low hundreds. Food, basic medical supplies, defensive weapons, and communications equipment are also certainly here.

Getting a Look Inside: There is no public admittance to this facility and trespassing is prohibited, although there are no warning signs other than "private." The front gate is electrically operated but unmanned.

Getting There: The facility can best be seen from southeast of Boonsboro on Highways 67, 17, or 40 Alternate; the closest public road is Reno Monument Road and the access road to the facility; the access road begins near a monument to General Jesse Reno, a Civil War hero. The area is known locally as Fox's Gap.

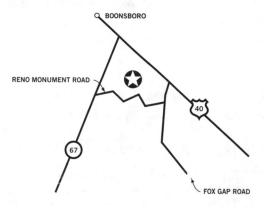

Roads to Continuity of Government Facility, Boonsboro

Continuity of Government Facility, Hagerstown

Southeast of Hagerstown is another FEMA Continuity of Government (COG) facility. This facility is also believed to be intended for housing civilian second-tier government officials (such as cabinet department undersecretaries) instead of senior-level officials.

Like the Boonsboro facility, this is part of the fallout shelters built around Washington in the 1950s and 1960s to house essential government personnel and support staff in case of a nuclear war.

What's There: This facility is believed to be very similar to the Boonsboro facility described previously.

Getting a Look Inside: There is no public admittance to this facility and trespassing is prohibited.

Getting There: This facility is located in a wooded area between Highways 66 and 17; the access road is not marked from either highway but is locked and marked with "no trespassing" signs.

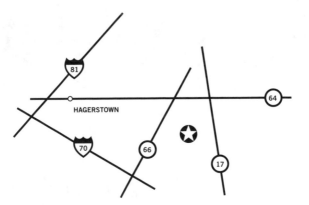

Roads to Continuity of Government Facility, Hagerstown

EG&G, Gaithersburg

EG&G is one of the Top Secret Government's favorite companies. It provides high-tech products (like X-ray security devices) and what are nebulously called "asset management services" to the Department of Energy, NASA, the Department of Defense, etc. But EG&G also does stuff like provide the security for Area 51 and run the airline that flies workers from Las Vegas to Area 51.

Edgerton, Germeshausen & Grier (EG&G) is a company that was born in the early days of the Top Secret Government. Harold Edgerton, a professor at the Massachusetts Institute of Technology, developed the "strobe light" techniques of high-speed photogtaphy in 1931. He formed a consulting business with a former MIT student, Ken Germeshausen, to commercialize the process. Later they added another former MIT student, Herbert Grier, to the consulting business.

During the Manhattan Project, the nascent Top Secret Government realized it needed a method to photograph the different stages of an atomic explosion. They turned to Edgerton, Germeshausen, and Grier, and the memorable sequence of photos of the first atomic bomb test in 1945 were all taken by equipment they designed and installed. Soon the three incorporated as EG&G and were busy photographing atomic tests in Nevada and the Pacific. They won additional government contracts to develop instrumentation to monitor atomic tests and provide support services for nuclear weapons testing and manufacturing. EG&G went public in 1959 and began to acquire additional companies, such as Reynolds Electrical and Engineering (REECo), which for years was the prime contractor at the Nevada Test Site. In 1993, EG&G won a major contract to provide management and technical support for the Kennedy Space Center and the Space Shuttle program, including security, fueling, testing of the Shuttle's systems, and managing Kennedy Space Center during Shuttle flights.

EG&G never strayed far from its Top Secret roots. Beginning in the 1960s, it started providing security services for various government facilities, including the Nevada Test Site and what became known as Area 51. As Area 51 grew, EG&G began operating its own airline, known as "Janet Airlines," to shuttle workers between their homes in Las Vegas and Area 51. Janet flights later expanded to include routes between Las Vegas and the Tonopah Test Range in Nevada as well as Plant 42 in Palmdale, California.

As EG&G grew, it became involved in more civilian engineering and research projects. Among its discoveries was the prostate-specific antigen (PSA) test for early detection of prostate cancer. EG&G also developed the high-speed microsensors used to trigger air bags in case of an auto crash. In 2002, EG&G was acquired by URS Corporation, the largest engineering firm in the United States. Its current activities are buried under broad categories such as "engineering and technology services," but EG&G's job listings indicate it is still heavily involved in classified projects (numerous positions require a Top Secret or higher security clearance along with a background investigation and polygraph), especially those involving the Department of Homeland Security and unmanned aerial vehicles, such as those tested in Nevada at Area 51 and the Tonopah Test Range.

What's There: EG&G's corporate headquarters is a typical suburban office complex. For details on the EG&G facilities at Plant 42 in California and in Las Vegas, see the descriptions for those sites.

Getting a Look Inside: Uninvited visitors are distinctly unwelcome at any EG&G facility. People have been threatened with arrest for merely stepping into one of their parking lots to take a photo of their buildings. In other words, make sure you are always on public property when near an EG&G facility.

Getting There: EG&G's corporate headquarters is at 200 Orchard Ridge Drive in Gaithersburg, with additional offices at 900 Clopper Road. Directions to Plant 42 in California and the Las Vegas Janet Airlines terminal are given in the entries for those states.

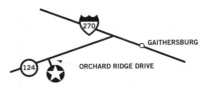

Roads to EG&G, Gaithersburg

National Geospatial Intelligence Agency, Bethesda

"Geospatial intelligence" is the process of analyzing multiple satellite images to determine what is present, and what is happening, at a given point on the Earth. For years, the main targets of the National Geospatial Intelligence Agency (NGIA) and its predecessor agencies were foreign nations. But that was before the September 11 attacks. Today, more and more targets in the United States are being analyzed. And, yes, NGIA cooperates with domestic law enforcement agencies such as the FBI, DEA, and even local police.

The National Geospatial Intelligence Agency was created in 2004 by combining the National Imagery and Mapping Agency with various geospatial intelligence functions in other government agencies. NGIA was created to provide more efficient and accurate analysis of satellite imagery as well to develop commercial applications of geospatial intelligence. NGIA headquarters is in Bethesda, but it has operations in northern Virginia, Washington, DC, and St. Louis, MO.

One of the main tasks of NGIA is to develop and maintain the most highly detailed and accurate maps in the world. Maps are maintained in digital form for rapid processing and comparison by computers. For example, suppose the CIA learns from an informant that a wanted terrorist is hiding in a "safe house" in a Middle Eastern country, but this informant has no street address or other definitive identifying details of the house's location. But if the informant could supply some other details—such as the house's size, color, type of roof, whether it has a fence, whether it has trees in the front or back, etc.—then NGIA computers could identify houses in the area meeting those criteria. Further examination of those "suspect" houses would then be done to determine traffic patterns around them, whether people and vehicles entered and left the house, when the lights were on and off in the houses, what type of heating was being used and when (this could be determined by the infrared emissions from the houses), etc. By this process, it would be possible to soon identify a small number of houses that could be the "safe house" and target them for human surveillance or possible military action.

Such capabilities are great when the targets are terrorists or hidden caches of nuclear, biological, and chemical weapons. But does NGIA ever turn its "eyes" on the United States? The answer is yes.

Some of the NGIA's geospatial intelligence of the United States is undeniably helpful. For example, it has produced imagery of forest fires and flooding that proved valuable in firefighting and disaster relief efforts. NGIA also helped identify critical security lapses in such vulnerable infrastructure as nuclear power plants, dams, and electrical transmission systems. But the NGIA admits it has also collected and analyzed image data on political demonstrations (such as those during the 2004 political conventions) and has offered what it terms "passive assistance" to law enforcement agencies. According to Bert Beaulieu, director of NGIA's Americas office, an example of such passive assistance could be NGIA checking to see whether they have an image showing a certain vehicle in a given location on a specific day and time. But, Beaulieu added, "I can't remember a single case where we actually had such an image for that day."

NGIA can only specifically track targets (such as homes and businesses) in the United States when national security and anti-terrorism issues are involved. However, it is much easier for law enforcement agencies to raise such issues in the post-September 11 environment. So if you're doing something unusual—like having all the lights in your home on at 3 a.m.—you might find yourself a NGIA target.

What's There: The NGIA headquarters is your standard-issue brick government office; only the guardhouse at the entrance road indicates Top Secret Stuff is going on inside.

Getting a Look Inside: Forget it!

Getting There: The main NGIA building is at 4600 Sangamore Road in Bethesda.

Roads to National Geospatial Intelligence Agency, Bethesda

National Security Agency, Fort George Meade

If it's an international telephone call, fax, or e-mail that travels by satellite or microwave link over any part of its journey, it may well be intercepted by the National Security Agency (NSA). The same thing goes for cell phone calls (there are orbiting NSA satellites that do nothing but intercept cell phone calls), radio transmissions, and other electronic communications that cross international borders—and domestic communications can be, and have been, monitored with equal ease. NSA has the most advanced computers in the world, and their text and speech recognition software scans all intercepted communications for key words and phrases; if they detect any of these, then the entire communication is analyzed. And don't think that using e-mail encryption or telephone scrambling gives you security. NSA can easily crack such encryption, and using it only makes the NSA more curious about you.

In the spring of 1999, reports began to appear in the media about a new system called "Echelon," a network of spy satellites and world-wide listening posts run by the National Security Agency (NSA). The May 27, 1999 issues of both *Business Week* and *The New York Times* carried stories about Echelon, and its sinister ability to intercept telephone calls (including cell phones), faxes, e-mail, and radio signals and then analyze their contents with powerful supercomputers to look for key words or phrases. As *Business Week* told its readers, "Just get used to the fact—Big Brother is listening."

The reaction of those who had been following the NSA for years was a bit different—it was "so what else is new?" The only thing noteworthy about the Echelon revelations was that we finally know the code name of the NSA's worldwide snooping system and the extent to which foreign nations, particularly the British, are involved. But the functions of Echelon have been carried on for decades. The only thing that has changed has been the NSA's capabilities for widespread eavesdropping. As computer hardware and software have improved, so have the efficiency and pervasiveness of NSA's snooping. In fact, it's safest today to assume that any communication you make via electronic means—by phone, fax, the Internet, radio, etc.—may be intercepted and analyzed by the National Security Agency.

The NSA doesn't, to be the best of our knowledge, actually install wiretaps on phone lines. It doesn't have to, because most electronic communications today involve some wireless links. Cell phone and long-distance calls use satellites; many local calls use microwave relays beyond your local switching office. And when something is sent via wireless, the NSA is listening to it, storing it, and processing it. If there is something in the communication that catches the NSA's interest, like a certain word or phrase or the use of encryption, the NSA analyzes it to see if it has any "national security" implications. If the analysis yields something suspicious, or if the NSA can't figure out what the communication is about, the parties involved may be targets of more intensive surveillance, including possible wiretaps authorized by the Foreign Intelligence Surveillance Act (FISA) Court (see entry in DISTRICT OF COLUMBIA).

While it is the NSA's interception of telephone calls and faxes that upset most people, the NSA also tracks everything sent electronically, including e-mail, financial transactions (like stock trades and credit card sales), travel reservations, etc. If it involves a wireless link at some point along the way, the NSA is trying to intercept and analyze it. In addition, recent reports have claimed that the NSA is tapping into undersea cables and network access points that local Internet service providers (ISPs) use to connect to the Internet.

In addition to its own signal intercept facilities, the NSA also serves as a central clearinghouse for all intercepts by the military and the various civilian agencies of the federal government. The results of all signals intelligence activities by the U.S. Army, Navy, Air Force, and Coast Guard are all sent to the NSA for its processing and analysis. The same thing happens with signals intercepted by the FBI, Customs Service, Drug Enforcement Administration, the Federal Communications Commission, etc. If it's anything that appears remotely connected to "national security" (or if the intercepting agency can't figure out what it is), it winds up in the NSA's lap.

To keep track of all the stuff it intercepts and receives from other agencies, the NSA has developed what has to be the most impressive (and scary) computing capabilities in the world. Its main headquarters at Fort George Meade houses perhaps the most awesome collection of physical and human computing resources anywhere. The NSA has what is reported to be the second most powerful collection of super-computers in the world (and that might be an understatement). Its computer scientists and programmers have developed incredibly sophisticated software capable of analyzing digitized phone calls and documents to find certain words or phrases or patterns in the use of words. When these are found, the file is then more intensively analyzed, including the use of human analysts.

Make no mistake about it: despite some recent attempts to "humanize" it, the NSA is a scary outfit. For years, it was so secret that its very name was classified (the joke was that "NSA" stood for "no such agency"). That cult of secrecy still pervades NSA. The details of its budgets and special access programs (SAPs) are unknown to all but a handful of members of Congress, and even they only have a cursory knowledge of what those involve. In fact, the size of the NSA's annual budget and number of employees is not accurately known because so much of its funding is hidden in SAPs. Estimates of the NSA's budget range from $2.8 billion to over $10 billion and its number of employees has been pegged at anywhere between 38,000 to 52,000.

The NSA was not created by an act of Congress, and no statute establishes the agency or defines the permissible scope of its activities (this is in sharp contrast to the CIA, which was created by an act of Congress and thus has clearly defined missions and accountability). The NSA came into being on November 4, 1952, as a result of a National Security Council Intelligence Directive issued by President Harry Truman under the authority of the National Security Act of 1947. President Truman's directive consolidated the various signal interception and analysis activities of the U.S. government, including those of the military, under the umbrella of the NSA. The directive itself was classified Top Secret until the 1970s.

The NSA's operating authority is to gather "foreign intelligence" for the purposes of "national security." However, those terms have never been precisely defined and are open to broad and creative interpretation. No law has ever been enacted by Congress to prohibit the NSA from engaging in any activity; however, Congress has enacted numerous laws prohibiting anyone from divulging information about the NSA or its activities.

The lax definitions of "foreign intelligence" and "national security" resulted in the NSA turning its attention to surveillance of American citizens in the 1960s and 1970s. Senate hearings chaired in 1975 by Idaho Senator Frank Church revealed that the NSA began to compile "watch lists" of American citizens in 1962. The purported intent of snooping on American citizens was to determine if any "foreign powers" were lending support to the civil rights movement. These lists and surveillance efforts against Americans were greatly increased in 1967, as the NSA targeted antiwar groups and more civil rights organizations. Among the Americans whose names appeared on NSA watch lists during that era were Dr. Martin Luther King, Jane Fonda, Joan Baez, Eldridge Cleaver, and Abbie Hoffman. The NSA also began to get requests for surveillance from other government agencies, like the CIA and the Bureau of Narcotics and Dangerous Drugs (the forerunner of today's Drug Enforcement Administration), that were prohibited by law from conducting such surveillance.

The NSA's program of domestic spying was finally ended by Attorney General Elliott Richardson in October 1973, as the rapidly-unraveling Watergate scandal threatened to expose it. In the wake of Watergate, NSA Director Lew Allen finally revealed the NSA's surveillance efforts against Americans to the Church committee in 1975. This was accompanied by promises to establish safeguards to prevent such abuses in the future.

One such safeguard put into place after the Church hearings was to protect the privacy of U.S. citizens who were not targeted or otherwise under suspicion but had been a party to an intercepted communication. In such cases, the U.S. citizen is supposed to be referred to simply as "American Citizen" in all summaries, transcripts, and records of the communication. However, there have been numerous reports that the NSA can get around this self-imposed restriction by allowing a foreign partner, such as the Canadians or British, to do the analysis of the communication.

The NSA still fights Congressional efforts to control its activities. In 1999, the House Permanent Select Committee on Intelligence attempted to investigate how the NSA handled intercepted communications involving American citizens. The committee requested legal opinions, decisional memoranda, and policy guidelines the NSA used to handle intercepted phone, fax, and e-mail communications from citizens. The NSA responded by claiming an attorney/client privilege between the NSA director and its general counsel, thus exempting the requested documents from Congressional review (this was the same tactic President Nixon tried with John Dean during the Watergate scandal). Even right-wing Republicans on the committee were outraged by the NSA's response. Representative Bob Barr (R-Georgia), a former CIA analyst, called the NSA claim "bogus" and said it was an attempt to "deny the chairman and committee members proper information with which to carry out their oversight responsibilities." Despite such protests, the NSA steadfastly refused to provide the request documents and the committee could only protest in its final report.

Senator Frank Church said it best in his committee's 1975 hearings: "I know the capacity that is there to make tyranny total in America, and we must see to it that this agency [NSA] and all agencies that possess this technology operate within the law and under proper supervision, so that we never cross over that abyss."

The NSA in Action: A United Press International (UPI) story by Richard Sale, dated February 13, 2001, gave insights into how the NSA operates today. The article concerned the NSA's efforts to locate Osama bin Laden through his telephone communications. Sale reported that when UPI wanted to send some information about one of bin Laden's associates to a former CIA official using e-mail, the official replied, "My God, don't put that in an e-mail." The official explained that such an e-mail would get him on NSA's watch lists and he didn't want that to happen.

The UPI story explained that the NSA maintains computerized "dictionaries" of personal names, political groups, crime organizations, phrases, and other words. All intercepted communications are checked against these dictionaries. If there is a match between any of the dictionaries and the intercepted communication, both the sender and receiver of the communication are placed on a watch list. All future communications to and from the sender and receiver are then intercepted and analyzed. For example, suppose someone sends you an e-mail with something that matches a name, word, or phrase in one of the dictionaries. You are then placed on a NSA watch list. People you send e-mails to are added to the list; so are other people that send you e-mails. You get off the watch list when it is determined that you do not pose a threat to national security. Who determines if you no longer pose a threat to national security? The NSA. And no, the NSA does not have to tell you that you are under surveillance nor do they need any warrant to monitor your communications.

Foreign Partners: The NSA maintains close links with Canada's Communications Security Establishment (CSE), Britain's Government Communications Headquarters (GCHQ), Australia's Defence Signals Directorate (DSD), and New Zealand's Communications Security Bureau (CSB). These nations are part of a formal signals intelligence alliance with the NSA. However, the alliance is curiously one-way; the foreign agencies allow the NSA to operate listening facilities in their countries, and forward signal intercepts from their military and civilian agencies to the NSA for processing and analysis, but the NSA is under no obligation to share all of the intelligence it gathers with its partners. However, NSA generally shares enough to keep its partners happy (such as intelligence about nations in the South Pacific for Australia and New Zealand, for example) processed and analyzed by NSA's supercomputers. In addition, the NSA has also entered into agreements with Japan and South Korea, but these nations are decidedly junior partners; they seldom get to see any intelligence gathered by the NSA or the "Anglo Alliance." Instead, intelligence they gather is processed and returned to them; the NSA may also share it with the "Anglo Alliance" without informing Japan or South Korea.

Key Facilities: The main NSA facilities at Fort George Meade and other locations in Maryland are reported to occupy over 3.5 million square feet of space. The main NSA facilities at Fort George Meade are two high-rise office complexes and smaller support buildings, including a technical library and engineering laboratories. A 1992 report entitled List of the World's Most Powerful Computing Sites said the NSA facilities at Fort George Meade had the world's second most powerful collection of supercomputers; however, it is widely believed this site may be actually the world's most powerful. In addition, the NSA leases office space at the National Business Park, across the Baltimore/Washington Parkway from the main NSA facilities, and at Airport Square Technology and Industrial Park near the Baltimore/Washington International Airport. It is believed the functions carried on at these two sites are considerably less sensitive than those at the main NSA site. It is reported that the NSA employs approximately 20,000 persons in Maryland.

NSA maintains two communications satellite interception stations in the continental United States: at Sugar Grove, West Virginia and Yakima, Washington (see entries for these facilities under those states). The Sugar Grove facility processes intercepts from communications satellites over the Atlantic while Yakima does the same for Pacific satellites. In addition, almost any military site in the United States with communications receiving equipment is a potential source of input for the NSA. It is also known that U.S. embassies and consulates abroad have signal interception capabilities; one major intelligence coup of the 1960s by the U.S. embassy in Moscow was the interception of the crude radio-telephones installed in the limousines of Politburo members. As noted earlier, intercepted communications from the military and civilian agencies are forwarded to the NSA for processing and analysis.

Overseas, the NSA and GCHQ jointly operate a mammoth listening complex at Menwith Hill, near Harrogate in Great Britain. This station mainly intercepts signals from Russia and the rest of the former Soviet bloc. Misawa Air Base at Misawa, Japan, is the NSA's main base for eavesdropping on China and North Korea. The U.S. and Australia jointly operate a large facility at Pine Gap, Australia, that targets southeast Asia.

Getting a Look Inside: The National Cryptologic Museum was opened in December 1993, adjacent to NSA headquarters. The Museum has displays of mainly historical signals intelligence and codebreaking (largely from World Wars I and II) but nothing on current activities and techniques. The museum is near the intersection of the Baltimore/Washington Parkway and Route 32; hours of operation are 9 a.m. to 4 p.m. Monday through Friday and 10 a.m. to 2 p.m. Saturday. Its phone number is (301) 688-5849.

Unusual Fact: In 1999, the NSA sent around a memo to employees banning the then-popular "Furby" toys from all NSA facilities. The "Furby," which resembled a big-eyed, cute-faced stuffed owl, had an internal chip that allowed it to record and repeat words and phrases it heard; one of the appeals of the Furby was that it could be "taught" to speak. The NSA was worried that Furbies could overhear classified conversations, memorize them, and repeat them to unauthorized personnel. The memo advised any NSA employees who had a Furby in their office, or spotted a Furby on NSA premises, to immediately "contact their Staff Security Office for guidance."

Getting There: From the Baltimore/Washington Parkway, take the exit for Route 32/Fort Meade. Watch for the sign for Colony 7 Road; turn onto it and follow the signs to the National Cryptographic Museum. If you continue on Route 32, you will see the main NSA headquarters between Canine and Emory roads; there will be stoplights at the intersections of these roads and Route 32. From Route 32, NSA headquarters appears to be two ordinary high-rise glass and steel office buildings; the antennas on their roofs are the only indication something unusual is going on inside them. The area is heavily patrolled, however, and people taking photographs of the buildings have been stopped by security guards.

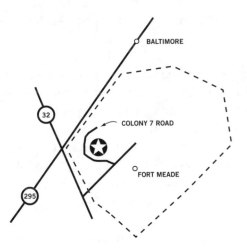

Roads to National Security Agency, Fort George Meade

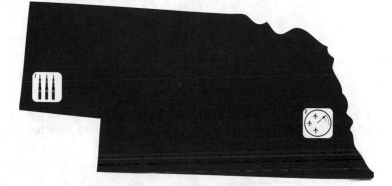

NEBRASKA

1. Kimball County, Kimball 2. U.S. Strategic Command Center (USSTRATCOM), Bellevue

Kimball County, Kimball

This small, quaint county on the high plains of western Nebraska was once best known as being the location of the highest point in Nebraska and the site of the first oil discovery in Nebraska (in 1950). But in the 1960s, the "Oil Capital of Nebraska" became the ICBM capital of America as silos were constructed to house the then-new Minuteman missiles. Today Kimball County is the "Missile Capital of the World," with over 200 Minuteman III ICBMs, all carrying multiple nuclear warheads, located in its immediate area.

Kimball County is located on the high plains of southwestern Nebraska. The high point of the state (5424 feet) is located in the extreme southwestern corner of the county and the flat, open plains around the town of Kimball are actually several thousand feet in elevation. Originally established as a railway stop, Kimball later added ranching and oil to its economy. But it was the development of ICBMs that put Kimball on the map of Top Secret America. Kimball had a lot of advantages as a location to base ICBMs, such as plenty of open land and a low population density in case the Soviets decided on a pre-emptive strike. The first Minuteman ICBM silos were constructed in 1962, and today the spacious open grasslands of Kimball County (along with adjoining territory just across the borders of Colorado and Wyoming) are pockmarked with silos housing Minuteman III missiles, each of which contain multiple warheads.

What's There: Kimball itself is a modest town of about 2,500 people and is the county seat. The silos themselves can be detected as fenced areas in the distance; power lines and gated roads can be seen leading to many silos. Most silos are on private land and trespassing is generally prohibited, and any attempt to enter the area of any silo would certainly result in arrest or possibly the use of lethal force. In other words, you can look but you'd better not touch.

Key Facilities: Since you can't see an actual missile or silo close up, you might want to drop by Gotte Park in downtown Kimball to see an actual Titan I missile. However, this missile was never in service in Kimball (it was based near Chico, California instead) and—at the time this book was written—the top section of the missile was missing because of wind damage. But hey, it's better than no missile at all!

Getting a Look Inside: There's no way you'll ever see the inside of the missile silos here. Instead, you'll have to be content with cruising the country roads while armed with a pair of binoculars in case you spot a distant silo. Maybe you'd enjoy finding an isolated spot along a road, pulling over, turning off the engine, listening to the wind, looking at the vast open skies, and thinking to yourself, gee, there's enough firepower around me to annihilate every living thing on the whole goddamn planet.

Getting There: Kimball is located in the southwestern "panhandle" of Nebraska near the junction with Colorado and Wyoming; it can be accessed from an exit off Interstate 80.

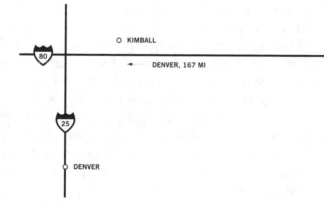

Roads to Kimball County, Kimball

U.S. Strategic Command Center (USSTRATCOM), Bellevue

When the President gives the order to launch our nukes, here is where the attack will be coordinated from. Previously the home of the Strategic Air Command, this site now will command and direct all nuclear weapons delivered by manned bomber, missiles, and submarine-launched missiles. And there's also an airborne command post here ready to command and direct an attack in case this facility gets nuked itself.

The U.S. Strategic Command Center (USSTRATCOM) is where the Really Big One will be directed. It is a two-level reinforced concrete and steel building occupying over 14,000 square feet. Twenty-four hours a day, it is commanded by either an Air Force general or a Navy admiral, and they are ready to command and direct all use of U.S. nuclear weapons should the President authorize their use.

USSTRATCOM is located on Offutt Air Force Base near Bellevue. Offutt was a former Army fort, Fort Crook, until June 1946. During World War II, Fort Crook had been the site of a factory producing B-26 and B-29 bombers. In a sense, Offutt has already been responsible for a nuclear attack—the B-29 bombers that dropped the atomic bombers on Hiroshima and Nagasaki were built at the factory here.

Offutt became the home of General Curtis LeMay's Strategic Air Command (SAC) in November 1948. Offutt's selection was the result of it being located in the middle of the country, well out of range of the bombers and missiles then in existence. At first, manned bombers were stationed and directed from Offutt. In the late 1950s, the first

Atlas missiles were deployed in Iowa and Nebraska, and these were commanded from here. In 1971, an airborne command post named "Looking Glass" was added to provide an alternative nuclear command in case Offutt got knocked out by one of those pesky Soviet missiles. Looking Glass was a specially-outfitted EC-135 jet that was in the air 24 hours a day, seven days a week, 365 days per year; when one Looking Glass craft landed, a replacement took to the air. Each plane had an Air Force general aboard and equipment for direct communication with the President and other military officers. If an incoming missile was detected heading for Offutt, Looking Glass would fly to safety and the counter-attack (if any) would be directed from aboard it.

SAC was deactivated on June 1, 1992, and was then replaced by USSTRATCOM. While SAC was strictly an Air Force operation, USSTRATCOM includes all branches of the military. However, its command is top-heavy with senior officers from the Air Force and Navy, since those services have a monopoly on strategic nuclear weapons. Looking Glass is still in operation (it's now a modified Boeing 707) and always carries either an Air Force general or a Navy admiral. In fact, except for a change of name and the addition of officers from other services, USSTRATCOM still operates much in the same way that Curtis LeMay envisioned.

What's There: USSTRATCOM is located underground at Offutt, so there's not much to see from the outside. Battle commanders and senior staff work in the lower level, while lower-level officers and support staff work in the upper level. In case of war, the entire facility would be sealed off and continue to operate from emergency power, water, and food supplies. The facility is reinforced to protect against the electro-magnetic pulse produced by a nearby nuclear explosion; the pulse could damage electronic equipment without such added protection.

Inside USSTRATCOM is the Alternative Processing and Correlation Center (APAC), a missile tracking and warning center that would take over if Cheyenne Mountain Operations Center (see entry under COLORADO) was destroyed or otherwise unable to function. If USSTRATCOM is activated for war, the APAC will provide it with data on enemy missiles.

Key Facilities: The interior of USSTRATCOM includes numerous workstations with video monitors and secure telephone systems. Eight large wall screens are capable of displaying video and still images. In the event of war, battle information and data would be displayed on the wall screens as well as on individual video monitors. Numerous high-powered computer systems are here along with an extensive telephone network—the USSTRATCOM commanders have direct telephone access to over 200 U.S. military facilities around the world, including missile silos. Direct lines also go to the President, Secretary of Defense, and the Chairman of the Joint Chiefs of Staff. Other lines link USSTRATCOM to military computing centers and communications facilities. The communications demands of USSTRATCOM forced the construction of massive telephone lines and switching facilities going into and out of Offutt. Satellite and radio communications facilities are used to link USSTRATCOM with Looking Glass and other sites, such as Navy submarines.

Getting a Look Inside: Forget about getting a look inside USSTRATCOM or Offutt itself; the security at the base is very tight and people parked near the base or walking in the area have been questioned and told to move along by local sheriff's deputies.

However, there is a Strategic Air Command museum in the area open to the public. Opened in 1998, the museum is located at Exit 426 off Interstate 80. It occupies over 300,000 square feet and includes displays of 31 aircraft and six missiles, including the SR-71 Blackbird spy plane. Most of the exhibits deal with the history of SAC, and several of them are interactive. As their motto says, their purpose is "to educate, inspire, and entertain." Global thermonuclear war—you can't get more entertaining than that!

Listening In: Offutt uses shortwave frequencies to keep in touch with Looking Glass. If you have a shortwave radio capable of receiving upper sideband (USB) transmissions, listen for them on 4724, 6739, 8992, 11175, 13200, and 15016 kHz. Offutt will identify as "Offutt" and Looking Glass will identify as that. Although you may hear some encrypted communications, many routine communications will not be scrambled.

Unusual Fact: The massive telephone line and switching infrastructure necessary to support USSTRATCOM has made this area a leading telemarketing and "800" call response center. When you call long-distance information, or receive a sales call from a major company out of state, the odds are good that it is made from, or routed through, the Bellevue area.

Getting There: Offutt Air Force Base is located southwest of Bellevue off Highway 75.

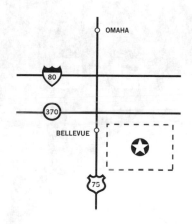

Roads to U.S. Strategic Command Center (USSTRATCOM), Bellevue

NEVADA

1. Area 51, Rachel 2. Base Camp Airfield, Warm Springs 3. Fallon Naval Air Station (NAS), Fallon 4. Janet Airlines Terminal, Las Vegas 5. Nellis Air Force Base 6. Nuclear Weapons Storage Facility Facility, North Las Vegas 7. Nevada Test Site (NTS), Mercury 8. Nuclear Emergency Search Team (NEST), Nellis Air Force Base 9. Project Faultless Test Site, Nye County 10. Tonopah Test Range (TTR), Tonopah

Area 51, Rachel

The original and still the best! If you can visit only one site of the Top Secret Government, this is the one. Most of what you have heard about this place is false, most of what you haven't heard is true, and no one wants to talk about the things that aren't entirely true but aren't entirely false either. No matter how much you've read about this place, nothing prepares you for the impact it makes when you visit in person. Even if you consider yourself a levelheaded skeptic, you will probably have a few moments where you wonder if you haven't stepped into a parallel universe. And you might get to catch a brief glimpse of a top-secret aircraft undergoing tests!

If you come here wanting to see UFOs, then you will see UFOs. If you come here wanting to see secret aircraft being tested, then you'll see them. Area 51 will reflect your expectations of it like a mirror.

Perhaps no place is both so well known and so secret. Yes, you can drive or hike right up to its borders. And, yes, you will almost certainly be arrested and fined if you step across the border. No one who really knows what's going on inside its boundaries will talk about such things. But it's clear something extraordinary is still going on there based on the sonic booms, low-flying jets, and bewildering display of lights over it most nights.

Area 51 was born because the CIA needed a place to test its new U-2 spy plane, and the area around Edwards Air Force Base (see entry in CALIFORNIA section) had become too populated for tests of truly top-secret aircraft. The need was for a new site with a large, hard dry lake bed that could be used for take-offs and landings. In early 1955, several isolated lakebeds in the West were evaluated. Groom Lake, adjacent to the Nevada Test Site, met the CIA's requirements. It also had the advantage of being adjacent to the Nevada Test Site; the CIA figured that fear of radioactive fallout would help keep adjacent areas lightly populated and discourage people from attempting to enter the area. In a matter of weeks, aircraft hangars, housing units, support buildings, tracking and navigation aids, and a paved runway had been added and the U-2 was able to take its maiden test flight out of Groom Lake on August 4, 1955. Training of U-2 pilots began the next year at Groom Lake.

Originally, the facility at Groom Lake was known as "Paradise Ranch," a name that was a bitter commentary on the lack of amenities there. A 1960 map of the Nellis Range Complex showing its section placed the Groom Lake facility within "Area 51" on the map. While the facility was a closely guarded secret throughout the 1960s, military and civilian pilots knew something was going on there because its airspace was off-limits to all military and civilian traffic; military pilots training at Nellis or Tonopah quickly discovered that accidentally slipping only a few hundred feet inside the restricted airspace brought disciplinary action. The Groom Lake area became known as "Dreamland" among military pilots because that was the radio call sign used by its air traffic control.

Paradise Ranch/Dreamland/Area 51 still remains the premier test facility for highly advanced aircraft and other aerial weapons systems. The U-2 was only the first in a long line of remarkable aircraft tested at Area 51, including the SR-71 spy plane and the F-117 Stealth fighter. It is widely assumed that new secret aircraft, such as the next generation of Stealth aircraft and unmanned aerial vehicles (UAVs), are currently being tested there. In addition, there is much speculation and some evidence that other advanced weapons systems, such as directed energy weapons, are also being tested inside Area 51.

But most visitors to Area 51 come hoping to see UFOs. It's impossible to discuss UFOs and Area 51 without mentioning the Papoose Lake area, known as "S-4." S-4/Papoose Lake is immediately south of Groom Lake/Area 51 and, according to reports, is the scene of the most amazing UFO-related activity the Top Secret Government is trying to keep hidden. Unfortunately, those reports are almost certainly bullshit.

The legend of S-4 began in November 1989, when a man named Bob Lazar came forward claiming he was a physicist who had worked on UFOs being tested at S-4. Lazar said the UFOs were being reverse-engineered from alien technology recovered from crashed UFOs; their power source was a mysterious "element 115" used to power anti-matter reactors. He said he had seen golf balls bouncing off "gravity waves" emitted by the reactors, that he had read autopsy reports of aliens killed in UFO crashes, and that the government knew the UFOs came from Zeta Reticuli. Lazar said he held advanced degrees from MIT and Caltech, was previously a staff scientist at Los Alamos National Laboratory, and had been hired at S-4 as a result of a personal recommendation by Dr. Edward Teller, the developer of the hydrogen bomb.

Lazar's claims caused a sensation in Las Vegas, and he was extensively featured on local television and radio stations. His story spread like wildfire within the UFO world and got play in several supermarket tabloids. He was soon a regular on the late night talk radio circuit, and television crews came from Europe and Japan to interview him. Lazar was a persuasive speaker. He spoke authoritatively, used scientific terms and engineering jargon, and seemed familiar with military projects. He admitted there were aspects about the saucer program he didn't know or understand. He didn't seem like the stereotypical wild-eyed UFO buff; his manner was calm, sincere, and rational.

And Lazar claimed the best places to see these UFOs being tested was near the gate of a secret facility he called Area 51. His preferred viewing spot was near a black mailbox along Highway 375 (known ever since as the Black Mailbox, even though it was later painted white). In fact, he said he had escorted people up to Area 51 and the Black Mailbox in the months before he went public, and these witnesses supported Lazar's claims that strange lights and disc-shaped objects could be seen in the night skies near Rachel.

Unfortunately for him and those who wanted to believe his story, Lazar's credibility soon crashed to Earth like the wrecked UFOs he claimed to have seen. The first big hit came in April 1990, when he was arrested in Las Vegas on charges of pandering for prostitution (he was later convicted). With that, some previously credulous reporters finally began looking into his past. It turned out he didn't have degrees from MIT or Caltech, but instead had attended (but not graduated from) Pierce Community College in California. He had indeed lived near Los Alamos, but had been employed as a photo-finishing technician, not as a scientist at the national laboratory. His biggest claim to fame in Los Alamos was apparently his attempt to mount a jet engine on his Honda CRX (he had vanity license plates that read JETUBET). His record after he moved to Las Vegas raised more questions, such as the fact that he had filed for bankruptcy in 1986 as a result of a failed photo-finishing business and had married his second wife before divorcing his first.

Amazingly enough, there are still people who believe Lazar is telling the truth and such unpleasant facts were fabricated and planted as part of a campaign by the Top Secret Government to discredit him. Others believe Lazar was a patsy set up by the Top Secret Government to ridicule the whole notion of UFO tests at S-4/Area 51 and allow those tests to continue without close public scrutiny. And others believe that Lazar was just an articulate, personable con man who knew how to tell a good story to an audience eager to be fooled.

If nothing else, Lazar must be credited with launching the entire Area 51 mania. This section that you're reading is a perverse tribute to his sense of drama and keen insight into the human need to believe in the unbelievable.

What's There: As an American citizen, you can be arrested and imprisoned for taking a fuzzy, indistinct photograph of the Area 51 facilities from a mountaintop over 20 miles away. Fortunately, some Russians got angry and you can now buy one-meter satellite photos of the area from an American company (and the satellite was launched from Vandenberg Air Force Base in California).

Space Imaging, of Denver, CO, operates the IKONOS satellite and sells high-resolution photos made from space. Space Imaging includes many former military brass among its managers, and had announced that it would not sell photos of restricted military areas such as Area 51. Moreover, U.S. law prohibited U.S. companies to sell satellite photos of restricted military areas. As such, requests to Space Imaging to purchase photos of Area 51 were routinely declined.

In March 2000, Space Imaging released "before and after" photos of Chechnya after an assault by the Russian army. A few days later, the Russians released a photo of Area 51 taken in early 1998 by their SPIN-2 satellite. While the Russians did not publicly comment on why they made the Area 51 photo available, it is believed they were angry over the Chechnya photos and the release of the Area 51 photo was in retaliation. Shortly after the release of the Russian photo, Space

Area 51 as photographed by a Russian satellite.

Imaging released its own one-meter resolution photo of Area 51 that was taken in April 2000. No reason was given for this abrupt reversal in policy (and violation of federal law), but it was clear that the Russian release (and the photo orders the Russians were receiving) must have been the major factor. Whatever the reasons for their release, these photos give us valuable new information about Area 51.

The centerpiece of Area 51 is a runway, reportedly built sometime in the early 1990s, that is 11,960 feet long and 140 feet wide. The length and width of this runway is far beyond what is required for normal military and civilian aviation; such a runway would be ideal for short-winged aircraft that needed to achieve a high speed before obtaining enough lift to become airborne. Tire skid marks on this runway show it is heavily used. There are also shorter runways, including one used by the "Janet" flights from Las Vegas and elsewhere (see entry in this section) and a terminal where the Janet flights arrive.

There are numerous aircraft hangars at Area 51, with the most interesting being one that has become known as Hangar 18. From the photos, it is estimated that its doors are over 100 feet high. Several hangars are of the "scoot and hide" variety, meaning they can be moved. These are used to conceal certain aircraft and activities during times when spy satellites are due to make a pass overhead. Fuel tanks, radar and satellite dishes, and aircraft maintenance facilities are numerous.

A large building with a white roof adjacent to the Janet airlines terminal is believed to be an engineering facility for employees who fly in from Las Vegas, Palmdale, or other locations. What is believed to be the base headquarters building is located near the original hangars built for the U-2 project. There are also housing units for personnel that do not commute daily on Janet airlines. Most of Area 51 is laid out in a grid-like pattern; from space, Area 51 looks a bit like a neat housing subdivision adjacent to an airport. There are also several parking areas and a surprising number of cars even though all personnel arrive by either plane or bus; as far as is known, personnel are not allowed to drive their private cars into Area 51.

While personnel who lived inside Area 51 on previous projects (like the F-117 Stealth fighter) do not talk about projects they worked on, they do talk about the living and recreational facilities. A baseball diamond and tennis courts are visible in the satellite photos, and an indoor swimming pool, bowling alley, and gymnasium are available to on-base personnel. The dining facility (named Sam's Club, after the last CIA director of Area 51) offers fresh seafood such as shrimp and lobster along with a well-stocked bar. However, duty at Area 51 is generally difficult. Since most tests are conducted at night, many personnel keep a vampire-like schedule. The secrecy of the projects here means that personnel cannot discuss their work with their families or co-workers; they may be ordered inside or told to look away when a secret aircraft or other project is scheduled to come into view. Personnel are restricted to only those sections of Area 51 essential for their work and living and are not permitted to wander the base freely.

Several of the mountains inside Area 51 have radar domes and communications facilities on their summits. The most widely visible of these is atop Bald Mountain, a 9,380-foot-tall peak that dominates much the western skyline along Highway 375 near Rachel.

The boundary of Area 51 is patrolled by a legendary security force that has become known as the "Cammo Dudes" because of the camouflage clothing they often wear (although you may sometimes glimpse them in khakis). At the time this book was written, the Cammo Dudes are employees of EG&G (see entry in the MARYLAND section) but in the past have been employees of Wackenhut (see entry in the FLORIDA section). For years, their vehicle of choice has been a white Jeep Cherokee, although they have also used tan Ford pickups that blend in well with the desert. They are heavily armed, including automatic weapons, and they are authorized (just like the warning signs say) to use deadly force to stop trespassers. While the Cammo Dudes work inside Area 51, they are restricted to its perimeters and probably know nothing more about its inner workings than the average person.

When Area 51 first burst into national attention in the early 1990s, the Cammo Dudes were famous for their aggressive behavior toward visitors, even those on public land miles from the actual boundary. They would leave Area 51 to challenge any approaching visitors, such as those driving the gravel road from Highway 375 to the Main Gate. Such visitors would find their cars closely followed or the road ahead blocked by one of the Jeep Cherokees; the local sheriff was invariably called and a deputy would soon arrive. Even though nothing could be done to such visitors as long as they remained on public land and roads, such tactics discouraged all but the most determined visitors. Those who hiked on foot to then-public areas from which Area 51 could be viewed were routinely followed by Cammo Dudes, and occasionally buzzed by low-flying helicopters. Campers on public land near the boundary could expect a middle-of-the-night visit from Cammo Dudes. Area 51 folklore was full of tales of firearms being brandished by the Cammo Dudes and even tires of cars approaching the boundary being shot out.

Now that Area 51 is a tourist attraction, the Cammo Dudes are likely to leave you alone so long as you remain in plain sight on the main access roads (however, they routinely photograph all cars and visitors near the Area 51's gates). However, you will still be followed if you hike away from the road toward the base; you might even get treated to a helicopter zooming a few feet over your head. Campers near the boundary can expect to have Cammo Dudes wandering around their campsite during the night (since it's public land, they have as much right to be there as the campers). If you do encounter them on public land or roads, the encounters will usually be friendly ("Do you need any help?" has replaced "What are you doing?" as their standard greeting) but make no mistake—these guys are intent on keeping you from entering Area 51 or getting a good look at what's going on inside. (The use of "guys" in that last sentence is not sexist language but just a reflection of reality; there are more credible reports from reliable witnesses of UFOs at Area 51 than there are of female Cammo Dudes.)

Notable landmarks outside of Area 51 itself include the Black Mailbox made famous by Bob Lazar and the town of Rachel. The Black Mailbox is located on Highway 375 approximately 19.5 miles south of Rachel and five miles north of the turnoff for the Main Gate of Area 51. It's the only thing resembling a mailbox for miles and is unmistakable. As mentioned previously, it has been painted white since it was named. It is an actual working mailbox belonging to the Medlin family, which operates a ranch adjacent to Area 51. From this spot, you do have a good view of the airspace over Area 51 and S-4 (although even better viewing spots can be found along Highway 375). The dirt road at the mailbox eventually leads to an intersection with Groom Lake Road, the road leading to the Main Gate of Area 51. However, it is easy to take the wrong turn on this road and end up somewhere else (see "Unusual Fact" below for a well-known and funny example).

You are more likely to have an encounter with local sheriff's deputies at the Black Mailbox than you are along the boundaries of Area 51. The Medlin family has been ranching here since long before anyone had heard of Area 51 but visitors cruising through their ranch operations have disrupted their lives; even their mail has sometimes been stolen. You may be told to move (or even cited) by local deputies if you are parked here, block access to the mailbox, or disturb the ranching operations. Best advice is to stop for a quick look and photograph, and then move on.

The "town" of Rachel is little more than a collection of trailers in the high desert; total population hovers at slightly over 100. The main attraction in Rachel is the Little A'Le'Inn. The Little A'Le'Inn caters to those who come to Area 51 looking for UFOs; its walls are plastered with UFO photos and posters and it carries an extensive selection of UFO merchandise for sale. It also has a restaurant and operates the "Dreamland Resort," a Spartan motel cobbled together from trailers that provides the only accommodations for over 50 miles. The Little A'Le'Inn now has a melancholy air compared to its heyday in the 1990s; one of its co-owners died in 2003 and it gets only a fraction of the visitors/customers it once did. Another UFO-related Rachel business, the Area 51 Research Center, closed in 2002 (although attempts have periodically been made to open similar businesses on the same site). While the UFO fanatics seem to be losing interest, Area 51 and Rachel still draw visitors interested in trying to glimpse still-secret aircraft undergoing development and testing.

Secret Stuff: Despite the number of visitors to its boundary, most of Area 51 is still safe from prying eyes and it will likely remain the main test and development facility for secret aircraft and other exotic weaponry well into the future. Other than the UFO stories, most of the speculation about things under development at Area 51 revolves around Stealth aircraft, a rumored hypersonic craft named the "Aurora," unmanned aerial combat vehicles, and flight tests of fighter aircraft from Russia and China.

It is almost a sure bet that any new generation of Stealth vehicles would be undergoing tests at Area 51. The two known Stealth craft in America's inventory, the F-117 fighter and B-2 bomber, completed their flight testing over two decades ago and it is almost inconceivable that more advanced Stealth designs are not being tested, especially since Russian and Chinese radars are developing the capability to detect the F-117 and B-2. In addition to improvements on radar-scattering designs of existing Stealth planes, it is widely speculated that tests of daytime stealth technology are going on here. In addition to radar-scattering, daytime stealth would involve electroluminescent surfaces that would change to match the color and brightness of the background sky and low-noise engines. Many reliable witnesses have reported silent lights that abruptly change color, and these may be tests of such advanced Stealth techniques.

No other aircraft rumored to be operational at Area 51 has attracted as much attention, and rumors, as the now-legendary Aurora. The Aurora was supposedly a Mach 6 (over 4000 miles per hour) spy plane to replace the Mach 3 SR-71 spy plane, which was retired in 1990. On January 10, 1988, the *New York Times* reported that the Air Force was developing a new reconnaissance aircraft capable of travel at Mach 6. The name "Aurora" came about as a result of a 1987 Pentagon budget request that included a request for a project with that name in the amount of $2.3 billion dollars; the "Aurora" project was in the same category as budget requests for the U-2 and SR-71. In the 1998 budget request, however, there was no mention of Aurora. It was widely assumed that Aurora was the name of the Mach 6 plane in the *Times* story, that it was mentioned by accident in the 1997 budget document, and that it had gone into operation when the SR-71 was retired.

In 1988 and 1989, a sound variously described as "the sky being ripped open," "a deep, throbbing roar," and "a pulsing like the lowest notes on a pipe organ" was reportedly heard around Edwards Air Force Base in California. This "Aurora roar" was reported in the hours between midnight and 5 a.m. Speculation was that this was a new type of jet engine, known as a pulse-detonation wave engine, which literally exploded liquid methane for propulsion. In 1991 and 1992, a series of "skyquakes" were heard in southern California. These skyquakes were not earthquakes, but were detected on seismographs as if they were. An analysis conducted by the seismological laboratory at the California Institute of Technology in Pasadena found these skyquakes similar to the ones made by the Space Shuttle when it landed at Edwards Air Force Base, but were made by objects traveling at Mach 2 to 4 and traveling toward the Nellis Range Complex in Nevada (which includes Area 51). During this same period, the "Aurora roar" was also being heard in Rachel, including daytime instances when the sky was overcast.

However, there was never a reliable eyewitness sighting of the Aurora nor were any photographs taken of an airplane matching any of the reported descriptions of the Aurora or similar hypersonic craft. And the skyquakes and Aurora roar stopped being reported in late 1993. Some stories claimed the Aurora project had been moved outside the United States, but the most likely explanation is that some sort of hypersonic vehicle was being tested in the early 1990s but is no longer flying for some reason (for example, it didn't work as expected). Both NASA and the Air Force have conducted research into hypersonic vehicles since 1993 and have plans for their eventual development, so the existence of Aurora, and the results obtained from the project, could remain classified until hypersonic aircraft military are operational and publicly known. (There is a precedent for this; it wasn't until the F-117 Stealth fighter was publicly acknowledged that details of earlier Stealth aircraft prototypes, such as "Tacit Blue," became known. Such prototypes were built and tested, but never became operational.)

In early 2006, *Aviation Week & Space Technology* magazine reported that a secret manned spaceflight program was operating out of

Area 51 and may have been responsible for the Aurora reports. According to the magazine, a rocket-powered "space plane" carrying a single pilot—similar to the old X-15 rocket plane—was taken aloft by a "mother ship" airplane similar to the prototype B-70 bombers of the 1960s. The space plane and pilot were launched from the "mother ship" on a sub-orbital flight to elevations of about 100 miles. While *Aviation Week & Space Technology* is normally considered a reliable source, this report was widely ridiculed by aviation experts and journalists. The consensus is that such a "rocket plane" system may be undergoing tests at Area 51, but is likely unmanned and not fully operational.

Perhaps the hottest area of testing these days at Area 51 involves unmanned aerial vehicles, like the Predator. The new generation of UAVs rumored to be undergoing testing at Area 51 are supposedly faster than the Predator (some are reported to be jet-powered), fly at a higher altitude, and incorporate a form of neural network computing to give it the ability to monitor its operating environment and make adjustments without human intervention. This new generation of UAVs could replace manned bombers for many combat missions in the future.

One of the most closely guarded secrets of Area 51 during the Cold War era didn't involve American airplanes but Soviet ones. Beginning in 1967, an Air Force program known as "Red Hat" was established to test captured, stolen, and otherwise surreptitiously obtained Soviet aircraft to determine their capabilities and weaknesses. Among the craft tested here were the MiG-17, MiG-21, MiG-23m Su-22, and S7-27. Efforts are still being made to obtain the latest military aircraft from both Russia and China (usually by bribing corrupt officials). In fact, Red Hat has never been officially acknowledged to exist, but numerous daytime photographs of Soviet aircraft in the air over Area 51 (and a photo of a MiG-21 on the Area 51 runway, taken from an area now closed to the public) have provided conclusive proof that such craft are here.

There are rumors of many other weapon systems, such as "directed energy" weapons, being tested here but those reports can't be confirmed. It is more likely that such weapons are actually tested in other areas of the Nellis Range Complex.

Getting a Look Inside: It's easy to get badly lost in the maze of gravel roads around Area 51. Copies of maps and viewing guides are for sale at the Little A'Le'Inn and are a must if you decide to travel off either of the two main roads leading to the base.

The only look "inside" Area 51 is now from the summit of Tikaboo Peak, a 7,800-foot-high mountain located approximately 26 miles from Groom Lake. The top of Tikaboo offers a view of the facilities at Area 51 and much of the Nevada Test Site. However, the climb to the summit of Tikaboo Peak, while not requiring mountain-climbing skills, is strenuous and you need to need to be in good physical condition before attempting it.

It cannot be stressed enough that you must not cross over the boundary of Area 51 under any circumstances; even if you do so by accident, you can expect to be detained by the Cammo Dudes and turned over to the Lincoln County sheriff's department for arrest. When this happens, you will be fined at least several hundreds of dollars and any film, videotapes, or other recording media you have will be confiscated. Away from the roads, the boundary is marked with orange posts spaced apart at distances ranging from ten feet (near the road) to 200 feet in the open desert. An accidental crossing of the border, even if the border is not clearly marked, will not be accepted as an excuse. Motion detectors are known to be in use along the border. Unless you are absolutely certain of where the border is, it's always best to keep a safe distance.

Most visitors content themselves with simply driving to the border of Area 51 and glimpsing the warning signs and Cammo Dudes. The closest entrance to Rachel is the so-called "North Gate." The road to the North Gate begins approximately 1.4 miles south of Rachel near mile marker 11.4; on maps this may be identified as Valley Road or Groom Road (do not confuse this with Groom Lake Road!). While the road is generally well maintained, slow, careful driving is recommended since large rocks can cause flat tires. Follow the road for a little over ten miles until the guardhouse comes into view. Watch carefully for the warning signs as you approach the guardhouse; you will need to stop well before the guardhouse to avoid entering Area 51. If you are speeding, or fail to note the signs (a very real possibility if you are approaching at night), you may cross over the border without realizing it.

The North Gate is the newer entrance to Area 51 from Highway 375. It seems to be the preferred entrance for trucks and other heavy vehicles. While visiting the North Gate when researching this book, I was parked along the access road just short of the Area 51 border. In my rearview mirror, I noticed a large 18-wheeler truck traveling down the road toward the border and me. This was not your typical truck. It was painted (both cab and truck) gleaming white and I could see no markings of any sort. As it approached closer to my parked car, it began veering closer and passed me with only a couple of feet of clearance between our vehicles. As it passed, it kicked up a lot of dust, making it impossible to see the driver. I searched for any lettering on the side of the cab and truck but could see none. However, I did notice that the truck had a U.S. government license plate. Judging from the "brushback" he gave me, the driver was not too pleased to see me near the gate.

The Main Gate is located south of Rachel and is the most visited place on the Area 51 boundary. The easiest way to reach the main gate is via the Groom Lake Road, a graded gravel road similar to the one leading to the North Gate, located approximately 24.5 miles south of Rachel on Highway 375; it is a little over five miles south of the Black Mailbox. Groom Lake Road is unmistakable; it is a long, straight road leading toward the west and Area 51. Satellite photos indicate that this road continues through Area 51 into the Nevada Test Site and eventually to Highway 95.

It is also possible to reach the Main Gate from the road beginning at the Black Mailbox, but this is not recommended. That road will eventually take you to an intersection of three different roads, and failing to take the correct road will send you away from the Main Gate (see "Unusual Fact" below for an example of the possibly hilarious consequences of the wrong choice).

The distance from Highway 375 to the Area 51 border is just short of 14 miles. While there are several other gravel roads intersecting with Groom Lake Road, you travel straight on the road and make no turns. As you approach the border, the surrounding terrain will get hilly and you can often see the glint of reflected sunlight from a Cammo Dude truck on one of the hills inside area 51. Slow down and be alert for warning signs on both sides of the road; the boundary is not blocked by a security gate (as is the case at the North Gate) and the guardhouse is not visible from the Main Gate border—it is around

Area 51 Main Gate.

a bend in the road approximately a half-mile past the boundary. Once again, you should not cross past the warning signs under any circumstances! If you drive past them to the guardhouse, you will be detained and placed under arrest. Stop short of the border, turn around, and park well over to the side of Groom Lake Road so as not to block traffic.

You will be under both video and human surveillance at the Main Gate. During daytime, you usually won't be bothered by the Cammo Dudes as long as you don't act suspiciously or hike away from the road area (you might even find them hospitable; I have looked at them through binoculars while they looked back at me through their binoculars, I waved at them, and received a friendly wave back). But you are likely to be photographed or videotaped at the Main Gate. I have managed to videotape a Cammo Dude pointing what seemed to be a video "handy cam" at the Main Gate area, panning back and forth in a way that allowed him to capture the license plates of cars and faces of me and other visitors.

The Cammo Dudes get more active and aggressive if you hike away from the road or visit at night. The "rules of engagement" seem to be that anyone approaching the border on foot or at night is presumed to be intent upon crossing the border. If you hike toward the border on foot, you will be followed by Cammo Dudes and may encounter some along your path. If you drive toward the Main Gate at night, or are parked near the boundary at night, you may find yourself followed by a Cammo Dude truck or have a Cammo Dude truck park behind you. You may also be buzzed by low-flying helicopters.

There is also anecdotal evidence that the Cammo Dudes get more aggressive when some exceptionally secret activities are going on at Area 51. People have found Groom Lake Road blocked by Cammo Dude trucks, have been closely followed, or have been subjected to questioning and intimidating behavior (such as display of weapons) when parked near the Main Gate. And campers on land near the boundary have been awakened in the middle of the night by Cammo Dudes near their campsites. Such incidents are comparatively rare, however.

Area 51 Cammo Dudes.

Prior to 1995, it was possible to get a good view of the facilities at Area 51 from two hilltops known as Freedom Ridge and White Sides. Trails to these viewpoints were described in some guides to Area 51, and directions to these hilltops can still be found on some Web sites. However, these hilltops were added to Area 51 in April 1995, and it is now illegal to hike to them. Warning signs have been placed at the beginning of the old trails to Freedom Ridge and White Sides and orange posts mark the border. Do not attempt to climb to Freedom Ridge or White Sides as these are heavily monitored!

As mentioned earlier, Tikaboo Peak is the only spot left to get a look inside Area 51. It is a backpacking trip with no established trail (rock "ducks" mark the route) and, depending on the condition of the road to the trailhead, a four-wheel drive vehicle may be required. Snow is common during the winter. At the summit, you will need high-power binoculars (such as 20x magnification) or a spotting telescope to see any detail. Haze or other weather conditions may make getting a decent view impossible. On clear days (and nights), however, you will get an unobstructed view of Area 51 and the airspace above it as well as a large portion of the Nevada Test Site. Scanner radio reception is also excellent from the summit.

It is possible to get a good view of the airspace over Area 51 and S-4 from several locations on Highway 375 south of Rachel. During the day, you'll see readily identifiable military aircraft (and hear an occasional sonic boom) but there have been no reliable reports of UFOs, or even possibly secret aircraft, in daylight. The real action here takes place at night. Even if you don't believe in UFOs (or secret aircraft), the skies are filled with military aircraft performing combat maneuvers, flares, and other sights that are fascinating. There is often a myriad of unusual lights on most nights, especially after midnight. Depending on your perspective, these lights are conventional military aircraft and weapons systems, top-secret aircraft undergoing tests, UFOs, or maybe all three. The most active time to see things is during the normal Monday to Friday workweek, with late Wednesday night and early Thursday morning reportedly being best. This would make sense for testing programs; Mondays and Tuesdays could be used to set up the tests, and the results could be evaluated on Thursdays and Fridays.

Area 51 warning signs.

Unusual Fact: Area 51 was officially pronounced closed and abandoned in the June 1997 issue of *Popular Mechanics* magazine; according to that article, the Air Force had shifted its top-secret aircraft tests to the Green River Launch Complex in Utah (see the entry for it in the UTAH section). But, as the satellite photos prove, Area 51 is still very much in business and (as any visitor will quickly discover) as heavily guarded as ever. So what got into *Popular Mechanics?*

Jim Wilson, the science and technology editor of *Popular Mechanics*, wrote the article. According to his report, Wilson turned at the Black Mailbox toward Area 51. He followed the road to its end and found no guardhouse, no Cammo Dudes, no warning signs other than generic "no trespassing" signs and warnings that the area was used for live bombing practice. There was only a cattle gate—"the sort you can buy at K-Mart," as he described it—closed with weathered locks and rusting barbed wire. The road disappeared shortly after the gate. From such evidence, Wilson concluded Area 51 had been closed and was no longer used.

When the magazine hit the newsstands, Internet chat rooms and message boards were quickly abuzz with speculation. Since Area 51 was still in operation, was the article a piece of Air Force-sponsored disinformation? Was the Air Force laying the groundwork for a possible relocation of Area 51? Was Jim Wilson some sort of covert government operative? (Certainly, the Top Secret Government had to have been pleased by anything that discouraged visitors to Area 51.)

The truth turned out to be simpler and much funnier: Jim Wilson got lost and instead arrived at the gate for Area 61, a section of the Nellis Range Complex used for live bombing missions. He had driven down the road from the Black Mailbox, chose the wrong road at the intersection, and drove away from Area 51 and toward the gate to Area 61! Surprisingly, Wilson mentions using a map and a compass in trying to find Area 51 in his article. Since these skills are not often required in the New York City metropolitan area (unless your cab driver arrived last week from Bangladesh), perhaps he was a bit out of practice.

Area 61 is located south of Area 51 and you could, in theory, travel across it to Area 51. However, you would run into the same heavy security that you do when you approach Area 51 from any direction—provided that you managed to get that far. Area 61 is littered with live, unexploded bombs and shells, and there's a good chance that anyone trying to cross it on the way to Area 51 would be blown to bits long before running into the Cammo Dudes.

What was the aftermath of this story once Wilson's huge blunder became widely known? Did *Popular Mechanics* run a retraction or correction of the story? No. In fact, the article was still proudly posted on their website over five years later as an example of the outstanding journalism and accurate reporting you can find each month in the pages of the magazine. But let's be fair in this analysis. Maybe *Popular Mechanics* isn't the best place to look for information on Area 51, but I would never buy a riding lawnmower without first consulting their reviews.

Getting There: From Las Vegas, take Interstate 15 east until you reach the intersection with Highway 93. Travel north on Highway 93 for a little over 90 miles until you reach its intersection with Highway 375 north of Ash Springs. Look for the "Extraterrestrial Highway" signs at the intersection and follow Highway 375 north.

From Tonopah, take Highway 6 east for 50 miles and then turn south on Highway 375 for 60 miles to Rachel.

All routes into Rachel involve travel over roads with few gas stations, and gas is not always available in Rachel, especially at night. It's wise to top off your tank before leaving for Rachel and at every opportunity along the way, especially if you're traveling at night. Your car also should be in good working order with a full-size spare or an emergency tire inflation kit; extra water, food, and warm clothing can make the difference between an irritating delay and a life-threatening situation. This is very isolated country—as a brochure from the Nevada Commission on Tourism notes, "If a dozen cars traverse the 98-mile stretch of U.S. 375 in a day, it qualifies as rush-hour traffic." You will be out of cell phone coverage for much of the road. This is not the sort of trip you should make on the spur of the moment from Las Vegas—plan ahead!

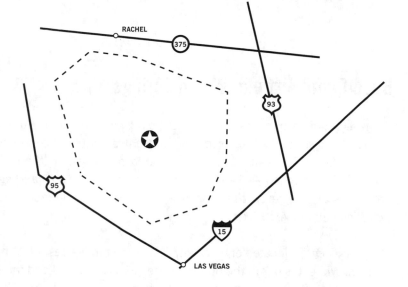

Roads to Area 51, Rachel

Base Camp Airfield, Warm Springs

A top secret airstrip located along a public highway? It's true! Built in the 1960s to support a proposed new nuclear test site, this was taken over by the Air Force in 1985 and declared off-limits. In the early 1990s, Stealth fighters were seen practicing "touch and go" landings here. It is also believed that this is an emergency landing strip for test flights out of Area 51.

Base Camp is located on Highway 6 about ten miles east of Warm Springs. While it is out in the open, the area is very isolated and miles from the nearest town and gas station. Highway 6 gets very little traffic even on weekends; a top-secret aircraft could land there in the middle of the night—or in the middle of most days—and not be noticed.

The name "Base Camp" was originally given to this site by the Atomic Energy Commission when it was planning to establish a new nuclear testing site in central Nevada. After that idea was abandoned, Base Camp was unused until the Air Force took over the area in April 1985 and began making improvements, including a new runway. According to the Air Force's official land use statement, Base Camp is used for "collecting data for Air Force testing programs conducted in the vicinity of the Tonopah Test Range (TTR) and the Nellis North Range." It is also reported that Base Camp is used as a recreation site for personnel at the Nellis Range Complex (although what "recreation" is available here is not readily apparent) and as an emergency landing site for flights out of the Nellis Range Complex, including Area 51.

What's There: Base Camp has a runway measuring 7,300 feet, radar domes and other navigation aids (including a radio-beacon), and fire-fighting equipment. There are several buildings that are mounted trailers and other mobile facilities; most appear to be office or administrative buildings although some are apparently used for housing. Rumors are that less than a dozen personnel work here at any given time.

Getting a Look Inside: There is no public admittance to this facility and trespassing is prohibited. However, Tybo Road runs through Base Camp, effectively cutting the facility in half, and the public is allowed access to this road. Tybo Road leads to the ghost town of Tybo: you should have a high-clearance four-wheel drive vehicle before attempting to drive the entire way to Tybo. In the mid-1990s, this road was incorrectly marked with "No Trespassing—U.S. Government Property" signs and security guards tried to prevent cars from using this road. The signs are now down and you may travel freely on the road. However, if you are parked along the road, expect a visit from a security guard. They are polite ("Are you having some trouble with your car, sir?") but very interested in why you are parked along the road.

Listening In: The aeronautical beacon here operates on 113.90 MHz and transmits "AEC" in Morse code every 30 seconds. "AEC" is almost certainly a relic from this site's ownership by the old Atomic Energy Commission. Interestingly, you won't find this beacon in any civilian list of aeronautical beacons.

Getting There: Base Camp is located on Highway 6 about 60 miles east of Tonopah and ten miles east of Warm Springs. Tybo Road is marked and the facility is unmistakable from Highway 6.

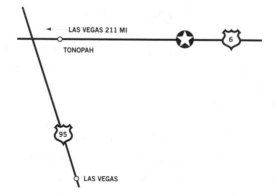

Roads to Base Camp Airfield, Warm Springs

Fallon Naval Air Station (NAS), Fallon

Located southeast of Reno in the high desert, Fallon NAS is the new home of the Navy's "Top Gun" school made famous in the movie of the same name. But the nearby town of Fallon is becoming famous for something else. Since the early 1990s, several children in this town of 8,300 have been diagnosed with acute lymphocytic leukemia, including eight new cases in 2000 alone. What's causing this concentrated outbreak? Vicki Badder, whose five-year-old son was diagnosed with leukemia, has a theory. "I think it has to do with the base," she says.

The U.S. Navy relocated its "Top Gun" fighter pilot school from San Diego to Fallon NAS in 1994. The sparsely populated area around Fallon was far better suited to its requirements than urbanized southern California; there is plenty of room here to practice maneuvers that might create sonic booms and to use live ordinance in drills. The relocation of "Top Gun" was the latest in a near-continuous expansion of Fallon's activities since it was founded in World War II. Today, it is arguably the Navy's most important aviation training and practice facility.

But something else arrived in Fallon in the early 1990s—a sudden, inexplicable outbreak of acute lymphocytic leukemia among the children of Fallon. By 2001, many outsiders (including the University of California's Arsenic Health Effects Research Program and Senator Hillary Clinton) focused on the high levels of arsenic in Fallon's water supply. The levels of arsenic in Fallon's water are truly scary; at 90 parts per billion, they are the highest of any municipal water supply in the nation and nearly double the highest levels generally considered safe.

Dangerously high levels of arsenic in Fallon's water supply have been present in Fallon's water since its founding in 1896. "If [high arsenic levels] were causing this," testified Randall Todd, the state epidemiologist for Nevada, "then we would have expected to see a cluster develop a long time ago." And indeed Fallon's rate for cancers of all types was not abnormal until the 1990s.

But maybe there is something deadly in the water of Fallon besides arsenic. David Toll, in his book *The Complete Nevada Traveler*, notes, "The Navy's use of the air space over a big part of the country to the east, to train pilots in combat techniques, has made the region uninhabitable. Oil and fuel spills, as well as bomb drops, have accumulated enormous environmental damage. Fallon is one of America's unsung Navy towns, but no one had this kind of impact in mind when the landing strip was built to help prevent a Japanese invasion."

The Navy rejects the notion that it is releasing anything into the environment that is responsible for the leukemia cluster. "Nothing has migrated off base and nothing is in the drinking water we've been able to detect," says Anne McMillin of Fallon NAS' public affairs office.

That may be true. But Fallon NAS started making bottled water available to Navy families in 1999.

To be fair to the Navy, they are not the only ones who may have unleashed something deadly into Fallon's groundwater. Fallon was the site of an underground atomic test on October 26, 1963. "Project Shoal" was part of a short-lived effort by the Atomic Energy Commission to test atomic weapons at sites other than the Nevada Test Site. The Project Shoal explosion measured 12 kilotons and was located 1,200 feet underground. While there was no known aboveground leak of the radiation, the underground particles from that test would still be heavily radioactive for thousands of years. Curiously, the AEC didn't monitor groundwater for radiation leaks, and neither did its successor, the Department of Energy, until February 1999. By that time, the cluster of cancers in Fallon was starting to attract national attention.

What's There: Fallon NAS is your standard-issue Navy base, complete with family housing, recreational facilities, etc. Perhaps the most remarkable facility at Fallon is a 14,000-foot-long runway.

Getting a Look Inside: Fallon NAS has no facilities open to the public, and tours are only offered to groups; such tours must be scheduled several months in advnace. However, Fallon NAS has an air show scheduled for June each year, and the base is open to the public at that time.

Unusual Fact: The Navy has proposed a "population mixing" theory to explain the cluster of childhood leukemias at Fallon. Quote from an official Navy press release: "The Population Mixing Theory suggests that Acute Lymphocytic Leukemia (ALL) clusters may be associated with unusual mixing of people, often in relatively isolated rural areas. Some researchers believe that exposure to a variety of infectious agents (i.e., virus, and/or bacteria) may trigger an unusual and rare reaction that affects a very small number of children within the susceptible population." However, there are several other areas, mainly military facilities, where "unusual mixing of people" takes place "in relatively isolated rural areas." If this theory is valid, there should be other similar clusters of childhood leukemias near them. Moreover, Fallon NAS was established in 1944 and has been a major command facility since 1972, so why did any "population mixing effects" not show up until the 1990s and the arrival of "Top Gun"?

Getting There: Fallon is located about 400 miles north of Las Vegas on Highway 95 and 60 miles southeast of Reno on Alternate Highway 50 East.

You can also visit the site of Project Shoal. From Highway 50, take the Sheelite Mine Road for five miles and then turn onto the crumbling asphalt road that heads toward the west. Only piles of rubble and a few thick iron posts set in concrete remain at the site, although the private Center for Land Use Interpretation has placed a descriptive plaque there.

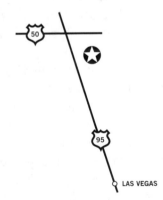

Roads to Fallon Naval Air Station (NAS), Fallon

Janet Airlines Terminal, Las Vegas

Janet Airlines is the Top Secret Government's official passenger airline and Las Vegas is its hub. Each day, its planes transport over 1000 workers from their homes in Las Vegas and Palmdale, California (see entry for Plant 42 in the CALIFORNIA section) to Area 51 and the Nellis Test Range in Nevada. It is also rumored that some Janet flights go to White Sands Missile Range in New Mexico.

Janet Airlines gets its name because "Janet" is the identifier heard used by its airplanes when communicating with air traffic control facilities. (It is rumored to stand for "Joint Air Network for Employee Transportation.") However, don't look for that name on any of its aircraft. Janet Airlines uses aircraft painted white with a single red stripe running down the length of the fuselage; the identifying numbers indicate the planes are registered to the Air Force. Janet uses mainly Boeing 737s along with some smaller Beechcraft planes. In Las Vegas, Janet Airlines flights depart from a private, secure terminal near McCarran Airport on Haven Street while flights at Palmdale are boarded at a facility on Plant 42 property adjacent to the Palmdale Airport.

Janet Airlines is operated by EG&G (see entry in the MARYLAND section). This is known because public records indicate the terminal facility is leased to EG&G. As noted above, the actual planes belong to the Air Force. It is not known whether the pilots are civilian or military, but the most likely scenario is that they are former military pilots now employed by EG&G. The passengers are all civilian employees of companies with projects underway at Area 51, Nellis, and other locations in the Southwest. The exact number of employees who commute this way is not known, but over 1,000 cars have been observed in the terminal's parking lot.

Those who travel on Janet Airlines work some unusual hours. Cars generally begin arriving around 3:30 a.m. and continue to arrive for about an hour later. (Even though they arrive when it's dark, most cars turn off their headlights as they approach the guard shacks at the entrance to the parking lots.) Flights load and take off quickly, far faster than commercial flights. Janet usually operates only on Monday through Friday; any weekend flights are generally considered a good sign that something exceptional is going on at one of the facilities serviced by Janet.

What's There: The Janet terminal looks very much like an ordinary general aviation facility, except for the high fence (topped with barbed wire), two guard shacks, and security guard patrols. Do not attempt to trespass on this property; trespassers have been arrested. Individuals in cars parked on Haven Street have had their license plate numbers taken by security guards and have also been told to move by Las Vegas police; presumably the police were acting at the request of terminal security guards. There are apartments on neighboring streets that offer unobstructed views of the terminal and the cars entering and leaving it.

Getting a Look Inside: The fences and security guards will keep you from actually walking inside. However, you can get a good view of the terminal, parking lot, and Janet airplanes arriving and departing from many high-rise hotels on the strip near McCarran. If you have a room facing McCarran in the Mandalay Bay, Luxor, Excalibur, Hacienda, MGM Grand, or Tropicana, you can watch activity at the terminal, including arrivals and departures, from your hotel room!

Listening In: Frequencies used by Janet aircraft to communicate with air traffic control in Las Vegas include 118.00, 118.70, and 133.95 MHz.

Unusual Fact: Among the job openings sometimes found on the EG&G website are what seem to be Janet Airlines flight attendant positions. These positions, based in Las Vegas, require candidates to have experience on 737 jets and hold a current Secret, or higher, security clearance; among the duties these flight attendants must perform include "manifesting passengers per security requirements" and "occasional overnight support as required."

Getting There: The Janet Airlines terminal is located on Haven Street at the northwest corner of McCarran Airport. From the Las Vegas Strip, take East Hacienda Avenue toward McCarran. Haven Street is the first right immediately after Bethel Lane.

Nellis Air Force Base Nuclear Weapons Storage Facility, North Las Vegas

Just off Interstate 15, north of Las Vegas, is a storage facility currently holding over 200 nuclear weapons. When nuclear weapons were being tested at the Nevada Test Site (NTS), this is where those weapons were kept prior to being transported to the NTS.

Officially known as Area 2 of Nellis Air Force Base, this nuclear weapons storage installation is located about a mile north of the main Nellis site. In addition to being a storage facility for nuclear and "unconventional" (whatever that means) weapons, Area 2 is also the site of a minimum-security federal prison.

What's There: The nuclear weapons are kept in numerous underground bunkers covered with earth; from a distance, they resemble the burial mounds created by Native Americans. Several tall security fences surround these bunkers; presumably the fences are electrified. Floodlights illuminate the entire area at night, and what appear to be security cameras and motion detectors are along the fence. The federal prison is located away from the nuclear weapons storage area.

Getting a Look Inside: There is no public admittance to this facility and trespassing is prohibited. However, it is very well lit at night and easily visible from Interstate 15.

Unusual Fact: According to former Air Force personnel who have been assigned here, each nuclear warhead is stored inside a heavy lead container resembling a coffin. Who says the Top Secret Government doesn't have a sense of humor?

Getting There: Area 2 is located northeast of Las Vegas on Interstate 15 and becomes visible soon after the intersection with Ann Road. It is located away from the highway, however, and you'll need binoculars to get a good look during the day. As noted above, it is easily spotted at night because of the security lighting.

Nevada Test Site (NTS), Mercury

Located about 65 miles north of Las Vegas is the most heavily-nuked piece of real estate on this planet. But in 1992 a moratorium on nuclear testing went into effect. So what do you do with a chunk of land bigger than Rhode Island (site #3 in Top Secret America) that has blast craters like those on the moon and areas of high radioactivity if you can't test atomic bombs there? Well, you do hazardous chemical spill tests, "environmental technology studies," "emergency response training," and build a germ "factory" to produce microbes for germ warfare research. Plus you also turn it into a prime Top Secret Tourism destination by offering guided tours!

The Department of Energy describes the Nevada Test Site (NTS) as "a unique national resource."

The NTS was established in December 1950, and occupies over 1,350 square miles. Its eastern boundary is Area 51, making their combined area among the most secretive and closely guarded pieces of real estate on this planet. Between 1951 and 1962, 126 atomic bomb tests were conducted aboveground within the confines of the NTS. In that era, a highlight for many vacationers to Las Vegas was not seeing Frank, Dean, or Sammy at The Sands, but instead driving up north on Highway 95 to see a real, live atomic bomb explosion. Atmospheric nuclear testing was banned by international treaty in 1962. Underground tests were still permitted, and over 800 were conducted here until 1992. Since then, underground "subcritical" tests have been conducted here that use amounts of fissionable material too small to sustain a chain reaction.

All these tests have left NTS "hot." According to a report in the October 23, 2000 *Las Vegas Sun*, the soil of the NTS is contaminated with over four tons of plutonium. In most areas of the NTS, however, the concentration of plutonium is too small to pose a health risk. That's good, because it will still be radioactive for another 500,000 years.

While the NTS may not be doing much nuclear testing these days, it is doing a good bit of testing of other hazardous substances. In fact, it seems that the NTS is pitching itself as a place to test things away from the prying eyes of the media and the Environmental Protection Agency. According to a marketing sheet prepared by the Department of Energy to generate business from private companies, "The Nevada Test Site also serves the nation as a proving ground for alternative energy research and Department of Defense projects that require the isolation, complex infrastructure, and technical expertise we can provide. As a National Environmental Research Park, the Nevada Test Site is home to important environmental activities including technology development, clean up and remediation of contaminated environments, and waste management. The Test Site is a unique outdoor laboratory where federal agencies and private industry conduct large-scale open-air experiments with hazardous and toxic chemicals and test remediation and emergency response techniques." It further continues, "The Nevada Test Site offers an enormous amount of space, including more than 1,000 miles of completely undisturbed land available for new projects. The vast site also offers security. The boundary and security areas are guarded, and the area is isolated from population centers." Sounds like a terrific place to do something you'd rather not have people know about.

What's There: More than 1,100 buildings and laboratories are located at the NTS along with 400 miles of paved roads, 300 miles of unpaved roads, two airstrips, ten heliports, and power transmission and generation facilities. There is also housing for 1,200 people (although most employees commute from the Las Vegas area via shuttle buses), a hospital, a cafeteria, a post office, a fire station, and a substation of the Nye County sheriff's department (who are there mainly to place arrested trespassers and haul them to the county jail). In fact, the population of the NTS makes it the second largest "city" in Nye County (the biggest is Pahrump, former home of radio talk show host Art Bell). The NTS is Nye County's biggest "industry," with the second largest apparently being several legal brothels and massage parlors near Pahrump.

The NTS is divided into different areas, and employees are able to enter only those areas for which they have the proper security clearance. The areas visible from Highway 95 require only relatively low-level security clearances, while those areas bordering Area 51 require very high-level clearances. Immediately adjacent to it inside the Nevada Test Site is Area 15. Area 13 is where plutonium dispersal tests were conducted in the 1950s. The most isolated region of the NTS, Area 19, is the subject of much speculation; it is actually more remote than the fabled Area 51. Topographic maps show that several large power lines lead into Area 19, but official NTS maps show no facilities located there. However, satellite photos do indicate that some buildings are inside Area 19. So what is going on there that requires so much electric power? One possibility would be high-power lasers or some form of directed energy weapons.

Key Facilities: The Device Assembly Facility (DAF) is a 100,000 square-foot building located in Area 6 where the atomic bombs to be tested underwent final assembly. Since testing stopped, it is used for disassembly of atomic weapons being withdrawn from America's stockpile. All aboveground portions of the DAF are covered with at least five feet of soil and the building includes decontamination stations, testing laboratories, bridge cranes, and—even though it is located entirely inside the NTS—its own guard stations and security cameras. The interior of the building is divided into five assembly "cells." As official NTS literature says, the DAF is "designed to minimize release of nuclear material in the unlikely event of an accidental explosion."

The Hazardous Material (HAZMAT) Spill Center, according once again to official NTS literature, "allows live releases of hazardous materials for training purposes, field-test detection, plume dispersion experimentation, and equipment and materials testing." In other words, this is a place where laws and regulations to protect the environment don't apply, and they're damn proud of it. The HAZMAT Spill Center is located in Area 5 of the NTS.

The Big Explosives Experimental Facility (BEEF—get it?) is, like its name implies, a place to test really big conventional explosives. The BEEF is in Area 4 and is a converted aboveground nuclear explosion monitoring facility, complete with a reinforced concrete bunker, cameras, and monitoring and diagnostic electronics.

The U1a Experimental Facility is located in Area 1 and is an underground complex originally built for an underground nuclear test that was never conducted. The complex includes a vertical shaft going down to 960 feet below the surface, where it then connects to horizontal tunnels over a half-mile long; a mechanical hoist carries equipment and people down to the 960-foot level and the intersecting tunnels. On the surface, the U1a facility is marked only by trailers and other temporary structures. What is U1a used for? Official NTS literature vaguely says that it permits "scientists to gain more knowledge of the dynamic properties of aging nuclear materials" (whatever that means). But, the literature continues, "the complex will provide a high degree of safety for NTS workers and the public and will minimize environmental impacts."

While not exactly "facilities," there are several additional points of interest inside NTS. There are several lunar-like craters, all of them produced by underground atomic tests of devices located not far under the surface. The most famous is the Sedan Crater, measuring 1,280 feet wide and 320 feet deep. It was produced as part of the "Plowshare Project," a program to see if nuclear explosions could be used as a cheap way to excavate land for construction projects (don't laugh). Sedan Crater is on the National Register of Historic Places.

Other somewhat surreal areas of NTS are the so-called "Doom Towns," built to test the impact of nuclear explosions and fallout on civilian structures. One Doom Town was a replica of early 1950s American suburbia. In the 1950s, these camera-rigged homes, many with cars parked in front, were filled with typical home furnishings (including bric-a-brac and fresh food) and populated by department store mannequins so the effects of nearby atomic explosions could be studied. (You may have seen the grainy black-and-white films of these tests, the ones in which the blast wave from the explosion shatters living room windows and knocks "Dad" from his recliner, sending him flying across the living room in a disturbingly prophetic vision of the looming 1960s social upheavals.) The other Doom Town was a startling sight: a Japanese village in the middle of the Nevada desert. This Doom Town was used to study the dispersion and spread of fallout, and used the data gathered from the actual explosions at Hiroshima and Nagasaki to study the fallout-producing capabilities of new bomb designs. Today, only a handful of structures remain at these two Doom Towns.

Various areas inside the NTS are fenced off and access roads are gated to prevent entry by those without the proper level of security clearance. The gates are numbered, and the most famous is Gate 700. It controls access to the road leading from the NTS into Area 51.

Secret Stuff: In 1953, the Nevada Test Site played the key role in the United States government's nuking of John Wayne.

"Harry" was the code name for a nuclear test at the NTS on May 19, 1953. This device used a newly designed hollow fissionable core and the device was located atop a tower 300 feet aboveground. The new core design and elevated location produced an unexpectedly heavy amount of fallout; long before the Clint Eastwood movie, this test became known as "Dirty Harry."

The prevailing winds at the time of the test took the main fallout plume over St. George, Utah, a town in southwest Utah near the Arizona and Nevada borders. At least five residents of St. George developed radiation sickness, and the Atomic Energy Commission (AEC) had to order residents to stay indoors for several hours after the test. Hundreds of sheep in the area died after eating grass contaminated by the fallout, and for months afterward livestock in the area had an exceptionally high number of stillbirths.

Shortly after the "Harry" test, the movie *The Conqueror* was filmed around St. George. In addition to John Wayne, the movie also starred Susan Hayward and Agnes Moorehead; it was directed by Dick Powell. All four were to die of cancer. A total of 220 people were in the cast and crew, and 91 of them had developed cancer by 1980. According to the AEC, this was all just a coincidence.

The NTS was the scene of the most serious nuclear accident in American history when the "Baneberry" underground test went awry on December 18, 1970. Although the bomb was located 900 feet below the surface, its yield was greater than expected; the explosion created fissures in the surface through which clouds of radioactive dust escaped. Since the explosion and all radioactivity were supposed to be contained underground, most workers in the area were caught without protective clothing and received substantial does of radiation. The Department of Energy maintains that only 86 employees were exposed and that (in the DOE's words) "none received exposure that exceeded the guideline for radiation workers." However, over 300 workers claimed to have been exposed; at least that many showed clear symptoms of radiation poisoning, such as hair loss and passing blood. Many who claimed exposure filed lawsuits against the DOE. However, most of those suits against the DOE were never settled because the majority of the plaintiffs had died by the mid-1970s (leukemia was the most common cause of death). The depositions taken for those suits repeatedly contained details of how key evidence of the actual exposure workers received, such as the radiation-monitoring badges workers were required to wear, had been destroyed after the test.

Even though the Baneberry incident is much less well known than 1979's Three Mile Island accident, the radiation released by Baneberry was several thousands of times greater than at Three Mile Island.

Is there still potentially dangerous, or even deadly, secret stuff going on at NTS? The probability seems quite high. Giving credence to the notion that something hazardous is still happening at NTS is supported by the Community Environmental Monitoring Program (CEMP), a network of 20 monitoring stations in Nevada and Utah that are located in areas downwind from NTS. Sponsored by the Department of Energy, these stations are supposed to check for evidence of "manmade radioactivity" but the stations, in the DOE's own words, "collect a variety of environmental data." But why is it necessary to check for radioactivity now since the last underground test was several years ago? The answer, obviously, is that the CEMP stations are monitoring more than just radioactivity drifting from the NTS. Given that the NTS boasts of its facilities for testing hazardous materials spills and other accidents, it seems almost a certainty that sort of activity is underway at NTS and those are the sorts of hazards CEMP is designed to detected. The next "Dirty Harry" or "Baneberry" accidents could well be chemical or biological instead of nuclear.

Evidence for such speculation was provided on September 4, 2001 by a story in the *New York Times*. According to the report, a germ-making "factory" was built during the late 1990s in the "Camp 12" (was this supposed to be Area 12?) section of the NTS. According to the *Times*, the facility was built by the Defense Threat Reduction Agency to assess how difficult it would be for a rogue nation or terrorist group to construct a germ warfare facility (it turned out it would be easy, as all components used in the plant were obtained from hardware and construction supply stores). The facility was used to determine if such a factory would have tell-tale "signatures" (such as chemical or infrared emissions) that could be detected by surveillance planes or satellites. While the facility was fully capable of producing lethal organisms such as anthrax, officials say it was only used to produce ordinary microbes and was strictly defensive in intent.

An interesting footnote to the *Times* story was that the White House and Congress were never notified of the project, supposedly because of its small scale and low cost.

Getting a Look Inside: Incredible as it might seem, the Nevada Test Site offers guided tours.

Tours are currently offered monthly and always take place Monday through Thursday. Visitors are shuttled to the site aboard buses departing from the Department of Energy Nevada Operations Office. Because of security considerations, you must register in advance and provide a variety of personal information, including social security number, date and place of birth, your employer's name, address, and telephone number; you will need official photo identification (driver's license, passport, etc.) and tour admission may be denied to anyone deemed a security risk. Visitors are not allowed to bring or use cameras, video recorders, binoculars, telescopes, tape recorders, make sketches, take any rock, soil, or plant samples, or remove any metal objects; basically, you're allowed to look and that's it. Visitors are forbidden to wear shorts or sandals, and pregnant women are discouraged because, in the words of the NTS, "the long bus ride and uneven terrain" may pose health hazards.

So what do you get to see in exchange for being treated like a fourth-grader on a school trip? Quite a bit, actually. Tour stops include the HAZMAT Spill Center, Sedan Crater, the Low-Level Radioactive Waste management Site, Control Point 1 (the command post used for aboveground atomic tests), Frenchman Flat (site of the first aboveground test at NTS), and the American "Doom Town." To find out the dates of upcoming tours and to register, write U.S. Department of Energy, Nevada Operations Office, Office of Public Affairs and Information, Visit Coordination Staff, P.O. Box 98518, Las Vegas, NV, 89193-8518.

The entire area of NTS is restricted and unauthorized entry is strictly prohibited; trespassers are routinely arrested. However, there are unmarked gravel roads leading into the NTS and the border may not be clearly indicated. Before security was increased after the September 11 attacks, I drove past an open gate and several hundred feet into NTS before I spotted a sign telling me I was inside the NTS. Since I had no desire to spend the evening as a guest in the Nye County jail,

I turned around and got the hell out. It's still a good thing for America that I'm just some epicene writer instead of an international terrorist.

Unusual Facts: The Nevada Test Site was the scene of the first live telecast of an atomic bomb explosion. On May 17, 1953, the "Annie" test was broadcast live across America on NBC's *Today* show. The television crew was located 11 kilometers away on a hilltop that became known as "News Knob." The test was conducted just before dawn and entertained families gathered around their breakfast tables in the eastern and central time zones.

And we can't say goodbye to the NTS without noting it is now officially a "National Environmental Research Park." If that isn't an unusual fact, nothing is.

Getting There: The Nevada Test Site is located about 65 miles northwest of Las Vegas on Highway 95. The exit for Mercury will take you to the main entrance for the NTS. However, the "town" of Mercury only exists within the NTS; there are no services at this exit other than the NTS gate. Since this area is very isolated, you should top off your gas tank in Indian Springs or Amargosa Valley before visiting the NTS.

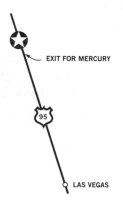

EXIT FOR MERCURY

95

LAS VEGAS

Roads to Nevada Test Site (NTS), Mercury

Nuclear Emergency Search Team (NEST), Nellis Air Force Base

Suppose Uncle Sam receives a report that a terrorist group has planted a nuclear device somewhere on American soil. If that happens, the Nuclear Emergency Search Team would be dispatched to locate and disarm it.

The Nuclear Emergency Search Team (NEST) is an outgrowth of the Air Force's experience in retrieving nuclear weapons from crashed bombers during the 1950s and 1960s. NEST was formed after the 1991 collapse of the Soviet Union, which greatly increased the possibility of a nuclear weapon falling into terrorist hands. Its funding was substantially increased after the 1993 World Trade Center bombing. While that attack used conventional explosives, a nuclear weapon could have just as easily been concealed in the terrorists' van parked in the Center's garage. This realization was the impetus for NEST to greatly expand its capabilities, especially the ability to be rapidly deployed to search for hidden nuclear weapons.

The NEST staff consists of volunteers from Nellis AFB and from the Los Alamos and Sandia National Laboratories in New Mexico and the Lawrence Livermore National Laboratory in California. Their areas of expertise mainly include nuclear device fabrication and dismantling, with other members having skills in radiation detection, conventional explosives and firearms, and field security.

Nellis was apparently selected as the NEST headquarters because of its long experience in matters related to nuclear weapons. For many years, Nellis is where devices tested at the Nevada Test Site underwent final assembly, and, as noted earlier, it is a storage facility for atomic weapons. Training missions are held at the NTS, including locating hidden nukes and their disassembly. The identities of all NEST members are classified.

What's There: The NEST headquarters building is located in a remote part of Nellis AFB, away from public view. It is known that a military cargo plane is kept in a constant state of readiness at Nellis for their use; the plane includes radiation detectors, vans, disassembly tools, protective clothing, communications and computing gear, electrical generators, and other items that would be needed to locate and disarm a nuclear device.

Secret Stuff: Remember the Los Alamos National Laboratory spy scare back in 1999, involving Chinese-American scientist Wen Ho Lee? He was arrested late that year and charged with 59 felony counts of espionage, most involving downloading of data from the Los Alamos computers to his personal computer. Eventually, the government dropped the espionage charges and Lee pleaded guilty to a single count of mishandling classified information. U.S. District Court James Parker, who presided over the case, said the government's handing of the Lee case "embarrassed our entire nation" and admitted he was misled by the FBI and the Justice Department. Some of the information Lee was charged with stealing was data used by NEST, including design, assembly, and technical data for all the known nuclear weapons in the world, U.S. and foreign, and how to neutralize such devices.

Getting a Look Inside: Nellis AFB can arrange tours for groups through the public affairs office with at least 30 days advance notice; however, the NEST facilities are not part of any such tour.

Unusual Fact: In addition to training exercises at the NTS, NEST has also conducted simulations in various American cities in which members try to locate a hidden "nuke" (actually a mildly radioactive object that can be detected with their highly sensitive instruments). It has been reported that some NEST members were mugged during one such simulation when the object was hidden in what was described as "a depressed urban area."

Getting There: Nellis AFB is located northeast of Las Vegas on Interstate 15 off the East Craig Road exit.

Roads to Nuclear Emergency Search Team (NEST),
Nellis Air Force Base

15

EAST CRAIG ROAD EXIT

LAS VEGAS

Project Faultless Test Site, Nye County

The site of a one-megaton hydrogen bomb test on public land that you can freely visit—I'm kidding, right? Nope! But be sure to obey that sign that tells you not to dig or take any soil, okay?

By the mid-1960s, the atomic bomb tests at the Nevada Test Site were no longer tourist attractions for Las Vegas. In fact, they were the opposite—some people were afraid to visit Las Vegas, and conventions were being cancelled in the city, because of fears that a test could go awry and destroy the city. While all tests after 1963 were conducted underground, they did produce earthquake-like effects (including swaying buildings) in Las Vegas. Pressured to find a new test site, the Atomic Energy Commission selected a tentative new site in the northeastern corner of Nye County, about 30 miles from the intersections of Highways 6 and 375. To determine whether this site had the proper geology for underground testing, a "calibration" hydrogen bomb of one megaton was detonated at a depth of 3,200 feet on January 19, 1968. While the bomb was a success, the test was a failure because the land was shown to be too geologically fragile to reliably contain the radioactivity from an underground test. However, that same site today is not restricted and can be visited by anyone.

The test site was approximately 75 miles east of Tonopah, and there was strong public opposition there and among ranchers in the area to the proposed tests. To counteract such opposition, the AEC decided on a policy of openness instead of the secrecy that cloaked tests at the NTS. A group of civilians from the region would be allowed to observe the first test, called "Project Faultless," from a location "safely" away from ground zero. Economic benefits, such as an influx of highly paid nuclear scientists needing gasoline, food, and housing, were stressed by the AEC in an attempt to build support among the many unemployed miners and ranchers in the region.

But Project Faultless didn't work as planned. The land above ground zero bulged 15 feet upward at the moment of the blast and quickly began to collapse back as the explosion created an artificial cavern. In several places, the ground collapse measured ten feet below the previous level; the total depressed area is about 4,000 square feet. Fault lines running thousands of feet north and south of ground zero formed. And the shock wave from the blast was strong enough to shatter windows 90 miles away even though it was contained underground.

The resulting public outcry, from both in and outside of Nevada, forced the AEC to cancel all future tests at the Faultless site (the next one was to have been a five-megaton test). After the test, the AEC sealed off the other tunnels that had been drilled for additional tests, removed soil they said was contaminated, and eventually opened the area for public access. In January 2001, the Department of Energy announced that employees who had worked at the Project Faultless site had been added to the list of those eligible for medical expenses and other compensation for any medical conditions produced by exposure to toxic substances. However, the DOE also says it's safe for the public to visit this site. Is there a contradiction in those two statements?

What's There: At the site you will see what is often referred to as the "Monument," which looks like a ground-mounted water tank on a concrete slab. This is actually a "plug" for the tunnel in which the bomb was placed. On the side of the "Monument" is a plaque identifying this location as the site of the Project Faultless test and warning, "No excavation, drilling, and/or removal of materials is permitted without U.S. Government approval within a horizontal ground distance of 3,300 from surface ground zero." When I visited, someone had painted "body shadows" on the "Monument" similar to those produced by bomb victims at Hiroshima and Nagasaki.

You will notice the ground at the site is depressed compared to the surrounding land. You will also note other markers in the areas with cryptic lettering (such as "UCI-I-2 N1414 32407") that may have been used to define boundaries or areas. The other tunnels dug for future tests are now covered by thick concrete "caps" and look more like something from an irrigation project than an atomic test.

Getting a Look Inside: Look around all you want; it's now public land although some older maps may indicate this belongs to the AED or DOE.

Getting There: The Project Faultless site is located off Highway 6 and the nearest town is Tonopah. Take Highway 6 east approximately 75 miles from Tonopah (25 miles from Warm Springs and the intersection with Highway 375) until you see a sign to "Moore's Station" near mile marker 76.5; take the graded dirt road on the left. Follow this road about 12.5 miles until you reach a stop sign. Continue straight ahead past the stop sign, but the road beyond this point can be rough; if you have a low clearance vehicle, you may want to walk the remaining 1.5 miles to the site. Look for the "Monument" as you approach the site; you can usually drive right up to it. This is very isolated country. You should fill up with gas in Tonopah and your car should be in good mechanical condition and have a full spare; extra food, water, and warm clothing should also be taken in case of a problem since you are a long way from help out here.

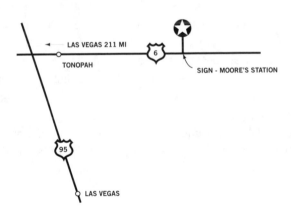

Roads to Project Faultless Test Site, Nye County

Tonopah Test Range (TTR), Tonopah

Less known than Area 51 or the Nevada Test Site, the Tonopah Test Range was the location for the first F-117 Stealth fighter group back when the plane was still top secret. Originally used by the Atomic Energy Commission for nuclear weapons research, it's now shared with the Air Force. After the Stealth fighter became publicly known, the group at Tonopah relocated to Holloman Air Force Base in New Mexico and the Air Force relegated their operations at Tonopah to "caretaker status." Recently, however, new roads and buildings have recently been constructed, and rumors say TTR is going "blacker," possibly to handle some still-secret aircraft that are now operational.

The Tonopah Test Range (TTR) was the perfect place to station the first operational F-117 Stealth fighter group back in 1984. It is almost as isolated as Area 51 and farther from Las Vegas or other significant population area. TTR borders on Area 51, and it is believed that many projects under development there are tested on the TTR radar range.

TTR occupies 625 square miles at the north end of the Nellis Range Complex. It was first opened in 1957 as an adjunct facility for the Nevada Test Site for research connected with the test at NTS. The Air Force first began using TTR in 1979 and began a major construction program to house the F-117 Stealth fighter being developed at Area 51. Later, additional facilities to support Air Force programs were added. However, TTR is still administered by the Department of Energy through Sandia Labs.

TTR proved to be an ideal location for the first Stealth fighters. The area north of TTR is the isolated Great Smokey Valley, a sparsely populated area that was perfect for the first nighttime training missions of the F-117. In addition to its isolation, the citizens of nearby Tonopah were reticent to talk about the strange aircraft they saw cruising their nighttime skies. It was common knowledge in Tonopah during the early 1980s that something big and secret was going on at TTR, but the citizens kept silent about what they were seeing and hearing because TTR employees were a desperately needed source of revenue.

TTR was also a site during the 1980s for tests of Soviet aircraft, such as the MiG-21 and MiG-23, which the United States had obtained through clandestine means (the fact that the United States had such aircraft is no longer classified, but the means by which they were obtained still is). Like the F-117, these were mainly tested at night. These tests continued at TTR until the early 1990s.

In addition to its air base facilities, TTR includes the Tonopah Electronic Combat Range (TECR), an extensive system of camera and radar systems to record data from aircraft and missiles tested there and simulate threats (such as surface-to-air missiles) from enemy defenses. In fact, TTR is known to have several Russian and Chinese radar systems obtained through various means (such as purchases via third countries and bribes paid to military and industrial officials connected to those nations) that are used to test the radar "invisibility" of various weapons systems.

After the F-117 fighters were transferred from TTR in 1992, activity here dropped greatly. However, there has recently been a flurry of new activity, especially on the eastern side near an area known as Cedar Ranch. The road leading to the Cedar Ranch entrance to TTR was recently repaved and security has been increased there. This may be a better place to get a close-up look at still-secret aircraft than Area 51.

What's There: The runway at TTR is over 12,000 feet long—a few feet longer than the runway at Area 51. When the first F-117 squadron arrived at TTR, a hangar was built for each craft. As a result, there are 54 hangars here. There are also extensive barracks and other facilities. When the F-117 was still secret, great efforts were made to keep TTR as self-contained as possible so personnel would not have to leave the base. Thus, TTR had accommodations and recreational facilities superior to those found in Tonopah or other towns within reasonable driving distance. The "barracks" were hotel-like and far superior to housing found on other military bases; they included "blackout" curtains and soundproofing since almost all Stealth operations were conducted at night and personnel slept during the day.

The TECR is located south and east of the base facilities. While electronic warfare is the stated purpose of this area, it is believed that many other activities are conducted from behind the "screen" provided by Tolicha Peak. Satellite photographs show several buildings there, including some that strongly resemble aircraft hangars, but no landing strip.

Secret Stuff: "Janet" airplanes (see entry in this section) have started landing at TTR and can sometimes be seen from the main gate. The presence of Janet airplanes is a good indication that something connected with Area 51 and Plant 42 (see entry in the CALIFORNIA section) is now going on here.

Getting a Look Inside: There are currently no tours of the TTR, and no facilities open to the public. However, you can get a surprisingly good view of the runway from the main entrance of the TTR.

Unusual Fact: Giving credence to reports that TTR is a hotbed of electronic warfare were several strange incidents in the northern areas of Las Vegas on February 20, 2004. On that date, car dealerships and locksmiths were flooded with reports of sudden failures of keyless car lock systems. Even personnel at Nellis Air Force Base were not immune. "Maybe it's those little green men up north," said Mike Estrada, a spokesman for Nellis. "I've been trying to figure it out. It happened to me after lunch." Some car dealers reported over 100 calls from customers "zapped out" of their cars, while others were forced to use their keys to gain entry and triggered their car alarms as a result. Since there were no thunderstorms in the Las Vegas area on that day and no abnormal sunspot activity, that left an apparently too successful test of an electromagnetic pulse weapon in the southern region of the TTR as the most likely culprit. The Los Angeles office of the Federal Communications Commission—the office responsible for Las Vegas—seemed to agree. "Who knows what the military could be using at any given time?" said Paul Oei, a spokesman for the Los Angeles FCC office.

Getting There: The main entrance to the TTR is via a paved road located about 15 miles east of Tonopah on Highway 6; a sign shaped like a rocket marks the road. The road travels approximately 20 miles south toward the TTR. The road leads to a guard gate that is manned 24 hours a day. Caution is required as you approach this gate, as the TTR boundary is before the gate and guardhouse; the boundary is poorly marked and it's easy to stray across into the TTR if you're not careful. The boundary area is highly developed and you can see numerous hangars, barracks, and support buildings from its perimeter.

The new Cedar Ranch entrance into the TTR leads to the TECR.

This entrance is from the eastern side of the TTR and is located off Highway 375 just before the Queen City Summit marker. This road is marked on some maps as the Cedar Ranch Road. Formerly a dirt road leading to an unguarded gate, the road is now paved and a manned guardhouse has been added a few hundred feet inside the secured perimeter. These enhancements are a strong indication that some new classified activity is going on in this part of the range. This part of the TTR borders on the Area 51 boundary and security is more active here than along the road to the main laboratory; there have been numerous reports of travelers along this road being followed and otherwise monitored by security. Along Cedar Ranch Road you can also see, not surprisingly, Cedar Ranch, a small cattle ranch that was abandoned in the 1950s because of fallout from the Nevada Test Site. Even though the ranch has been abandoned, several buildings are still standing and cattle graze in the area. The cattle frequently gather at the ranch because water is available, and care must be taken on Cedar Ranch Road to avoid hitting them in the road.

There is another entrance to the TECR from the west on Highway 95. The gate is manned around the clock and is located approximately 20 miles north of Beatty near a NASA satellite tracking station. The road to the gate is paved but unmarked; it heads east toward the TTR for about two miles before reaching the gate.

All of these entrances are located in isolated areas with the nearest gas stations or other services many miles away.

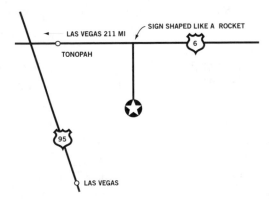

Roads to Tonopah Test Range (TTR), Tonopah

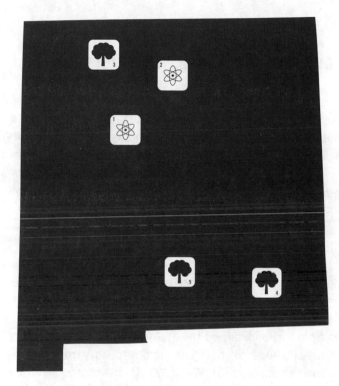

NEW MEXICO

1. Kirtland Air Force Base, Albuquerque 2. Los Alamos National Laboratory, Los Alamos
3. Project Gasbuggy Test Site, Rio Arriba County 4. Project Gnome Test Site, Eddy County
5. White Sands Missile Range, Alamogordo

Kirtland Air Force Base, Albuquerque

Kirtland Air Force Base is one of the high points of any tour of Top Secret America. It was one of the key transportation facilities for the Manhattan Project, and later became the world's first assembly plant for hydrogen bombs. Today it is home to two top-secret research labs and is also the world's largest known storage facility for atomic weapons. And don't forget the National Atomic Museum and its gift shop!

Kirtland Air Force Base covers 52,678 acres and over 20,000 military personnel and civilians work inside its secured boundaries. Kirtland has long been a major part of the Top Secret Government. Kirtland was founded in 1941 as an Army Air Field, and was one of the major transportation points for the Manhattan Project; C-54 cargo planes from Kirtland carried the atomic bombs eventually dropped on Hiroshima and Nagasaki from Los Alamos to Navy transport ships waiting in San Francisco. After World War II, it became a storage center for atomic bombs built in Los Alamos and later Kirtland served as the manufacturing site for the first hydrogen weapons until the Pantex nuclear weapons manufacturing facility was built in neighboring Texas.

For years, Kirtland was perhaps best known to the general public as the location of the Manzano Weapons Storage Area, a series of tunnels drilled deep for nuclear weapons storage. Weapons assembled at the Pantex plant in Texas were shipped to Kirtland for storage and eventual redistribution to other military bases. As a result, Manzano rapidly became the largest storage area for nuclear weapons in the United States and a lightning rod for nuclear disarmament and anti-war demonstrations in the 1960s. In 1994, the original Manzano facility was closed and replaced by a new facility inside the perimeter of Kirtland.

Several engineering projects that could not be accommodated at Los Alamos during the Manhattan Project were carried out at Kirtland. After World War II, Kirtland became a center for advanced weapons research. Current activities are carried out under the auspices of the Department of Energy's Sandia National Laboratories and the Air Force's Phillips Laboratory.

What's There: Kirtland is a big, busy place. Some of the less secret activities include the 150th Fighter Wing (consisting of about 30 F-16s) and the 58th Special Operations Wing, which trains all Air Force helicopter crews and C-130 transport crews. The Air Force Operational Test and Evaluation Center tests current Air Force weapons systems under various combat conditions to determine their effectiveness and areas for improvement. One interesting structure here is known as "the Trestle." This is the largest all-wood structure in the world, and was originally built to test how well an aircraft's electronics systems would be protected in case of a nearby nuclear explosion. There are also runways, hangars, support and maintenance buildings, housing, and related support facilities for the military and civilian personnel who work at Kirtland.

In addition to the Sandia and Phillips Laboratories, Kirtland is home to the Department of Energy's Albuquerque operations office.

Key Facilities: As mentioned before, the original Manzano facility was closed in 1994 and replaced by a new weapons storage installation known as the Kirtland Underground Munitions Storage Complex (KUMSC). Located in the southeast corner of Kirtland, the aboveground area of KUMSC covers 56 acres. However, most of KUMSC is underground deep within Manzano Mountain. Information about its structure and organization is classified, but it is known that KUMSC consists of multiple subterranean tunnels and storage areas. KUMSC is fenced off from the rest of Kirtland and has a special security force assigned to it. The exact number of warheads stored here varies, but usually over 2500 warheads are stored here inside lead containers. (Unconfirmed accounts by former Air Force personnel say the containers used to store the warheads closely resemble coffins.)

According to its official description, the Air Force's Phillips Laboratory "concentrates its research and development in six technical areas: geophysics, propulsion, space and missiles technology, lasers and imaging, advanced weapons and survivability, and space experiments." Phillips (and its predecessor organizations such as the Air Force Weapons Laboratory) has long been recognized as a world leader in laser research. One of their principal efforts has been the development of high-power lasers, such as those strong enough to shoot down incoming missiles.

Sandia National Laboratories can trace its origins back to the Manhattan Project, when a branch of Los Alamos was established at Kirtland to handle the transport of the first atomic bombs to San Francisco. After World War II, a branch of Los Alamos was established, and in 1949 it became an independent laboratory known as Sandia. The original focus was on atomic weapons research, but today Sandia is involved in perhaps the broadest range of semi-secret and secret research of any government laboratory. In addition to nuclear weapons, Sandia now conducts research in such areas as energy generation and distribution (especially electricity), "waste legacy" (that is, what to do with radioactive waste), solar energy, "remote sensing" of nuclear materials and warheads (how spy satellites and surveillance flights can detect hidden and clandestine atomic weapons), and "emerging threats," a broadly defined category that encompasses ways of detecting and neutralizing non-nuclear threats such as biological weapons, chemical weapons, large-scale terrorist activities, and "cyberwarfare," such as efforts to prevent hacking of military websites and networks. But nuclear weapons research is still the main business of Sandia. A 1994 report states that over one-ton of fissionable uranium and plutonium was at Sandia for use in their ongoing research activities.

Secret Stuff: Both Sandia and Phillips are currently working hard on "directed energy" weapons. Directed energy weapons are focused beams of photons (like lasers), microwaves, or atomic particles (neutrons, for example) designed to disable or destroy enemy weapons or personnel. The three main areas of research here seem to be lasers, microwaves, and charged particle beams. Lasers can temporarily blind humans even at modest power levels, and high-power lasers can destroy targets at a distance, primarily through heating effects. Microwave beams can cause heating injuries and damage like a souped-up version of your microwave oven. In addition, they can easily destroy the electronics of enemy weapons systems. Charged particle beams sound like something out of a bad 1950s science fiction film;

atomic particles are ionized, accelerated to high speeds, and then focused into a narrow beam of astounding energy. The main application foreseen for charged particle weapons is to blast enemy aircraft, rockets, and satellites out of the sky.

There is a "Directed Energy Directorate" at Phillips whose stated mission is to "conduct research into a variety of energies that might be transformed into future weapons systems." At Sandia, the emphasis seems to be on defensive measures against directed energy weapons as their research is under the "emerging threats" branch, which also conducts research into how to counter biological, chemical, and other unconventional weapons systems. However, in their "nuclear weapons" division Sandia is working on "pulsed power technology for defense applications," which sounds like a variation on the directed energy theme. It is believed that many of these weapons at being tested at White Sands (see entry in this section) and the Nellis Range Complex (see the entry under NEVADA).

Another division of Sandia covers "nonproliferation and materials control." Among their stated goals are to develop "new remote sensing technologies for aircraft and satellite deployment to detect and characterize proliferation activities" and to "track nuclear materials from dismantled weapons systems."

Sandia recently established an "energy and critical infrastructure" division. This division incorporates Sandia's long-established research into alternative energy sources (such as solar and fusion) with a new mission of (in their words) "preventing disasters resulting from threats to national and international systems that are essential to everyday life. We call these critical infrastructures. Examples are energy, transportation systems, health care networks, financial information systems, and communication networks." This is decidedly different from Sandia's traditional areas of weapons research, and it is not clear exactly what technologies are being developed (surveillance? "superhacking" of computer networks?) to help protect against such threats.

Getting a Look Inside: Kirtland offers group tours through its public affairs office, but these must include at least 20 people and be scheduled at least 90 days in advance. Naturally, the KUMSC is never on such tours. Admission to either Phillips or Sandia laboratories generally requires an official sponsor (usually one of their employees). However, the National Atomic Museum is open to the public from 9 a.m. to 5 p.m. each day except New Year's Day, Easter, Thanksgiving, and Christmas. To visit, park at the gates at either the Wyoming or Gibson entrances (see below) and present the guard with your driver's license, registration, and proof of insurance. You will then be given a pass good for travel to the museum, which is located on Wyoming Boulevard inside the base. Adult admission is currently $3.00.

Unusual Fact: The gift shop at the National Atomic Museum offers t-shirts, coffee mugs, key rings, and various other charming geegaws and doodads.

Getting There: Kirtland AFB is located on the southeast side of Albuquerque, next to the city's airport. It can be reached from Interstate 40 via the Wyoming South exit or from Interstate 25 via the Gibson Boulevard exit.

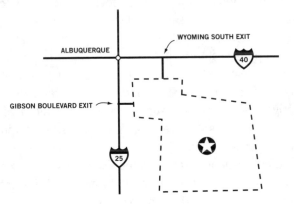

Roads to Kirtland Air Force Base, Albuquerque

Los Alamos National Laboratory, Los Alamos

This is the birthplace of the Top Secret Government. In the fall of 1942, the Los Alamos Ranch School (a boarding school for boys) was seized by the Army and converted into the headquarters of the Manhattan Project. It was here that the founding principles of the Top Secret Government—such as public deception in the name of national security, conducting activities in isolated areas, compartmentalization of information, withholding information from Congress and other branches of the constitutional government, surveillance and electronic eavesdropping without warrants, etc.—were developed and put into practice. But Los Alamos is not just a piece of history. It remains a major research center in its original area of atomic physics and has branched into other areas such as chemistry, life sciences, industrial technology, supercomputing, and what Los Alamos calls "international security and threat reduction." And almost all of the research conducted here is highly classified.

Los Alamos National Laboratory covers over 27,800 acres, employs approximately 9,600 persons, and conducts research into more than 50 technical areas. Like California's Lawrence Livermore National Laboratory (see entry in the CALIFORNIA section), Los Alamos is operated by the University of California under contract to the Department of Energy (DOE). Los Alamos is located in north-central New Mexico northwest of Santa Fe. Surprisingly, a few of the original buildings from the Manhattan Project are still in use.

Among the known programs at Los Alamos is the Stockpile Stewardship Program, which assesses the efficiency and safety of America's nuclear weapons in the absence of actual nuclear testing. It does so through research into such methods as x-ray analysis of weapons and measuring the minute leakage of radioactivity from such weapons. Closely allied to this effort is the Threat Reduction Directorate, which develops ways to detect hidden nuclear weapons and neutralize them and also track movement of fissionable materials around the world. (It was this directorate that was involved in the 1999 Wen Ho Lee espionage case; see the entry for the Nuclear Emergency Search Team in the NEVADA section.) This directorate recently expanded the scope of its activities to include threats from chemical and biological weapons.

The Strategic and Supporting Research Directorate conducts the bulk of the activities at Los Alamos. In its 2000 annual report, Los Alamos described the mission of this directorate as "scientific foundations for stockpile stewardship; to use neutrons, protons, and accelerators for scientific and national security purposes; to advance and apply high performance computing in Department of Energy missions; and to enhance the knowledge base and technologies for threat reduction, emphasizing bioagents."

A Strategic Computing Complex became operational in late 2001 and is believed to have the world's fastest supercomputers.

Key Facilities: The Main Technical Area, known as TA-3, is where 50% of Los Alamos' office and laboratory space is located and where most of its employees work. The facilities here include a Van de Graaff accelerator, laboratories for chemistry, physics, earth sciences, and material sciences, technical workshops for fabricating needed new items and equipment, a cryogenics laboratories, all computing facilities, and the offices of administrative personnel, including the Director.

The Plutonium Facility (TA-55) is where most nuclear activities and research are carried out. According to the official Los Alamos description, this is where "the complex chemistry associated with plutonium and other actinides in various physical states is examined using research and development in the fields of metallurgy, chemistry, engineering, and solid state physics." So what goes on inside this building? That's classified. What we do know is that this is one of the most heavily guarded facilities in the world, since it contains the largest supply of weapons-grade plutonium in the United States. In addition to elaborate electronic and physical security systems, it is reinforced to resist explosions and other physical assaults and its special security force is heavily armed and trained to repel terrorist attacks.

Near TA-55 is the Pajarito Site (TA-18). Research into the fundamental nature of nuclear reactions is conducted here. All experiments are conducted via remote control using robotic arms and viewed over closed-circuit television.

According to the official Los Alamos description, the biological and environmental research conducted at the Health Research Lab (TA-43) "provides information to analyze long-term health and environmental effects associated with energy and defense technologies." It is known that this is a center for human genome research.

The S Site is used for, again according to its official description, "environmental testing of nuclear weapons systems." It is also home of a new Weapons Engineering Tritium Facility; tritium is one of the key elements found in hydrogen bombs.

Secret Stuff: Although the exact quantity kept at Los Alamos is a closely-guarded secret, supplies of plutonium-239 and uranium-235—two highly fissionable isotopes used in the fabrication of atomic bombs—are stored here in large amounts. Plutonium-239 is also one of the most toxic substances known. It is normally stored in powder form and could be easily scattered by moving air, such as by being dumped into the ventilation system of a building.

Getting a Look Inside: The Bradbury Science Museum is the only building at Los Alamos open to the general public. Its numerous exhibits, including several interactive ones, cover the laboratory's history and current areas of research. Admission is free and the museum is open daily except for Christmas and New Year's Day.

While the other buildings at Los Alamos are not open to the public, it is possible to drive by many of them. Both the TA-55, the Plutonium Facility, and the Pajarito Site (TA-18) are located along Pajarito Road. The S Site is located on Highway 501 (known locally as West Jemez Road). TA-3, the Main Technical Area, is located near the intersection of Highway 501 and Pajarito Road.

Unusual Fact: On October 13, 2004, Roy Michael Moore was discovered living in a cave inside Los Alamos National Laboratory; the cave was down in a canyon less than 50 yards from the Los Alamos security office. Moore had apparently been living in the cave for several years; he had installed a glass front door, a wood-burning stove, a bed, solar panels for electricity, and a satellite radio system. He was also raising ten marijuana plants and had about 21 ounces of weed on hand. He was discovered when smoke from his stove attracted the attention of the laboratory's fire department.

"I don't know if anyone has tried squatting on DOE property before or not," said Bernie Pleau, a laboratory spokesman. "Pretty strange, don't you think?"

Yeah, Bernie, we think.

Getting There: East Gate, the main entrance to the laboratory, is located on Highway 502. Until 1957, Los Alamos was a closed city and only residents and approved visitors with a pass could enter through this gate. The Bradbury Science Museum is located at the intersection of Central Avenue and Thirteenth Street.

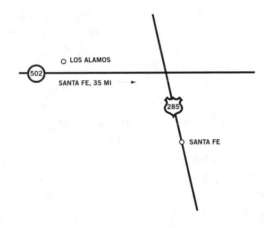

Roads to Los Alamos National Laboratory, Los Alamos

Project Gasbuggy Test Site, Rio Arriba County

Like Project Rulison (see entry under COLORADO), Project Gasbuggy was designed to stimulate production of natural gas and other hydrocarbons by using an underground nuclear explosion to shatter subterranean rock formations and free the gas. That was the theory, at any rate.

Project Gasbuggy was the second attempt—after Project Gnome—to stimulate production from a natural gas field by using an atomic weapon to shatter the underground rock in which the gas was trapped. In retrospect, the whole concept seems more than a little crazy: atomic bombs would be exploded, on a regular basis, inside subterranean salt formations, the salt would melt from the heat, water (either groundwater or piped in) would be converted to steam by the melted salt, and the resulting steam used to drive turbines and generate electricity. The Project Gasbuggy test used a 29-kiloton weapon placed 4,222 feet underground inside an already existing, but low-producing, natural gas well.

The bomb was exploded on December 10, 1967. The test had been scheduled several weeks earlier but was delayed for unspecified "technical reasons." A 1973 investigation by the *New York Times* uncovered those "reasons." Things began to go wrong almost immediately after the nuclear weapon had been placed into the well and the well sealed off with concrete. A water pump used for cooling the well failed, causing the temperature inside to soar and water inside the well to boil. Workers were pulled back from the area because no one—even the project scientists—knew what might happen next. (Apparently none of them had ever wondered what would happen if we stuck an atomic bomb in some boiling water.)

When the bomb was finally detonated, a ground wave seven feet high rose above the well. Observers two and a half miles from ground zero were knocked off their feet by the force of the wave. An underground cavern measuring approximately 160 feet in diameter and over

300 feet in height was created by the explosion, and fractures extended several hundred feet away from the cavern in various directions.

At first, Project Gasbuggy looked like a huge success; the amount of gas flowing was over five times greater than initially predicted. But a byproduct of the explosion was radioactive krypton which contaminated the gas as well as the soil and groundwater of the test area. The gas was burned away at the site, and soil and water was hauled away in barrels. Today the site is safe to visit, according to the Department of Energy.

What's There: A plaque on a concrete base sits in an open field. The plaque gives a brief history of Project Gasbuggy (although it incorrectly states it was the first attempt to stimulate production of natural gas through a nuclear explosion). It also states that any drilling, excavation, or removal of any materials is prohibited within a 600-foot radius from the plaque location.

Getting a Look Inside: The test site is on public land and you're free to visit and explore anytime.

Getting There: Take the F.S. 357 exit from Highway 64 and travel south for approximately seven and a quarter miles. You will then reach a fork in the road; go right and continue on F.S. 357 until you enter the Carson National Forest. The site is another six-tenths of a mile ahead.

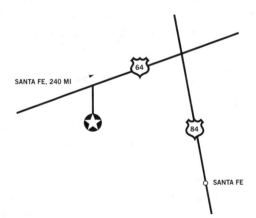

SANTA FE, 240 MI

64

84

SANTA FE

Roads to Project Gasbuggy Test Site, Rio Arriba County

Project Gnome Test Site, Eddy County

Back in 1961, the old Atomic Energy Commission (AEC) decided to detonate an atomic bomb here at a depth of over 1100 feet to see if nuclear explosions could be used to generate electricity from the resulting steam. You get one guess as to the outcome of this experiment.

Project Plowshare was a program by the old Atomic Energy Commission to find peaceful uses for atomic weapons (for more details about Project Plowshare, see the entry for "Project Rulison" under COLORADO). Several tests in the Project Plowshare program were conducted outside the Nevada Test Site, and, like Project Gasbuggy, Project Gnome was one of them.

Project Gnome was essentially identical to Project Gasbuggy. The Project Gnome test used a 3.1-kiloton weapon located 1184 feet underground inside a massive rock salt formation. The shaft drilled to place the weapon was meant to be self-sealing after the bomb exploded.

It wasn't. The test was conducted on December 10, 1961 at noon local time. Steam started to vent from the shaft two minutes after the explosion, followed five minutes later by a cloud of gray "smoke" that was laden with radioactive particles. The venting continued for a half hour, although steam continued to vent for another day. Radiation levels remained high enough to prevent the start of recovery operations until six days after the test. The salt chamber itself was not sampled until May 17, 1962. The temperature level inside the salt chamber had dropped to 140 degrees Fahrenheit by then and salt samples taken from the chambers were colored various shades of green, violet, and blue.

So what did we all learn from Project Plowshare? This: nuclear weapons are not suitable for everyday use.

What's There: A large plaque mounted on a concrete foundation marks the site and gives a sanitized history of Project Gnome that omits any reference to that unfortunate venting and release of radioactive materials. A second, smaller plaque tells you that any digging, drilling, or other excavation to any depth is prohibited within the test area. In other words, don't take a couple of shovels of the soil here as a souvenir—it might be "hot."

Getting a Look Inside: The Project Gnome test site is on public land and you're free to visit and explore anytime.

Unusual Fact: A report titled by the New Mexico Institute of Mining and Technology titled "A Proposal for Addressing Major Concerns for the Gnome/Coach Site in Eddy County, New Mexico" has this to say about a potential problem at the Project Gnome site: "Vandalism has been documented at this site and it would be very easy for an individual to cut the chain and open the valves allowing unabated access to the radioactive materials. Hazardous waste could then be removed from the cavity by pumping or by the use of a simple tethered bail." In other words, this is the ideal site to visit if you're a terrorist looking for the raw materials to make a radiological ("dirty") bomb.

Just remember—you didn't read the above here, okay?

Getting There: The Project Gnome site can be reached from Carlsbad by taking Highway 285 south toward Loving. Take the Route 31 exit until it comes to a junction with Highway 128, turn east (right) and proceed for a little over seven miles until the intersection with County Road 795 (Mobley Ranch Road) is reached; turn right onto this road. Continue 4.4 miles to a dirt road on the left. Take the dirt road and the site is about a quarter mile ahead. This is an isolated area. Be sure your car is in good mechanical condition before visiting, and don't leave for the site without a full tank of gas and a spare tire. The road may be impassible in winter or in rainy weather.

White Sands Missile Range, Alamogordo

The largest military installation in the country and site of the world's first atomic bomb explosion, White Sands is a must-see destination on any tour of the Top Secret Government. After World War II, White Sands is where captured German V-2 missiles were launched and the first American rocket weapons systems were developed and tested. Today, White Sands continues to be the prime test and development facility for smaller rockets (typically air-launched missiles) and many other secret weapons systems. NASA also uses White Sands for many civilian space projects. Rumors persist that operational but still-secret Stealth aircraft are based here. This is site #4 in Top Secret America that's larger than Rhode Island.

If Los Alamos can be considered the birthplace of the Top Secret Government, then White Sands Missile Range (WSMR) is where it came of age. White Sands was the first really large area (over 3,200 square miles) to be occupied by the Top Secret Government, and it's still the largest military installation in the country. This is where the Top Secret Government tested the world's first atomic bomb on July 16, 1945. It was later used for the first military rocket launches (initially using captured German V-2 missiles) as well as research into stealth technology. And secret stuff is still going on here 60 years later.

Prior to 1942, the area now occupied by WSMR was public land sparsely occupied by ranchers and miners. Beginning in 1942, many areas within the current WSMR were closed to the public and turned into bombing practice ranges and desert warfare training facilities. In August of that year, the U.S. Army launched the Manhattan Project to develop an atomic bomb, and a secure, isolated area was needed to assemble and test such a weapon. Its isolation and proximity to Los Alamos made the area around White Sands an ideal choice, and soon the U.S. Army Corps of Engineers was busy building the first facilities inside what was to become WSMR. The site of the first atomic bomb, known as Trinity Site, was located a little over 200 miles south of Los Alamos. It was the site of a ranch owned by the McDonald family which the government had purchased in 1942, and the ranch buildings, such as the ranch house and barns, were used for test and assembly of the first atomic bomb. Additional land was acquired and added to the existing bombing ranges, and by 1944 the current boundaries of WSMR were established.

While the Manhattan Project was reaching a climax in July 1945, a new mission for White Sands was just beginning. Numerous V-2 missiles and components, as well as German rocket scientists (notably Dr. Wehrnher von Braun), had been captured the previous spring when Germany surrendered. A large, isolated area was needed to conduct test and development work for military rockets based on the V-2, and White Sands was the obvious choice. On September 26, 1945, the first rocket launch was conducted at WSMR. Since then, WSMR has been the main testing location for almost all of America's short-range missiles, including the Nike family deployed in the 1960s, the Pershing missiles that targeted the USSR from West Germany in the 1980s, and the Patriot air defense missiles that are currently deployed in the Middle East. WSMR was also considered as a launch facility for the Space Shuttle, but that plan was not adopted. However, WSMR is an emergency landing site for the Space Shuttle and a flight landed there in March 1982 because of bad weather at the main landing sites in California and Florida.

WSMR continues to be used both by the military and NASA for rocket testing and development, but there is much more going on here. The Directed Energy Directorate of the Air Force Research Laboratory acknowledges it is conducting experiments with high-energy lasers and microwave beams here; such weapons, like the "death rays" of cheesy science fiction movies, could be used to destroy enemy aircraft and missiles. In fact, the most powerful laser in the world—the Mid-Infrared Advanced Chemical Laser (MIRACL)—is located at WSMR. (It is rumored that there are more powerful but still secret lasers being tested here.) WSMR includes numerous electronic warfare ranges for testing of new airborne weapons, and it is known that new unmanned aerial vehicles (UAVs) are undergoing development here. One good indication of the level of activity as WSMR is how often Highway 70, which runs along the south end of WSMR between Las Cruces and Alamogordo, is closed to traffic because of tests. Approximately 8,000 personnel work at WSMR. WSMR covers almost 3,200 square miles, with the north-south boundaries running over 100 miles.

What's There: Most of WSMR is empty high desert, which is just what you want under a rocket or experimental aircraft that might suddenly crash or explode. The longest runway is Northup Strip, located about 45 miles north of the Highway 70 entrance gate. It was used by the Space Shuttle for landing in 1982. There are also numerous launch pads for various rockets. Buildings and test facilities are scattered through WSMR, linked by a network of roads closed to the public. Much of WSMR is shielded from public view by the San Andreas and Sacramento mountain ranges. The administrative and personnel support facilities are located near the main gate.

Key Facilities: The High Energy Laser Systems Test Facility, operated by the U.S. Army's Space and Missile Defense Command, is where tests are conducted into the use of lasers to destroy incoming missiles and aircraft. The Nuclear Effects Facility is used to test for the impact of nuclear radiation, directed energy weapons (like lasers), high-energy electromagnetic pulses, high-power microwaves, and other exotic weapons on living organisms as well as military and civilian hardware, communications systems, etc.

Getting a Look Inside: The highlight of any tour of the Top Secret Government has to be a visit to Trinity Site, the spot where the first atomic bomb was tested. Currently, WSMR allows visitors to Trinity Site twice a year, usually in April and October when temperatures are moderate. Amazingly, no advance reservations are currently required. Visitors enter WSMR through the Stallion Range Center, located five miles south of Highway 380; the turnoff is about 12 miles east of San Antonio, NM. At the gate, visitors are given pamphlets about Trinity Site along with rules and regulations for visitors. You can then drive, unescorted, 17 miles to Trinity Site on a paved road. You can use a camera once you're at Trinity Site, but not while driving to or from it.

At Trinity Site, there is a stone monument, surrounded by a chain link fence, at "ground zero" for the first nuclear blast. The crater formed by the blast has been filled in over the years, although a portion of it has been left in its original state and can be viewed through a canopy; the canopy both protects the area from erosion and visitors from still-high-levels of radioactivity. You can also see the original Mc-Donald ranch house where the plutonium core of the first atomic bomb was assembled. The area is littered with pieces of "trinitite," a green rock formed from silica melted and fused by the nuclear explosion. Trinitite is radioactive and can fog conventional photographic film. Naturally, you're prohibited from taking any trinitite as a souvenir, and the same goes for any rocks, plants, or other material at Trinity Site.

If you're not in the vicinity of WSMR when tours of Trinity Site are being conducted, you can visit the WSMR museum and "missile park" (a display of full-size missiles tested at WSMR). These are located near the WSMT main gate and are usually open from 8 a.m. to 4 p.m. Monday through Friday.

Unusual Fact: Socorro, NM, is located on the eastern side of WSMR, and was the site of a famous UFO landing case on April 24, 1964. On that date, a Socorro police officer named Lonnie Zamora was pursuing a speeding car in an isolated area south of the town. Suddenly, he heard what sounded like an explosion and observed what he later described as a blue "cone of flame" coming from the direction where he knew there was a building where dynamite was stored. Thinking the dynamite in the building had exploded, he broke off his pursuit and took a dirt road leading in the direction of the "flame" and explosion. He followed the road several hundred yards until he came to the top of a hill, where he saw something that caused him to slam on his brakes: in a ravine about 150 yards away was a white, egg-shaped object resting on four legs. And around it were two human-shaped figures in what appeared to be white coveralls.

One of the figures seemed to have heard Zamora's car, as it turned and looked directly at Zamora and his vehicle. Thinking the figures were possibly in trouble, Zamora resumed driving toward the object and radioed the Socorro police station for assistance. (He reported a "10-40," the code for an accident, to the Socorro dispatcher.) He descended down the hill, and as he began to rise out of the dip he heard a loud roar and saw the object rising into the sky, with a blue flame coming out of the bottom. He saw not windows or other openings on the object, but did observe what appeared to be some red lettering on the side. However, the object was too distant for him to determine what, if anything, the lettering was. Thinking the object was about to crash, Zamora stopped his car again and took shelter behind it. Instead of crashing, the object gained altitude and flew off to the south-west, toward WSMR. Zamora continued on to the landing site, where he found "landing pad" prints in the desert sand along with scorched earth and bushes. Other officers arrived within minutes of Zamora's call and found smoke rising from the burnt bushes. By that evening, investigators had arrived from the New Mexico State Police as well as military investigators from WSMR. Air Force investigators arrived a couple of days later. All came to the same conclusion: Lonnie Zamora had seen something extraordinary, but they were not sure what it was. The "Socorro landing" quickly became one of the classic cases in UFO lore.

Initially, Zamora thought he had seen an experimental craft from WSMR. But official Air Force investigators could find no record of any experimental military craft being tested from WSMR that day, and even the lead Air Force investigator for the incident, Major Hector Quintanilla, later wrote in a then-classified report, "There is no doubt that Lonnie Zamora saw an object which left quite an impression on him. There is no question about Zamora's reliability. . . . He is puzzled by what he saw and frankly, so are we. This is the best documented case on record, and still we have been unable, in spite of thorough investigation, to find the vehicle or other stimulus that scared Zamora to the point of panic."

So Zamora saw an authentic UFO, right? Well, probably not. While there were indeed no military craft being tested at WSMR that day, it was discovered over 35 years later that NASA had been testing prototypes of the unmanned Surveyor lunar landing vehicle at WSMR on April 24, 1964. And the Surveyor vehicles (which later successfully made several landings on the moon) looked very similar to the object report by Zamora, down to the four landing legs. And NASA often used red paint on its prototype vehicles.

It now seems very likely that what Zamora observed was a Surveyor prototype undergoing tests at WSMR. It may have wandered off course and made an emergency landing, or perhaps was deliberately taken outside WSMR for launching toward WSMR airspace. So why was the Air Force unable to discover records for the Surveyor tests? As a civilian agency, NASA would not be required to furnish such information, and the presence of a Surveyor prototype outside WSMR would strongly suggest that something had gone wrong with the test, maybe something the personnel involved would prefer to keep secret to protect their jobs.

In other words, poor Lonnie—who was widely vilified by UFO de-bunkers for perpetrating a hoax—was probably right all along.

Getting There: WSMR is located east of Las Cruces on Highway 70. Much of Highway 70 between Las Cruces and Alamogordo parallels WSMR and many unusual lights, etc., can be observed from there during night hours. The main gate is located about 25 miles from Las Cruces on Highway 70; exit just after mile marker 169 onto Owen Road. The main gate is three miles down Owen Road.

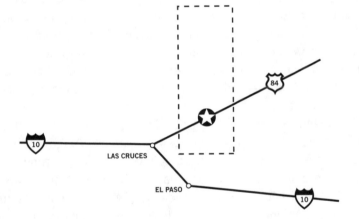

Roads to White Sands Missile Range, Alamogordo

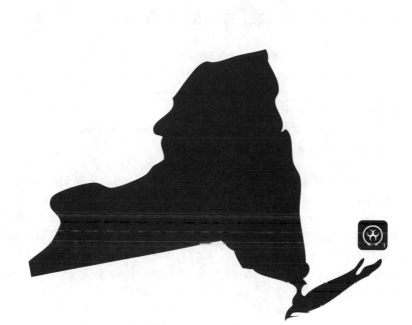

NEW YORK

1. Plum Island Animal Disease Center, Plum Island

Plum Island Animal Disease Center, Plum Island

This small island in Long Island Sound is where the federal government conducts research into exotic, deadly animal diseases such as foot and mouth disease, African swine fever, and the Nipah and Hendra viruses. Several of these diseases are also deadly to humans, and this facility is being upgraded to handle a greater workload and even more deadly diseases.

The Plum Island Animal Disease Center (PIADC) was founded in 1954 by the Department of Agriculture to study foot and mouth disease. Its isolated location in Long Island Sound was chosen to minimize the possibility of infecting animals or humans through airborne germs or viruses. Plum Island claims to have no incidents of infection of any animals or humans through accidental release of the pathogens studied there.

Among the activities carried on at PIADC are research into diagnostic methods for animal diseases, vaccine development, and training of veterinary and agriculture personnel in the recognition and treatment of animal diseases. During the Cold War, research was also conducted here into detection and treatment of biological warfare involving animal diseases. And, since the September 11 attacks, new programs have been launched into detection and vaccination methods for animal diseases (such as the Hendra virus) that also infect and harm humans. Despite frequent rumors, PIADC denies any research is being conducted into anthrax on Plum Island and says no stocks of anthrax are kept there.

Plum Island's laboratories are sealed from the outside world by air filtration and circulation systems; special clothing must be worn in the laboratories, and disinfecting showers must be taken when leaving the laboratories or moving between laboratories holding different infectious agents. All materials entering or leaving the laboratories are thoroughly fumigated or otherwise sterilized, liquid waste is heated to high temperatures before disposal, and solid waste is incinerated.

There are multiple backup power and filtration systems along with emergency medical personnel.

Even more secure laboratory facilities are currently being built at PIADC. These laboratories will require personnel to wear "space suits" with independent, self-contained air sources to totally isolate workers from pathogens. PIADC was transferred from the Department of Agriculture to the Department of Homeland Security in June 2003, and this has resulted in speculation that it will be emphasizing protection against biological terrorism in the future.

What's There: PIADC is located on the northeastern side of Plum Island and includes numerous laboratories, a power generating station, a sewage treatment station, waste processing and disposal facilities, a firefighting station, numerous roads, and landing strips for light aircraft.

Getting a Look Inside: Plum Island is off-limits to the public, with numerous electronic security systems and human guards. Any attempt to land on the island by boat will certainly involve arrest and prosecution. However, it is possible to sail by the island; its historic 1870 lighthouse, while no longer operational, is quite distinctive.

Getting There: Plum Island is located near the Gardiner's Bay section of Long Island Sound, approximately 1.5 miles from shore. The nearest town on Long Island is Orient Point in Suffolk County.

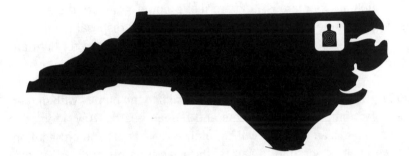

NORTH CAROLINA

1. Harvey Point Defense Testing Activity, Hertford

Harvey Point Defense Testing Activity, Hertford

Harvey Point is along the Atlantic Coast near the Outer Banks and Kitty Hawk. Originally established in World War II as a base for blimps conducting surveillance operations along the coast, it is now where the CIA conducts training exercises for its paramilitary forces.

Harvey Point is where the CIA sends its agents to learn paramilitary skills, such as use of explosives, advanced firearms and weaponry, sabotage techniques, "personnel snatches" (such as hostage rescue or kidnapping), and unconventional transportation methods (for example, use of jet skis for water transportation), techniques for being "inserted" and removed from hostile territory, and how to live off naturally occurring food sources and materials. In addition to individual training, guerrilla warfare training exercises are conducted here. In fact, Harvey Point is where the CIA trained Cuban exiles for the unsuccessful 1961 Bay of Pigs invasion.

Residents of nearby Hertford have become accustomed to being awakened by the sounds of explosions and low-flying aircraft—and yes, many are black, unmarked helicopters.

Harvey Point is surrounded by water, heavily wooded in places, and in a lightly-populated area, all of which makes for an ideal training environment. Many trainees are flown into and out of Harvey Point and have zero or minimal contact with local residents. When trainees are bused in through Hertford, they are usually in buses with blacked out windows. Unmarked trucks with U.S. government plates are also a frequent sight passing through Hertford.

What's There: Satellite photographs show landing strips, numerous buildings, and a network of roads through the facility. In addition to woods, there are several open areas.

Getting a Look Inside: Don't even think about it, okay?

Unusual Fact: While ordinary American citizens can't get a look inside Harvey Point, some foreign citizens can. For example, the *New York Times* reported in 1998 that security forces for the Palestinian Authority—in other words, Yasser Arafat's homeboys—have trained at Harvey Point. And, of course, there is absolutely no possibility whatsoever that those trainees later passed along their new skills to suicide bombers or other terrorists.

Getting There: Harvey Point is located about nine miles southeast of Hertford; the road ends at a guardhouse and a sign reading "Harvey Point Defense Testing Activity." That's as far as you can go.

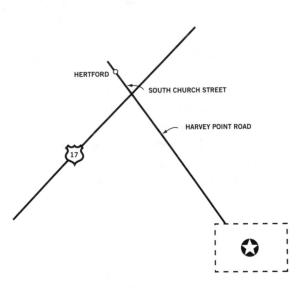

Roads to Harvey Point Defense Testing Activity, Hertford

OHIO

1. Wright-Patterson Air Force Base, Dayton

Wright-Patterson Air Force Base, Dayton

This the Air Force's premier research and development center; many of the super-secret aircraft and systems tested at places like Nevada's Area 51 and California's Edwards Air Force base are engineered here. Foreign military aircraft and weapons systems are also studied and evaluated here. The Air Force Institute of Technology is perhaps the foremost aeronautical engineering institution in the world, offering advanced degrees to career Air Force and Department of Defense personnel. From 1947 to 1969, this was home to Project Blue Book, the Air Force's official investigation into UFO sightings. And, if certain rumors are correct, this is also where the Air Force stores the bodies of dead UFO aliens in a building known as "Hangar 18."

Wright-Patterson Air Force Base (WPAFB) is located on the site where the Wright Brothers conducted some of their pioneering aviation work. It was named for Wilbur Wright and for Lt. Frank Patterson, one of the first military test pilots who died during a test flight. The first military operations began here in 1917 when the Army Air Corps began training pilots for service in World War I.

From its inception, WPAFB's prime mission has been aviation research and development. World War II greatly expanded WPAFB's operations and added foreign aviation technology research as a major activity. Following World War II and creation of the Air Force as a separate service, the Air Force Institute of Technology and the Foreign Technology Division were established at WPAFB. The latter often obtained actual items of foreign hardware (such as Soviet MiGs), took them apart, analyzed them, and even flew them to understand the capabilities and weaknesses of foreign aerial weapons. Sometimes the hardware was captured on the battlefield, but more often was acquired by bribing corrupt officials and military officers in Soviet client states. Such activities became among the most closely guarded secrets of the Cold War and secrecy greatly increased at WPAFB as a result. The Foreign Technology Division is still highly active today, analyzing Russian and Chinese aircraft, airborne weapons systems, radar systems, and electronic systems.

When UFOs (then known as "flying saucers" because of the most commonly reported shape) were first observed after World War II, a common theory was that they could be secret Soviet weapons, perhaps based on captured Nazi technology. Because of its mission to investigate foreign technology, WPAFB was the natural place for the official Air Force investigation into UFOs, which eventually became known as Project Blue Book. Established in 1947, this effort continued into 1969 when a Colorado University report, commissioned by the Air Force, concluded that almost all UFOs were the result of misinterpretation of ordinary aircraft, atmospheric phenomena, or astronomical objects and did not represent a national security threat to the United States. The report also concluded that Project Blue Book should be shut down; the Air Force complied soon after the report's release. However, rumors persist that UFO reports are still studied at WPAFB and secret investigative teams are dispatched from WPAFB to the sites of major UFO events such as reported landings and abductions.

The current employment at WPAFB is approximately 22,000, with about 10,000 being civilians. Over 6,000 Air Force personnel and their families live on the base.

What's There: For all of the Top Secret Stuff going on at WPAFB, it looks very ordinary. It consists of numerous aircraft hangars and large buildings (some dating from before World War II), smaller maintenance and administrative buildings, runways, and housing and other support buildings for personnel and their dependents. The most readily identifiable building complex is the Museum of the United States Air Force, three converted hangars that comprise the largest aviation museum in the world.

(Possibly) Secret Stuff: One of the persistent stories about WPAFB is that there is a building, known as "Hangar 18," containing wreckage from crashed UFOs, including the preserved bodies of space aliens in what is called the "Blue Room."

The UFO alien body story may have had its origins in WPAFB's connection to the Roswell, New Mexico "UFO crash" of 1947. It is known that debris and other material from the crash site was transported to WPAFB for analysis. While most investigators today—even those who were once convinced the Roswell crash involved an extraterrestrial spacecraft—now accept that the Roswell was a then-secret "Project Mogul" balloon, there are still those who believe the material sent to WPAFB in 1947 was a real UFO and its dead pilots, and that material is still held in storage there. As farfetched as that sounds, there were apparently some UFO-related activities at WPAFB that were being kept secret into the 1980s (see "Unusual Fact" below).

An alternative explanation for that secrecy is the theory that the Air Force—indeed, the entire U.S. government—has used the UFO mystery as a cover for other activities it doesn't want the public to know about or take seriously. This theory has some merit; most of the best UFO reports from experienced pilots, police officers, etc., turned out to have involved inadvertent sightings of then-secret government aircraft and projects (such as the U2 and SR-71 spy planes or the first Stealth aircraft). This theory holds that Project Blue Book was actually a disinformation effort designed to protect classified aircraft projects by categorizing them as "UFO reports," thereby ensuring they would not be taken seriously by the mainstream press and much of the public. In other words, Project Blue Book was actually a military exercise to manipulate public opinion in order to protect classified projects and activities.

And if that's true, then there might still be some "UFO-related" activities going on at WPAFB.

Getting a Look Inside: The Museum of the United States Air Force can be reached from Interstate 70 by taking Exit 44A, which leads to Interstate 675 South. Following this highway to Exit 15 (Colonel Glenn Highway) and turn right at the traffic light at the end of the exit. Drive to the third traffic light at Harshman Road/Wright Brothers Parkway and turn right.

Unusual Facts: Okay, so all the UFO stuff sounds like bullshit. Maybe it is. But, for whatever reasons, the Air Force kept some of the UFO information it compiled and stored at WPAFB secret even from Barry Goldwater, the former U.S. Senator from Arizona and a general in the U.S. Air Force Reserves.

In a letter dated March 28, 1975, to Shlomo Arnon of Los Angeles, Senator Goldwater wrote, "About 10 or 12 years ago I made an effort to find out what was in the building at Wright Patterson Air Force Base where the information is stored that has been collected by the

Air Force, and I was understandably denied this request. It is still classified above Top Secret. I have, however, heard that there is a plan underway to release some, if not all, of this material in the near future. I'm just as anxious to see this material as you are, and I hope we will not have to wait too much longer."

But Goldwater was still waiting on October 19, 1981, when he wrote to Lee Graham of Monrovia, California: "First, let me tell you that I have long ago given up acquiring access to the so-called Blue Room at Wright-Patterson, as I have had one long string of denials from chief after chief, so I have given up." And, in a letter dated July 12, 1986, to William Steinman of La Mirada, California, Goldwater wrote, "To answer your questions, I have never gained access to the so-called 'Blue Room' at Wright Patterson, so I have no idea what is in it. I have no idea of who controls the flow of 'need-to-know' because, frankly, I was told in such an emphatic way that it was none of my business that I've never tried to make it my business since." When Goldwater wrote these last two letters, the Republicans were in control of the Senate, and Goldwater was chairman of the Intelligence Committee and sat on the Armed Services as well as Science Technology and Space Committees. In other words, he had plenty of weight to throw around. Yet the Air Force refused to share the UFO information stored at WPAFB with the chairman of the U.S. Senate Intelligence Committee.

Makes you wonder what in hell they're keeping secret about UFOs at WPAFB, doesn't it?

Getting There: The Museum of the United States Air Force can be reached from Interstate 70 by taking Exit 44A, which leads to Interstate 675 South. Following this highway to Exit 15 (Colonel Glenn Highway) and turn right at the traffic light at the end of the exit. Drive to the third traffic light at Harshman Road/Wright Brothers Parkway and turn right. Drive to the exit for Springfield Pike and turn right at the end of the exit ramp. The museum is on the right; follow the posted signs to the entrance.

PENNSYLVANIA

1. Continuity of Government Facility, Mercersburg
2. Raven Rock Alternate Command Center ("Site R"), Waynesboro

Continuity of Government Facility, Mercersburg

This facility is another Continuity of Government facility designed to shelter essential government personnel in case of nuclear war or other catastrophe.

The Continuity of Government program built a "ring" of fallout shelters around Washington for the use of government personnel in case of a nuclear war. These shelters were intended to house essential government officials and necessary support staff. Unlike the legendary Mount Weather in Virginia, none of these "secondary" shelters were designed to withstand a direct nuclear hit but instead were meant to provide protection against radioactive fallout.

What's There: Aerial photographs show that most of this facility must be underground inside Cove Mountain. There are several surface-level concrete structures, including what appears to be a helicopter landing pad and antenna structure. A road runs from the front gate to what seems to be a surface entrance. This interior of this facility is believed to be very similar to the Mount Pony COG facility that was decommissioned in 1992. That would include shared bedrooms for high-ranking officials and shared "hot bunks" for the rank and file; the maximum number of people that can be accommodated here is believed to be in the low hundreds. Food, basic medical supplies, defensive weapons, and communications equipment are also certainly here.

Getting a Look Inside: Because of its isolation, visitors are definitely unwelcome here. There is a guarded gate with security cameras, and visitors are often brusquely turned away by guards with a lecture about national security regulations.

Getting There: This facility is located west-southwest of Mercersburg. It is reached by an unmarked eastbound road off Highway 45.

Raven Rock Alternate Command Center ("Site R"), Waynesboro

The "alternate command center" in its name tells what the purpose of this site is: this is where U.S. forces would be commanded if the Pentagon had been destroyed in the event of a nuclear war. After the September 11 attack on the Pentagon, several key military leaders, including Deputy Secretary of Defense Paul Wolfowitz, spent time here. Like Mount Weather (see VIRGINIA), this facility—also known as "Site R"—is underground and designed to be entirely self-sufficient for over 30 days following a nuclear catastrophe.

The Raven Rock Alternate Command Center, or Site R, is located approximately six miles of Camp David, the presidential retreat, along the Maryland-Pennsylvania border. It is located inside Raven Rock Mountain. The fenced surface area covers 650 acres.

Planning for a standby military command center near Washington began shortly after the Soviet Union tested its first atomic weapon in 1949. President Truman approved the selection of the Raven Rock site in 1950 and construction began in 1951. The facility became operational in 1953 and has been expanded and upgraded several times since then. From the beginning, communications capabilities were stressed and the facility is also known as an "alternate joint communications center" for the armed forces.

During the Cold War, Raven Rock/Site R was reportedly staffed full-time by 350 military and Department of Defense personnel. Support was provided by Fort Ritchie, a nearby Army base that has since been closed. After the collapse of the Soviet Union and the closure of Fort Ritchie, Site R went into a "maintenance" level of activity. However, Site R went back to a much higher level of readiness following the September 11 attacks. Helicopter and vehicle traffic to and from the site has greatly increased, as has security around the facility.

What's There: It is reported that Site R occupies approximately 700,000 square feet of underground space and is several hundred feet inside Raven Rock Mountain. It is reported there are five separate "buildings," each three "stories" tall, hollowed out of the granite under the mountain. Each building is connected by tunnels. Those who worked there in the 1950s and 1960s have said the facility contains much computing and communications equipment, living facilities (private rooms for VIPs, bunks/barracks for the rest), a dining hall (complete with numerous paintings of outdoor scenes), a medical bay with operating facilities, and even a barbershop. There are also power generating equipment and supplies of food and water to allow Site R to operate self-sufficiently for approximately a month.

The exact number of persons that can be housed inside Site R is not precisely known, with estimates ranging from several hundred to over 3000. Given the size of the facility, it is likely the number that can be housed is under 1000 persons.

Secret Stuff: There are reports that a tunnel runs from Site R to Camp David, which means the tunnel would have to be at least six miles long.

Getting a Look Inside: The best view of the surface facilities of Site R, including communications antennas, can be seen about ten miles west of Waynesboro, PA, on State Highway 16. Binoculars or a telephoto lens will help in making out details. Closer approaches to Site R will probably attract the attention of security guards, as described next.

Unusual Fact: Cell phones and GPS receivers often do not work near Site R, indicating some sort of jamming technology is employed to keep uninvited visitors from communicating or precisely locating the site. (GPS technology could also be used to guide in a hijacked airliner or other airborne weapon; the 9/11 hijackers used GPS receivers to guide their way to the World Trade Center and the Pentagon.)

Getting There: The closest town to Site R is Blue Ridge Summit, PA, but the easiest approach is an unmarked (but very well-paved) road off Highway 16 east of Waynesboro; the road intersects Highway 16 near an old stone church and heads uphill. However, this road is soon blocked by concrete barriers manned by military guards, and local police are summoned if visitors do not immediately leave; there have been several incidents of threatened arrest and confiscated film. There is also another entrance located on Harbaugh Valley Road off Highway 16; the intersection is just past a cemetery. Several homes are found along this road, but you will likely be stopped and questioned if you drive all the way to the guarded gate at the end of the road. There are also unconfirmed reports of two other entrances located off the twisting mountain roads in the area.

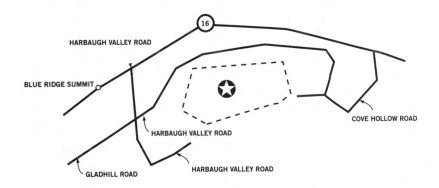

Roads to Raven Rock Alternate Command Center ("Site R"), Waynesboro

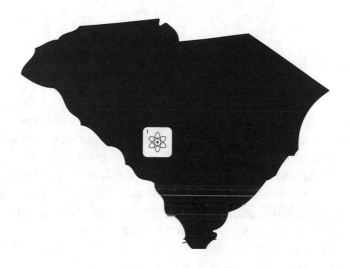

SOUTH CAROLINA

1. Savannah River Site, Aiken

Savannah River Site, Aiken

The Savannah River Site's mission is the "processing" of radioactive nuclear materials used in weapons and reactors. This involves the separation of useful quantities of tritium, plutonium, and uranium from waste products created during their production as well as the recycling of radioactive materials. It's also a storage site for several tons of uranium and plutonium as well as radioactive waste products, and "packaging" radioactive materials for storage is a big activity. During the Cold War, this was perhaps the biggest production facility for nuclear materials in the world; now it's where nuclear materials are stored until someone figures out what to do with them.

Located on the Savannah River along the South Carolina/Georgia border, the Savannah River Site (SRS) was established in 1950 to produce radioactive materials, mainly plutonium and tritium, for nuclear weapons. Its first reactor went operational in 1953, and the basic plant was completed by 1956. In 1963, SRS received its first shipment of spent nuclear fuel for processing from off-site reactors. As production of new nuclear weapons slowed down and eventually stopped after arms control treaties were negotiated, the reactors at SRS were shut down and processing/recycling of existing nuclear materials became SRS's main activity. Today, the SRS also provides storage of nuclear materials (including nuclear waste) and research into alternative energy sources with a nuclear angle, such as using the heat from nuclear reactors to separate water into its constituent hydrogen and oxygen atoms so it can be used as a fuel.

The SRS covers over 198,000 acres about 25 miles southeast of Augusta, Georgia and 60 miles southwest of Columbia, South Carolina. The site is entirely in South Carolina, however, and the closest city is Aiken, South Carolina. SRS employs around 20,000 people and is the largest single employer in the state.

One vital task SRS does is the recycling and "refreshment" of tritium, a radioactive material used in nuclear weapons that has a half-life of approximately 12 years. All nuclear weapons must have their tritium content periodically replaced, and SRS is the only American site for the production and recycling of tritium. The amount of fissionable nuclear material at SRS at any one time is classified, but it is believed there is usually about two tons of plutonium and over 20 tons of uranium in various forms stored at SRS.

Nuclear waste processed at SRS is often converted to glass through a process called "vitrification"; waste in glass form is more stable, compact, and easily handled (even liquid nuclear waste can be converted to glass). Over seven million tons of "vitrified" radioactive glass have been produced at SRS. There are still several million gallons of liquid nuclear waste stored in various tanks at SRS.

There are several classified projects underway at SRS. Several sources indicate research is ongoing into "mini-nukes" that could be transported inside ordinary luggage and carried by a single person. Research is also believed to be underway into the detection of such "mini-nukes," techniques for the disabling of nuclear weapons, and techniques for tracking the presence and movement of nuclear materials.

What's There: There were five reactors at SRS, although now all have been shut down and placed in standby status; all could be quickly reactivated if necessary. When new nuclear weapons were being produced, fissionable materials were separated in two facilities known as "canyons"; the F Canyon was used for plutonium and uranium production while the H Canyon produced only plutonium. Both canyons are now in standby mode.

The HB Line is a plutonium processing facility covering 28,000 square feet. Most of the operations here today involve recovery of plutonium from radioactive "scrap." Tritium processing functions are carried on in buildings 232H (extraction and purification of tritium), 233H (loading and unloading of tritium), and 234H (shipping and receiving of tritium).

Liquid nuclear waste awaiting processing at SRS is stored in the F-Area and H-Area tank farms. There are a total of 45 tanks in the two farms. The Solid Waste Management Facility has burial pits and vaults to store solid radioactive waste, and the newer (opened in 1994) E Area has over 100 acres of burial vaults for solid nuclear waste. PUFF is a 55,000-square-foot facility now used to store plutonium "pits" taken from decommissioned nuclear weapons. A 40,000-square-foot incinerator facility is used to dispose of any waste which can be safely burned. Testing, laboratory, and research buildings are scattered throughout the SRS.

Getting a Look Inside: Prior to the September 11 attacks, the SRS conducted tours by appointment for groups of ten or more. Tours were suspended at the time this book was being written, but may resume in the future.

Unusual Fact: In 1950, Ellenton, South Carolina was indirectly destroyed by atomic energy.

Ellenton was inside what is now the SRS, and once the decision was made to build the SRS its residents were given an ultimatum: take the government's offer for their property and move. More than 6000 people were evicted from the area, and several hundred homes and other buildings were leveled. Two graveyards were even relocated. In an attempt to compensate, the government established a community named New Ellenton near Aiken; it is located just before the intersection of Highways 19 and 278. New Ellenton never became a true community and is today a collection of small stores and a strip mall. Nothing was ever built inside the SRS on the site of Ellington, and recent photographs of the site show the crumbling brick and stone foundations of former homes and buildings as well as crumbling asphalt roads.

Perhaps the most fitting epitaph for Ellington was a hand-painted sign one resident nailed to a telephone pole during the final days before eviction. "It is hard to understand why our town must be destroyed," it read, "to make a bomb that will destroy someone else's town that they love as much as we love ours. But we feel that they picked not just the best spot in the US, but in the world. We love these dear hearts and gentle people who live in our Home Town."

Getting There: From Interstate 20, take exit 18 toward Aiken. The exit road turns into Highway 19 (Whiskey Road); follow it for approximately 15 miles to the intersection with Highway 278. After crossing the intersection, turn right on Savannah River Site Road 1 and take it to the entrance. Unless you are part of a tour or are otherwise invited to enter, you will not be able to enter the site. Highway 278 runs through the SRS, but its use by the public is restricted (although this fact is not made clear on some road maps and atlases) and you should not attempt to drive through the SRS on this road.

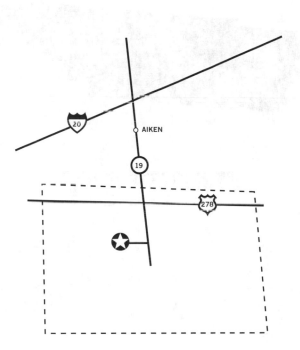

Roads to Savannah River Site, Aiken

TENNESSEE

1. Oak Ridge Reservation, Oak Ridge

Oak Ridge Reservation, Oak Ridge

The Oak Ridge Reservation, which includes Oak Ridge National Laboratory (ORNL), was known as "Site X" when it was established in 1942 as part of the Manhattan Project; many of those who knew about Los Alamos were unaware of Oak Ridge. It was here that methods of separating and producing fissionable uranium and plutonium were perfected along with other essential technologies for building nuclear weapons. While most of the activity involves non-classified research by ORNL, there is still some Top Secret Stuff going on. And, like the Savannah River Site (see SOUTH CAROLINA), there are big problems with nuclear waste cleanup.

The Oak Ridge Reservation, including Oak Ridge National Laboratory, is located on over 35,000 acres approximately 25 miles northwest of Knoxville. From its inception, the mission of Oak Ridge was research instead of production or operations. For example, the techniques for producing fissionable uranium and plutonium were developed at Oak Ridge, but large-scale production of those materials took place at Hanford Reservation (see WASHINGTON) and the Savannah River Site (see SOUTH CAROLINA). At one point during World War II, the then-largest building in the world was built at Oak Ridge to store uranium. Current employment at Oak Ridge is about 4,000 persons and over 1,200 buildings.

After World War II, Oak Ridge's activities expanded to include a wide range of advanced research areas, many of them non-military and non-classified. Today, the vast majority of Oak Ridge's activities are not secret, but substantial Top Secret Stuff—most dealing with nuclear weapons—still goes on here. And Oak Ridge is worth a visit for no other reason than it's one of the birthplaces of Top Secret America.

What's There: The remaining Top Secret Stuff at Oak Ridge is being carried on at the Y-12 National Security Complex, formerly known as the Oak Ridge Y-12 Plant. According to its official Department of Energy description, "Programs at Y-12 include manufacturing and reworking nuclear weapon components, dismantling nuclear weapon components returned from the national arsenal, serving as the nation's safe, secure storehouse of special nuclear materials, reducing the global threat from terrorism and weapons of mass destruction, and providing the U.S. Navy with safe, militarily effective nuclear propulsion systems." You can at least get a glimpse of this building on the public tour described below.

Building 2926 is the radioactive materials analytical laboratory, where small quantities of fissionable materials and much larger quantities of radioactive materials are stored and handled during tests. Building 3027 is the special nuclear materials vault; this is used to store radioactive materials other than uranium or plutonium, such as tritium.

One of the more interesting artifacts at Oak Ridge is the molten salt reactor housed in Building 7503. The molten salt reactor operated from 1965 to 1969, and reactor cooling and heat exchange functions were performed by salt heated to its melting point. The reactor was shut down when the molten salt was discovered leaking from several valves. In 1994, the uranium still inside the dormant reactor was found to have "migrated" within the reactor, creating the potential for release of radioactive gases, heat-generating chemical reactions, and, most ominously, runaway nuclear chain reactions. Corrective actions since 1994 have greatly reduced the possibility of runaway nuclear reactions but accidental release of nuclear gases is still a threat.

Getting a Look Inside: Oak Ridge offers public tours from May to September. Tours are conducted by bus, and include ORNL, the Y-12 complex (or at least a glimpse of its buildings from your bus window), and the East Tennessee Industrial Park, an area now devoted to civilian companies. The only place where the bus stops and you can get out is the Graphite Reactor Museum, the site of one of Oak Ridge's first reactors. The visitor services office has the latest tour schedule and other information, and their phone number is (865) 574-7199. Several Oak Ridge buildings, including the Y-12 complex, can be glimpsed from Scarboro Road, as described below.

Unusual Fact: In a series of reports appearing in August 1997 issues, the *Nashville Tennessean* described how several persons who lived near Oak Ridge, but who had never worked at the facility, were suffering from unusual patterns of illnesses and conditions their doctors could not explain. Symptoms included muscle tremors, memory losses, blurred vision, joint pain, skin rashes, slurred speech, and weakened immune systems. While there has been no known large release of radioactive materials at Oak Ridge, it is acknowledged that small quantities of such materials and non-radioactive toxins escaped into the area's water, soil, and air, especially in the early years of Oak Ridge's operation. Some have speculated that combinations of various materials are responsible for the conditions; there is very little data on the effects of long-term exposures to low levels of toxins, and virtually no data on the impact of long-term exposure to low levels of radioactive materials.

Unfortunately, the people living around Oak Ridge might be providing that data.

Getting There: From downtown Oak Ridge, travel south on Illinois Avenue; remain in the right lane. At the intersection of Illinois and Scarboro Road/Lafayette Road, turn right on to Scarboro. Along Scarboro you will see some Oak Ridge buildings on your right. Continue until you reach the intersection with Bethel Valley Road; turn right toward the visitor entrance. Unless you have been approved in advance for a tour or someone at Oak Ridge is expecting you, they won't be happy to see you.

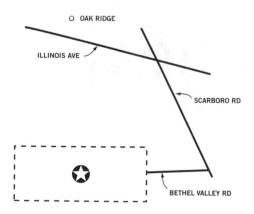

Roads to Oak Ridge Reservation, Oak Ridge

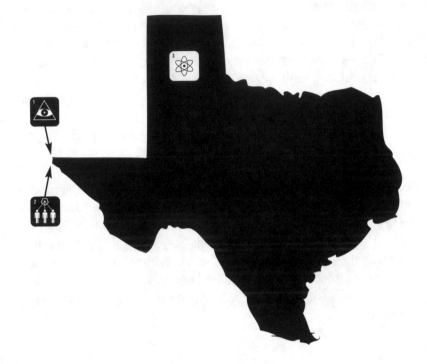

TEXAS

1. El Paso Intelligence Center, El Paso 2. Joint Task Force North, El Paso
3. Pantex Plant, Amarillo

El Paso Intelligence Center, El Paso

Established in 1974, the El Paso Intelligence Center (EPIC) collects and analyzes intelligence related to drug trafficking, including state and local drug investigations. If you've ever been arrested for a drug offense—or just happen to be a friend of someone arrested for a drug offense—you might be somewhere in one of EPIC'ss massive databases. In other words, this is the narc capital of the known universe.

The El Paso Intelligence Center was established in 1974 in response to a Department of Justice edict that called for increased drug and border enforcement along the U.S./Mexican border. It began with 17 employees, drawn from the Drug Enforcement Administration (DEA), the Immigration and Naturalization Service, and the Customs Service. Today, EPIC has over 300 employees from 15 federal agencies—including the FBI, CIA, Secret Service, Coast Guard, Department of State, Department of Defense, and Bureau of Alcohol, Tobacco, and Firearms—as well as the Texas Department of Public Safety (that is, the Texas state police) and the Texas Air National Guard. While EPIC's original focus was on the Mexican border area, it now targets the entire Western Hemisphere for its intelligence activities.

EPIC's stated mission is to collect data and produce intelligence analyses on drug activities/shipments and immigration violations. It gets this information from state and local law enforcement agencies in addition to federal agencies, and enters it into its own set of internal drug and immigration databases. Just what is in those databases and how it is used is not fully known. EPIC shares the information in its databases sparingly with state and local law enforcement agencies; the "flow of information" into EPIC from them is largely a one-way street. However, the collected intelligence is freely shared with federal agencies. As EPIC's official literature notes, "Member agencies have direct access to all EPIC information, with appropriate safeguards to provide for the protection and/or secure communication of highly sensitive or classified information."

However, EPIC conducts numerous training sessions for state and local drug enforcement officers. In their official literature, EPIC says it conducts classes on "indicators of drug trafficking," "concealment methods used by couriers," and "methods of highway drug and drug currency interdiction."

As with many other federal security agencies, EPIC expanded its activities after the 9/11 attacks under the guise of fighting terrorism. Speaking at EPIC in December 2004, DEA Administrator Karen Tandy said, "Drugs and terror frequently share a common ground of geography, money, and violence." She added that the DEA had identified 17 foreign terrorist organizations with "potential ties" to the drug trade.

What's There: EPIC is headquartered in the Enrique Camrena Building, named for a slain DEA agent. The building is clearly identified with a large sign reading "EPIC: El Paso Intelligence Center" but otherwise appears like a typical government office complex.

Getting a Look Inside: EPIC is located inside Biggs Army Airfield, and admittance is restricted to authorized personnel. It currently offers no scheduled public tours of its offices.

Unusual Fact: At her December 2004 address mentioned above, DEA Administrator Tandy said the U.S. military had used EPIC's databases and capabilities to check the backgrounds of civilian contractors hired to assist U.S. forces in Iraq.

Getting There: The main EPIC building is at 11339 Simms Street inside Biggs Army Airfield, which is adjacent to the El Paso international airport. However, Biggs is generally closed to the public. (See next map.)

Joint Task Force North, El Paso

Formerly known as Joint Task Force Six, Joint Task Force North (JTFN) coordinates military assistance to civilian law enforcement on everything from counterterrorism to drug law enforcement. The nature of this assistance includes training civilian law enforcement personnel to handle situations such as biological and chemical attacks, gathering and distributing intelligence to civilian law enforcement, and active military involvement in domestic law enforcement operations. The latter includes such activities as aerial surveillance, communications support, and construction of emergency roads and barriers. Rumors persist that JTFN would also coordinate any large scale military involvement in civilian law enforcement in case of a presidential declaration of national emergency.

JTFN's predecessor, Joint Task Force Six, was established on November 13, 1989 by President George H. W. Bush. Dick Cheney, then Secretary of Defense, said "I believe that our military forces have the capability to make a substantial contribution toward drug interdiction, and I am instructing them to make the necessary preparations to carry out that responsibility." Joint Task Force Six's original mission was to provide intelligence and operational support to local, state, and federal law enforcement agencies in the states of California, Arizona, New Mexico, and Texas; the stated goal was to stop the flow of illegal drugs from Mexico.

While Joint Task Force Six was created by the first President Bush, its activities really got rolling during the Clinton presidency. In the last two years of the first Bush presidency, it performed 1,260 missions; in 1995, it performed over 4,000 missions. The missions gradually evolved from simple reconnaissance and intelligence sharing to actual military patrols of border areas, including isolated roads, leading to frequent and often aggressive encounters with civilians. Residents of border areas, especially those who appeared Hispanic, complained that Joint Task Force Six troops would be present at traffic stops conducted by local police. Cars traveling roads in remote border areas complained about being followed by military helicopters.

This was a prescription for tragedy, and on May 20, 1997, a Joint Task Force Six patrol consisting of four Marines shot and killed Ezequiel Hernandez, an 18-year-old high school student, on his family's farm near Redford, Texas. He was tending his family's herd of goats, and, as was his custom, was carrying a .22-caliber rifle to kill any coyotes, rattlesnakes, wild dogs, or other pests he might encounter. Shortly before 6 p.m., Ezequiel's sister and neighbors heard a single shot. Hernandez was later found dead from a shot fired by the M-16 rifle of one of the Marines.

The Marines had been dressed in camouflage for the countryside around Redford, and also carried full combat gear. The Marines claimed Hernandez fired first and produced two spent .22 shells as evidence, but Hernandez was described by locals as someone with better sense than to deliberately fire on armed soldiers. Some speculated he may have seen some movement, not realized it was caused by the Marines because of their camouflage, and opened fire thinking it was caused by a coyote. Other locals, noting that no advance warning had been given about the patrols, suspected Hernandez may have thought the Marines were robbers or other out to harm him. The Marines released few details about the incident (such as whether they verbally warned Hernandez before opening fire) and a grand jury investigation did not charge the Marines with wrongdoing. Angry locals noted the grand jury contained several U.S. government employees and that its impartiality was compromised as a result.

After the Hernandez incident, Joint Task Force Six strove to minimize contact with civilians and operate more in the background. That changed after the September 11 attacks. Because of fears that terrorists might be attempting to enter the United States via Mexico, Joint Task Force Six began extensive and aggressive patrols of border areas, and its contacts with civilians became more frequent and often confrontational.

In 2004, Joint Task Force Six's responsibilities were expanded to include the entire continental United States instead of just the border states. Reflecting its new role, it was renamed Joint Task Force North (JTFN). JTFN's mission is to "detect, monitor and support the interdiction of suspected transnational threats within and along the approaches to CONUS; fuse and disseminate intelligence, contribute to the common operating picture; coordinate support to lead federal agencies; and support security cooperation initiatives in order to secure the homeland and enhance regional security." JTFN defines "transnational threats" as those activities "conducted by individuals or groups that involve international terrorism, narcotrafficking, weapons of mass destruction, and the delivery systems for such weapons that threaten the national security of the United States."

JTFN personnel are drawn from all branches of the U.S. armed forces as well as Department of Defense employees and contract personnel. Federal, state, and local law enforcement agencies must request assistance from JTFN; without such a request, JTFN can't intervene in domestic law enforcement activities unless ordered to do so by the President. When JTFN does assist civilian law enforcement, its activities include aerial surveillance (including the use of unmanned aerial vehicles such as the Predator), ground reconnaissance via patrol teams and detection devices such as motion detectors, ground and air transportation, communications, construction, and intelligence-gathering and analysis. As mentioned earlier, JTFN also conducts training sessions for civilian law enforcement personnel in such areas as weapons and marksmanship, responding to biological and chemical attacks, and interrogation techniques.

JTFN still engages in patrol along border areas, and there are reports that JTFN's real mission is to coordinate any large-scale military involvement in civilian law enforcement necessitated by a terrorist attack or a similar national emergency. For example, suppose it became necessary to quarantine a large city or even an entire state because of a biological terrorist attack (such as use of smallpox). In such a case, JTFN would likely take the lead in enforcing the quarantine or any other responses ordered by the President.

What's There: JTFN is headquartered at Biggs Army Airfield, a component of the sprawling Fort Bliss complex. JTFN facilities are typical, ordinary-looking Army buildings, including classrooms, aircraft hangars, housing and dining halls, and recreational facilities. One would never guess that an organization as interesting as JTFN is based at Biggs.

Getting a Look Inside: Admittance to Biggs Army Airfield is restricted to authorized personnel only. However, it is easy to see the buildings and vehicles of Biggs from surrounding public roads.

Getting There: Biggs Army Airfield is adjacent to the El Paso international airport.

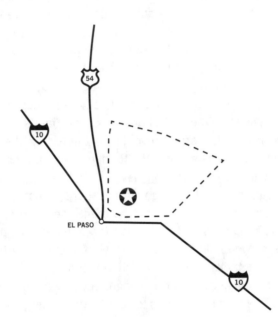

Roads to Joint Task Force North, El Paso and El Paso Intelligence Center, El Paso

Pantex Plant, Amarillo

On the high plains of the Texas Panhandle is America's only facility where atomic weapons are manufactured, disassembled, and undergo maintenance. While the exact number of nuclear weapons "in process" here varies over time (and it's classified), it's estimated that 300 to 400 nuclear weapons are here at any given time. Pantex is also the biggest storage location for radioactive "pits"—the fissionable cores of nuclear weapons, usually made of plutonium. You don't want to even think of what might happen in case of a major accident here.

The Pantex Plant was constructed as a munitions plant in World War II and its isolated location was no accident; accidental explosions were frequent hazards back then. After World War II, the United States needed a facility to construct nuclear weapons, and Pantex offered the isolation required. In 1951 the Atomic Energy Commission (now the Department of Energy) began construction of nuclear weapons here. Additional buildings and facilities were rapidly constructed, and today Pantex covers over 9,000 acres with employment of approximately 2,400 persons. There are 47 miles of roads connecting the different buildings and other facilities.

About one third of the Pantex Plant is devoted to the assembly and disassembly of nuclear weapons. While production of new nuclear warheads stopped several years ago, nuclear weapons require regular maintenance because some fissionable materials (like tritium) have short half-lives and the radiation from fissionable materials will eventually destroy the integrated circuits in the weapons' control electronics. Such maintenance requires the weapons to be disassembled and then reassembled. This "refurbishing" takes up the bulk of Pantex's budget and personnel. Pantex has numerous facilities devoted to different stages of the assembly/disassembly process.

Pantex also tests randomly selected nuclear weapons from America's active nuclear weapons stockpile. Various components are removed from the selected weapons and tested to determine the reliability and operational life of those components.

Nuclear weapons are "triggered" by conventional explosives which compress fissionable material (such as plutonium) into a critical mass. The reliability of such explosives is vital to the operation of nuclear weapons, and Pantex conducts active research into high-energy conventional explosives. This is probably some of the most highly classified activity at Pantex.

The fissionable material in a nuclear weapon is called a "pit." As the number of nuclear arms has been reduced, the number of pits has increased since weapons-grade fissionable material can't be used for peaceful purposes, such as in nuclear reactors. About the only thing that can be done with a pit is to store it in special facilities. Since the closure of the Rocky Flats facility in Colorado (see COLORADO section), Pantex has become the main storage facility for pits. Over 10,000 pits are stored here, even though the facility is described as being for "interim" storage. Since there is no other location capable of storing even a fraction of the pits found at Pantex, it's likely the storage of pits here will be more permanent than interim.

What's There: Pantex is divided into several different "zones," and each zone is devoted to a different function or task. Zone 4 is the weapons staging area; weapons arriving at or being shipped from Pantex are located here. Zone 10 is where the "pits" of disassembled nuclear weapons are stored. Zone 11 is devoted to something called "experimental explosive development." Zone 12 is where nuclear weapons are actually assembled or disassembled, zone 13 is a wastewater treatment facility, and zone 16 is devoted to administrative and managerial tasks at Pantex.

Getting a Look Inside: As you might expect, there are absolutely no public tours or other public admittance to Pantex. The facility is heavily guarded and you may be questioned by security personnel if you are parked near the facility.

Pantex does receive visits from VIPs, such as nuclear scientists and members of Congress. But even they have to complete a training course before going on their escorted tours. According to Pantex's official literature, some of the topics covered in the course are "emergency management," "hazard communication," "explosive safety," and, of course, "radiation training."

Getting There: The Pantex Plant is 27 miles northeast of Amarillo; it is bounded on the north by Highway FM 293, on the east by Highway FM 2373, and on the west by Highway FM683.

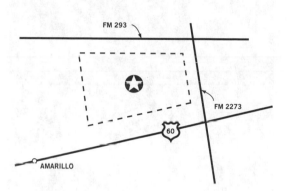

Roads to Pantex Plant, Amarillo

UTAH

1. Dugway Proving Grounds, Tooele 2. Green River Missile Launch Complex, Green River

Dugway Proving Grounds, Tooele

This mammoth installation—Top Secret America site #5 that's bigger than the state of Rhode Island—was established in World War II as a research facility for biological and chemical warfare agents and weapons. That is still one of its main missions, but today it is the main testing facility for military hardware of all types. Because of its size and isolated location, it is believed to be a major testing facility for next-generation weapons systems such as high-powered lasers, particle beams, and secret aircraft. There are also persistent, but unconfirmed, rumors of new chemical and biological weapons research here. In many ways, this place is just as mysterious as Nevada's better-known Area 51 (see NEVADA).

Dugway Proving Grounds was established in February 1942, as a testing area for offensive and defensive chemical weapons. In October 1943, testing of biological weapons agents began in an especially isolated area known as Granite Peak. Dugway's isolation from any significant population area made it ideal both from the perspectives of safety and secrecy, and those are still Dugway's main advantages as a weapons test site. It currently covers almost 800,000 acres and plans were underway at the time this book was being written to annex more adjoining acres, including much of the areas from which the public can observe some of the activities inside Dugway (especially moving lights at night). This has resulted in speculation that Dugway is being made into another Area 51 and that its role has expanded from a testing facility into a full research and development center for the most secret military projects.

Dugway was deactivated in August 1946, but was reactivated during the Korean War, finally being made a permanent U.S. Army facility in 1954. In addition to testing of biological and chemical warfare systems, Dugway became a center for testing how well weapons and equipment could survive battlefield conditions such as shock, vibration, heat, and other conditions in addition to chemical and biological warfare attacks. While administered by the U.S. Army, Dugway is also heavily used by the U.S. Air Force.

In the wake of the 2001 anthrax attacks against Congress, Dugway's role (and apparent funding) has been greatly expanded. The *Salt Lake Tribune* reported in its January 18, 2005 issue that a mock city was being constructed inside Dugway to serve as a training ground for responses to domestic chemical and biological attacks. The article also said Dugway was being considered as a test facility for rumored hypersonic (5,000+ miles per hour) aircraft that could cruise at altitudes in excess of 40,000 feet. It is also widely rumored that laser and particle beam weapons are being tested at Dugway. Beginning in late 2004, numerous observers have reported seeing bright vertical beams of light reaching skyward from inside Dugway during late-night hours. Strange aerial lights moving rapidly and performing unusual maneuvers have also been reported at night, leading to speculation that classified aircraft are being tested at Dugway. Security has been tightened recently, causing some observers to speculate that some projects formerly based at Area 51 (see entry under NEVADA) have been relocated to Dugway.

And, like Area 51, there are rumors of a UFO connection at Dugway. The March 3, 2005 issue of the *Tooele Transcript-Bulletin* reported that several persons observed strange flashing lights at close range near Dugway; the lights would abruptly appear and disappear. A few observers claimed that they suffered a mild sunburn and fatigue the next morning. Some felt they had been on the receiving end of a secret military weapons test; others felt they had been zapped by UFOs.

As is the case at Nevada's Area 51, people on public land adjacent to Dugway are kept under observation by security forces who make their presence known; security cameras and motion/vibration detectors have been added recently to supplement human security forces. Regardless of whether the activity is due to the Top Secret Government or aliens from space, it's clear something very unusual is now going on at Dugway.

What's There: Actually, not too much; Dugway is mostly lots and lots of barren high-elevation desert, including large salt flats, surrounded on three sides by mountains. And that's what you want for an area where weapons systems, including chemical and biological weapons, will be tested. Not only does the emptiness and isolation help prevent any accidental injuries to civilians, it also keeps military secrets safe from curious civilian eyes.

Key Facilities: There are over 600 buildings and other structures at Dugway. Among the best known are the Reginald Kendall Combined Chemical Test Facility, a 48,000-square-foot laboratory for the development and testing of chemical warfare detection devices and protective clothing. The Melvin Bushnell Materiel Test Facility is a 50 x 50 x 30-foot chamber capable of replicating temperatures from -40 to +150 degrees Fahrenheit, relative humidity from 4% to 95%, and a wide range of atmospheric pressures. It can also replicate the presence of various gases, particles, and other air contaminants. Most test facilities are located in the Ditto Test Area, approximately 12 miles from the main gate. Biological warfare test facilities are located in the most remote areas.

Secret Stuff: Did the anthrax used in the 2001 attacks on members of Congress originate at Dugway?

According to a report in the December 12, 2001 issue of the *Baltimore Sun*, for years small amounts of "live" anthrax had been produced at Dugway to test the effectiveness of protective clothing and other biowarfare defense measures. (The production of such small amounts to develop defensive equipment and techniques is permitted under international treaties.) Some of the test required finely milled anthrax like that sent to members of Congress. The genetic "fingerprint" of the anthrax produced at Dugway is indistinguishable from the anthrax mailed to members of Congress in 2001; it was identical at 50 genetic "markers" to the mailed anthrax.

In response to the *Sun* report, Dugway spokesmen pointed out that anthrax there had been stored and handled under similar security measures—including continuous video monitoring, multiple intrusion alarms, and double locks requiring two people to open—used to restrict access to fissionable nuclear materials such as plutonium. That was true. But there was a huge security flaw prior to the 2001 anthrax attacks. Before then, small samples of anthrax were routinely sent from Dugway to Fort Detrick in Maryland using ordinary Federal Express shipments. The shipments were done because Dugway lacked the necessary gamma radiation hardware to kill anthrax by irradiation; the resulting dead anthrax spores were then returned to Dugway to use in various tests that did not require "live" anthrax.

Recordkeeping for the shipments was sometimes sloppy prior to the 2001 attacks. While Dugway does not believe that any of its anthrax was used in the attacks on Congress, and there is no direct evidence linking Dugway to the attacks, the strong possibility remains that some of the finely milled anthrax sent on a regular basis to Fort Detrick may have been diverted (or lost) and later used in the Congressional attacks.

Getting a Look Inside: The guardhouse at the main entrance is about the only building inside Dugway that most of us will ever see. However, at night it is possible to see lights from various activities inside Dugway from public areas adjacent to the facility.

Unusual Fact: In March 1968, over 6,400 sheep were found dead in Skull Valley Goshute Indian Reservation, an area immediately adjacent to Dugway. Autopsies showed the sheep had been killed by a nerve gas known as "VX." While Dugway never admitted to being the source of the gas, the government did pay compensation to the owners of the sheep. There have also been numerous rumors that people living near Dugway have been affected by chemical and biological agents released, either accidentally or deliberately, from Dugway. The government denies these rumors, and, of course, they wouldn't lie about such matters.

Getting There: Dugway is located approximately 80 miles southwest of Salt Lake City. From the town of Tooele, take Highway 36 south from Tooele to its intersection with Highway 199; Highway 199 ends at the front gate of Dugway. Much of the perimeter area of Dugway is marked only with orange posts every ten to 20 feet, but is protected by motion and vibration sensors, as well as surveillance cameras, which are constantly monitored. Even accidental crossing of the boundary can result in your arrest, so take care when near the Dugway border.

Dugway and its environs are very isolated; your car should be in excellent mechanical condition before visiting and you should have a spare tire (or tire inflation kit), water, food, and, if you're visiting in late fall through early spring, warm clothing. Weather can be highly changeable here, with wide temperature variations between day and night and day to day. Cell phone coverage is spotty in many areas around Dugway.

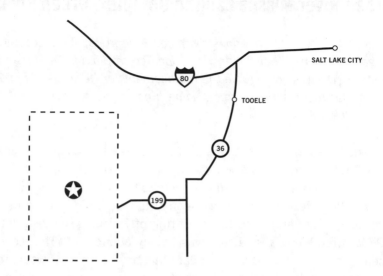

Roads to Dugway Proving Grounds, Tooele

Green River Missile Launch Complex, Green River

Back in June 1997, a hilariously wrong article in Popular Mechanics *magazine claimed that this facility—located in plain sight along Interstate 70—was going to be the replacement for Nevada's Area 51. While that report was incorrect, something might be stirring out in eastern Utah.*

The Green River Missile Launch Complex is a branch of New Mexico's White Sands Missile Range. From 1964 to 1973, over 140 Athena missiles were launched from here to the main White Sands facility in New Mexico to test new re-entry warhead designs for ballistic missiles. It was also used for test firing of Pershing missiles until 1974. After 1974, the facility was largely abandoned. The recent opening of Interstate 70 near it meant that any future tests would require shutting the highway for hours at a time, and there was concern over debris from failures raining down on environmentally sensitive areas like Canyonlands National Park. The structures at Green River were emptied and began to deteriorate. Soon this facility was forgotten by everyone but a handful of rocketry buffs and aviation historians.

But that was before the June 1997 issue of *Popular Mechanics* claimed that Nevada's Area 51 was being closed and future tests of top secret aircraft (and UFOs??) would be conducted in Utah at Green River. While the article was totally erroneous, it did bring Green River to national attention. (For more details of the *Popular Mechanics* article, see the listing for "Area 51" in the NEVADA section.)

What's There: Visitors to the Green River site in the summer of 1997 found it to be deserted. Ten large structures were still standing, but they were in various stages of deterioration. The main gate was open. Electrical conduits had been ripped open and the wiring removed. Some metal structures, like storage sheds and a radio tower, had collapsed. Concrete foundations of dismantled structures remained. Warning signs had faded, and the roads were in poor condition.

However, there were some improvements made at Green River by early 1998. The roads were improved and new warning signs (including those warning against any photography of the facility) were in place. New fences had been added around several areas and structures. While the facility was still deserted, these changes might indicate Green River is being kept in readiness for possible new uses (perhaps to support activities at Dugway Proving Grounds, as previously described).

Getting a Look Inside: Despite the new security signs and other improvements noted above, the facility was still vacant at the time this book was written. There was no full-time security patrol, although some occasional patrols may be made.

Unusual Fact: The *Popular Mechanics* article provoked an incredibly sarcastic response (for a government agency) from the White Sands public affairs office: "If you haven't seen the June (1997) issue of *Popular Mechanics* magazine, you are missing a fantastic example of voodoo journalism" was the opening sentence of their comments. It then tore apart each of the article's claims, and concluded, "Somehow *Popular Mechanics* has gotten away from those old articles on how to change your car's timing belt or how to build your own patio deck. This story reads almost like something out of the *National Enquirer*. Heaven help us."

Getting There: Green River is located parallel to Interstate 70 near the town of Green River. Take exit 162 south from Interstate 70 and turn left at the first intersection.

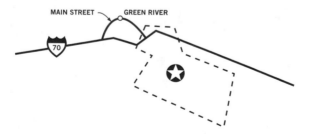

Roads to Green River Missile Launch Complex, Green River

VIRGINIA

1. Camp Peary, Williamsburg 2. Mount Weather (High Point Special Facility), Berryville
3. National Reconnaissance Office, Chantilly
4. Warrenton Training Center, Warrenton/Remington/Culpepper

Camp Peary, Williamsburg

Within the CIA, this place is known as "The Farm." It's the combined Harvard, Yale, and West Point of the spy business; this is where the CIA conducts training for its field agents and paramilitary forces.

To be a successful spy, you need to know more than how to wear a tuxedo or order a proper vodka martini. You also need to know how to open and re-seal letters, how to pick locks and figure out the combinations to safes, how to make a successful "brush contact" (that is, how to quickly pass documents to another person when you bump into them in a crowded public area like a subway platform), how to take clandestine photographs, and—of course!—how to make and use various disguises. They don't teach those skills at your local community college, but they do at Camp Peary. For reasons that are not entirely clear, this facility is known as "The Farm" to CIA personnel.

During World War II, Camp Peary was used to train the Navy's "Seabees" construction battalions. After the CIA was formed following World War II, Camp Peary was turned over to the CIA as a training facility for its field agents. As the CIA's mission grew over the years, so did the scope of activities conducted at Camp Peary, especially following the September 11, 2001 terrorist attacks. Camp Peary is now used to train the CIA's paramilitary forces. And, according to a report in the May 31, 2005 issue of the *New York Times*, questioning of some terrorist suspects (including some held at Guantanamo Bay, Cuba) has been conducted at Camp Peary. Camp Peary is also rumored to be the site of "deep secret" meetings with political opposition and rebel leaders from foreign nations where the CIA wants to bring about regime change.

What's There: Covering 9,275 acres, Camp Peary includes living accommodations, dining and medical facilities, and classrooms for students. Training facilities reportedly include a variety of indoor and outdoor environments where trainees can learn to function in everything from urban environments to deserts and rainforests. Special attention is given to "humint" (human intelligence) skills, and a variety of environments such as public transportation centers, restaurants, museums, stores, etc., are replicated so students can learn how to make contacts, pick up or leave documents, etc., in such public places. Satellite photos of Camp Peary show numerous buildings as well as some unnecessarily "twisting" roads; these are supposedly used for training in evasive driving techniques. The extensive woods are used for survival and paramilitary training, including "extraction" techniques from hostile environments. The basic espionage course that all CIA field agents take lasts 18 weeks.

There is also a landing strip at Camp Peary. Most of the traffic is from CIA headquarters in Langley, VA, but some is to and from the CIA's training facility at Harvey Point, NC. *The New York Times* report cited above said there have also been flights between Camp Peary and Guantanamo Bay, Cuba, since 2002.

Getting a Look Inside: Forget it!

Unusual Fact: Camp Peary was named for Robert Peary, who was credited in 1909 with being the first to reach the North Pole. However, there is considerable doubt whether Peary actually reached the North Pole because of his poor documentation and lack of a second trained navigator who could confirm his readings on his final journey to the Pole. Some doubters believe Peary made an honest mistake, while others believe he deliberately perpetrated a hoax. The issue will likely never be settled, making Robert Peary just as mysterious as the facility named for him.

Getting There: Perhaps no other top secret facility in this book is so easy to find. From Interstate 64, take exit 238; it is clearly marked "Colonial Williamsburg/Camp Peary." Follow the signs after exiting. However, the signs at Camp Peary itself simply identify it as "Armed Forces Experimental Training Activity."

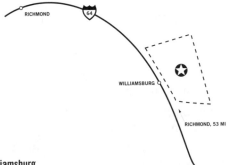

Roads to Camp Peary, Williamsburg

Mount Weather (High Point Special Facility), Berryville

At one time, this was maybe the biggest secret since the Manhattan Project. Built in 1958–60, this facility—located over 300 feet inside a mountain—was intended to be the ultimate bomb shelter for civilian government leaders (such as the president, vice president, secretary of state, etc.) in the event of nuclear war. It can sustain over 2,000 people for more than 30 days in complete isolation from the outside world; deep within Mount Weather is everything from a hospital to a crematorium to a radio-television studio. On the afternoon of September 11, 2001, Vice President Dick Cheney and several senior Congressional leaders were taken here by helicopter and automobile; this is where Vice President Cheney stayed in the weeks following the attacks. Rumors persist that FEMA maintains a parallel "government in waiting" here should everyone in the presidential line of succession be killed in a surprise attack. In other words, this is arguably the capital of Top Secret America!

Mount Weather is located approximately 75 miles southwest of Washington in the Blue Ridge Mountains. It got its name from the National Weather Bureau, who used the summit to launch weather balloons from 1893 to 1933. President Calvin Coolidge considered building a summer White House on the site. In 1936, Mount Weather was transferred to the Bureau of Mines, who tested new drilling and deep tunneling techniques in the mountain's solid, unfractured granite that was several hundred feet deep.

With the rise of the Soviet nuclear ICBM threat in the early 1950s, it became clear that a facility that was both located near Washington and capable of withstanding a nearby nuclear explosion was needed for the nation's top civilian leaders. Mount Weather was selected as the location for such a facility in 1954, and construction by the U.S. Army Corps of Engineers began soon afterwards. The first underground facilities became operational in 1958, and main construction was completed in 1960. Upgrades and improvements have continued since then, but most recent construction has been aboveground. The aboveground site covers 434 acres and includes conference centers, classrooms and training facilities, dormitories, dining and recreational facilities, and support functions (personnel, data processing, etc.) buildings. Over 900 persons are employed at the aboveground facilities; the exact number of employees working underground is unknown but is believed to be around 50 at most times.

Mount Weather has gone to "full operational" status several times, beginning with the 1962 Cuban missile crisis. On September 11, 2001, Vice President Dick Cheney, House Speaker Dennis Hastert, and several Cabinet members were taken to Mount Weather from Washington. Paul Bedard reported in the December 4, 2001 issue of *White House Weekly* that local residents near Mount Weather reported a motorcade with a police escort entering Mount Weather that afternoon. In the March 1, 2002 issue of the *Washington Post*, Barton Gellman and Susan Schmidt reported that several government helicopters, escorted by F-16 fighters, had taken several senior government officials, including Vice President Cheney, to an unidentified underground government facility on the afternoon of September 11. From their description of the site, it could have only been Mount Weather.

What's There: Much of what we know about Mount Weather comes from three sources: an article by Richard Pollack in the March 1976 issue of *The Progressive*, a report by Ted Gup in the December 9, 1991 issue of *Time*, and an article by Steve Emerson in the August 7, 1988 *U.S. News & World Report*. While some details differ, their descriptions of Mount Weather, mainly derived from anonymous former employees, do agree on main points.

The underground facilities at Mount Weather consist of 20 separate buildings, some three stories high (or maybe "deep"), all connected by sidewalks in tunnels. There are two 250,000-gallon water reservoirs, a sewage treatment plant, power generators, air and water purification and recycling equipment, a hospital, a crematorium, communications equipment, computers, cafeterias and dining facilities, meeting areas, a radio/television production studio, and apartments and dormitories. Private apartments are reserved for the president, vice president, Cabinet officers, senior members of Congress, and members of the Supreme Court; others would have to share dormitories or even cots. The door to the underground facilities is ten feet tall, 20 feet wide, and five feet thick; it weighs 34 tons.

Secret Stuff: Is there a "standby government" inside Mount Weather, ready to take over in the event the top civilian leadership is wiped out in a surprise attack? Maybe.

A report in the November 18, 1991, *New York Times* stated, "Acting outside the Constitution in the early 1980s, a secret federal agency [FEMA] established a line of succession to the presidency to assure continued government in the event of a devastating nuclear attack, current and former United States officials said today. The program was called 'Continuity of Government.' In the words of a recent report by the Fund for Constitutional Government, 'succession or succession-by-designation would be implemented by unknown or perhaps unelected persons who would pick three potential successor presidents in advance of an emergency. These potential successors to the Oval Office may not be elected, and they are not confirmed by Congress.'" A 1993 CNN report on FEMA identified such prominent Americans as Howard Baker, Jeanne Kirkpatrick, James Schlesinger, and Thomas "Tip" O'Neill as persons who had served as "standby" presidents. In the event of a national emergency wiping out the established presidential line of succession, the "standby" president would be taken to Mount Weather to direct the civilian government. The current status of any such "standby" presidential plans is unknown.

There are reports that similar standby plans exist for Cabinet officers. It is known that employee teams representing the Departments of Agriculture, Commerce, Defense, Health and Human Services, Housing and Urban Development, Interior, Labor, State, Transportation, and Treasury are rotated at regular intervals at Mount Weather; in the event of a national catastrophe, these teams could take over the functions of their departments until normal government operations can resume. It has been reported that each team is headed by a senior executive who would assume leadership of the department should its secretary be killed or incapacitated; this person has Cabinet-level rank and is addressed by subordinates at Mount Weather as "Mr. Secretary." Unlike regular Cabinet members, these "standby secretaries" can serve for an indefinite term and some have served under both Democratic and Republican administrations.

Getting a Look Inside: There's no chance of seeing the good stuff underground unless you have one those "above top secret" security clearances. However, many local and regional emergency response personnel without security clearances undergo training each year in the aboveground facilities. Since the September 11 attacks, the security around the perimeter of Mount Weather has been greatly increased; there have been reports that motorists driving in a slow or otherwise "suspicious" manner near the site have been pulled over and questioned by police.

Unusual Fact: The 1962 novel *Seven Days in May* was about an attempted military coup against the American government. The authors, Fletcher Knebel and Charles Bailey, were Washington journalists who had heard rumors about Mount Weather, and they created a "Mount Thunder" facility that sounded a great deal like Mount Weather. However, few readers at the time realized "Mount Thunder" was based on an actual place; the government did not acknowledge the existence of Mount Weather until 1975, and then only in response to Congressional queries.

Getting There: While "Berryhill" is the town most associated with Mount Weather, it is actually nearer to the town of Bluemont, near the intersection of Loudoun and Clarke counties. The address of the main entrance is 19844 Blue Ridge Mountain Road, and it can be reached from the intersection of State Routes 50 and 17, or from State Route 7, by following the signs for "Mount Weather EAC" (Emergency Assistance Center).

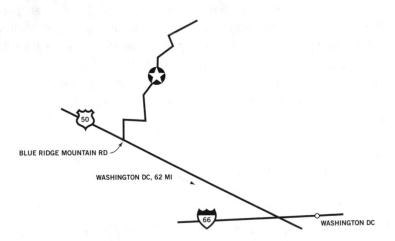

Roads to Mount Weather (High Point Special Facility), Berryville

National Reconnaissance Office, Chantilly

*For over three decades, the National Reconnaissance Office (NRO)
was one of the deepest secrets of the Top Secret Government. In fact,
the name "National Reconnaissance Office" was classified until September 18, 1992. The NRO coordinates all of America's spy satellite
operations, including those of the CIA, Air Force, and Department of
Defense.*

The National Reconnaissance Office was created on August 25,
1960, through an executive order issued by President Dwight Eisenhower. On August 12, 1960, America's first spy satellite, named
"Corona," successfully returned film capsules (which were recovered
in mid-air by Air Force planes) containing photos of the Soviet Union.
These photos had resolution down to two meters and were an intelligence breakthrough, giving previously unknown details of Soviet missile and nuclear facilities. A turf war quickly broke out between the
Central Intelligence Agency and the Department of Defense over who
would get to control the spy satellite program, and the NRO was created to address both civilian and military intelligence concerns.

When "Corona" proved successful in 1960, it was believed that
the Soviet Union was unaware of the new American intelligence-gathering tool (this assumption turned out to be correct; KGB documents
released since the collapse of the Soviet Union show it wasn't until
1963 the Soviets began to realize that their territory was being photographed from space). As a result, extraordinary measures were taken
to protect the secret. The very existence of the NRO was kept secret,
even from most members of Congress, until its existence was finally
disclosed in 1992. Its funding was hidden in budgets under code
names, cryptic references, or simply buried under "miscellaneous."
Even now, the exact amount of funding the NRO has received since its
founding is unknown.

While the NRO is not as secretive as before—for example, in December 1996, the NRO for the first time announced the launch of
one of its spy satellites—it is still far more secretive than the CIA.
The capabilities of the NRO's satellites are classified, although it's
safe to assume they now include signals interception and eavesdropping capabilities in addition to photography (it is also rumored that
real-time video, including infrared, is also within NRO capabilities).

The procedures, methods, and protocols of collecting, analyzing, and processing data gathered by spy satellites are likewise highly classified. In other words, there are still a lot of secrets in Chantilly.

What's There: The NRO seems to have followed a "hide in plain sight" philosophy for much of its existence, and its current headquarters (completed in 1992) is an example of that: it looks like an ordinary commercial office park that could be occupied by an insurance or financial services company. There are four buildings on 68 acres, and over 3,000 employees are believed to work in Chantilly. But while the facility looks ordinary and non-threatening, it is heavily guarded and under constant human, video, and electronic surveillance and any trespassing or other intrusion will be quickly noted. Those who loiter near the building or any of its entrance roads can expect a visit from security and/or local police.

Getting a Look Inside: Nope.

Unusual Fact: A 1994 audit by the General Accounting Office found the NRO had spent over $4 billion since 1961 that could not be accounted for in any way. While some observers felt this was evidence of sloppy management and poor accounting practices, others wondered if the funds had actually been redirected—as difficult as this might be to conceive—to even more highly classified activities.

Getting There: NRO headquarters is located at 14825 Lee Road in Chantilly. Chantilly is about 30 miles west of Washington.

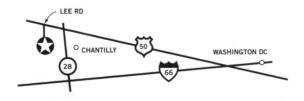

Roads to National Reconnaissance Office, Chantilly

Warrenton Training Center, Warrenton/Remington/Culpepper

Supposedly operated by the U.S. Army as a training and communications facility, this complex of four separate sites is actually used by the CIA for communications with agents in the field as well as for training of agents and personnel in the arts of clandestine and operations. It is also used for interception of electronic communications. There are underground tunnels and facilities here along with state-of-the-art computing and signal processing equipment. In fact, it's not clear exactly what is going on here; the only thing we know for is that the Top Secret Government doesn't want you to know about this place and what goes on inside it.

The Warrenton Training Center takes its name from Warrenton, the town closest to "Site A" and "Site B" of the facility. However, there are two other sites comprising the WTC. "Site C" is near Remington and "Site D" is near Culpepper. Signs at all four sites identify them as being part of the Warrenton Training Center and under control of the U.S. Army.

The Warrenton Training Center was established in 1951 as a communications training facility for the Department of Defense. It was transferred to the Department of the Army in 1973 and its mission was to support the National Communications System (NCS); the NCS was created in 1963 to coordinate radio and other electronic communications between the various branches and agencies of the federal government, including the CIA, FBI, FEMA, and the Department of State.

As Warrenton expanded during the 1960s and 1970s, it became clear that a lot of secret stuff was going on there. Ham radio operators and shortwave listeners managed to track various coded shortwave transmissions—known as "numbers stations"—to Site C. Coded transmissions by the Department of State's embassy radio network also originated from this site. Site D began adding radomes, satellite antennas, and antennas intended only for receiving during this time. Reports began circulating that Warrenton was the Top Secret Government's "communications central," a place where secret communications were transmitted, signals were intercepted, and personnel were trained in the art of preparing and breaking coded messages.

Several new buildings were constructed at Sites A and B during the 1980s, and Warrenton was still going strong at the time this book was written.

What's There: Site A is reportedly used for training, administrative, and residential purposes and—except for the armed guards and security fences—looks much like a small college campus. There are numerous buildings here and what seem to be, from a distance, homes. The latter are believed to be for use of instructors and others who must spend an extended period of time at Site A.

Site B is the largest of the four and is reported to be the headquarters for the Warrenton Training Center. It covers 346 acres and includes several multi-story buildings, some of which were constructed in the late 1980s. Also visible from the road is a microwave tower and a water tower. One of the buildings constructed in the 1980s is what appears to be a large mansion; the gate across the road leading to it has a sign reading "Brushwood." This is believed to be a conference center, although there are rumors this is a "safe house" for defectors.

Site C near Remington resembles a shortwave transmitting station like those used by the Voice of America. There are several large antenna towers at this location along with smaller buildings used to house transmitters and power distribution. While this site is guarded, it is likely that only a small number of people actually work here.

Site D near Culpepper also has some antenna towers like Site C, but not as many. Many of the antennas are like those at National Security Agency sites intended for satellite eavesdropping, and it's believed that this is a "listening only" location. There are more and larger buildings here than at Site C, and more people seem to be working here.

Secret Stuff: So what were those "numbers stations" that transmitted from Site C?

Beginning in the 1950s, some very unusual signals were being heard on shortwave radio on frequencies adjacent to those used by stations like the BBC and Voice of America. These stations transmitted nothing but blocks of numbers—in groups of four or five—read by a woman in an eerie, mechanical voice. On some especially strong, clear transmissions, listeners could hear a faint "click" sound between each digit, indicating the messages were produced by one of those devices used by the phone company when you reach a number that has been changed or disconnected.

Cryptology experts quickly recognized these number groups were part of a "one-time-pad" message system. The agent in the field would copy the number groups and then either add it to, or subtract it from, the corresponding group on a sheet from a "one-time pad." The groups resulting from the addition or subtraction are then compared to a master key list to produce the message. After the sheet from the pad has been used, it is destroyed (the CIA reportedly produced one-time pads whose pages would dissolve in your mouth). The one-time pad method sounds clumsy and low-tech, but messages produced by this system are virtually unbreakable so long as copies of the pads and master key list don't fall into the hands of the opposition.

At first, most of the numbers stations transmitted in English, German, or Russian. With the rise of Fidel Castro in Cuba, Spanish-language numbers stations began operating and soon became the most commonly heard such stations in North America. On any given night, shortwave listeners could hear dozens of numbers stations in Spanish, with a few English, German, and Russian language stations also heard.

Shortwave listeners quickly suspected the stations transmitting groups of five digits came from Cuba and other nations. In a few cases, audio from Radio Havana Cuba's shortwave broadcasts could be heard in the background of the five-digit Spanish stations, indicating they shared the same transmitter sites. And some Soviet agents, like CIA defector Edward Howard, were found to have shortwave receiving equipment and one-time pads containing five-digit groups in their possession when arrested.

The four-digit messages seemed to be coming from a source within the United States because they were uniformly loud and free of the distortion found on more distant shortwave signals. In 1984, a mathematics professor at a Connecticut college used a portable shortwave radio to conclusively determine that four-digit messages were being transmitted from Site C; he parked near the site and found the signals so strong that his shortwave radio "overloaded" and no other stations could be received, indicating he had to be within a few hundred feet of the station transmitter. His observations were confirmed by other shortwave hobbyists with portable radios.

Beginning in the early 1990s, a new type of numbers message started being transmitted from Site C. These became known as "3/2" messages, because they consist of five-digit groups was as distinct pause between the third and fourth digit of each group. This is believed to be part of a "book key" system, in which the CIA and the agent use a commonly available book to decode the message. The first three digits of each group are believed to be the page number, and the last two digits representing the position of a word on the page, counting from the first word in the upper left corner. This method does away with the problem of how to get one-time pads to agents.

It is now believed that the Internet is used for espionage communications, especially in areas where Internet access is common. This may be true, as the number of transmissions from Site C is down greatly from its peak in the 1980s. However, every day numbers groups are still broadcast from Site C and can be heard, with a little patient tuning late at night, on any shortwave radio.

Getting a Look Inside: Most of us have to be content with gazing at the four sites from the outside, but we can imagine what the inside looks like thanks to Del Miller, a columnist for *MacOpinion* magazine (a magazine for Apple Macintosh users). In his August, 2000 column, he recounted a visit he paid to the main site (presumably Site B) in 1986. At that time, he worked for a company that made advanced computing equipment, and the Warrenton Training Center was interested in buying such systems. Before he could visit, he underwent a background check that lasted three weeks (including interviews with people who had known him at least ten years). After arriving at the guardhouse at Site B, he was escorted to an underground location through what he described as tunnels drilled into granite; he said the walls were lined with old mainframe computers, some of which used vacuum tubes. His meeting with Warrenton personnel was different from the usual sales presentation in that they did not respond to any of his questions about their needs and requirements. Instead, they asked him very precise and narrow questions about the capabilities of his company's computing systems and never told him what they planned to do with the computers. The only response he could ever get about the intended applications was, "Listening, just listening."

If you're not as fortunate as Del Miller, you'll have to be content with glimpses from the roads adjoining the four sites. The antenna structures at Sites C and D are readily visible, but little else can be seen. Sites A and B are located in heavily wooded areas, and visibility will vary between seasons. You'll see the most in late autumn and winter after leaves have fallen and summer foliage has died.

Getting There: Site A is southwest of Warrenton at the intersection of Routes 744 and 802. Site B is northwest of Warrenton on Route 690 near Viewtree Mountain. Site C is southeast of Remington near the intersection of Routes 654 and 651. Site D is ten miles from Culpepper at the intersections of Routes 669 and 672. Do not take the well-paved road leading into Site B; there is a guardhouse just around the curve past the entrance and uninvited visitors can expect to be detained for questioning and possible arrest.

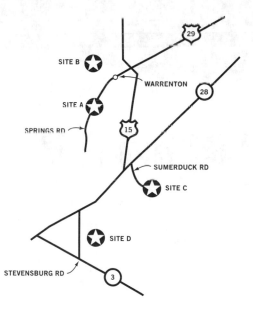

Warrenton Training Center, Warrenton/Remington/Culpepper

WASHINGTON

1. Hanford Reservation, Richland 2. Yakima Research Station, Yakima

Hanford Reservation, Richland

Built in almost total secrecy during World War II, this is where the plutonium for the world's first atomic bomb was produced. In the 1950s and 1960s, Hanford was the main production site for fissionable materials used in nuclear weapons as well as tritium for use in hydrogen bombs. Production of nuclear materials ceased here in 1991, but there was a little problem: over 50 million gallons of liquid radioactive waste, stored in slowly leaking drums, located yards from the Columbia River. Add in 2,300 tons of solid spent nuclear fuel, 12 tons of plutonium, 25 million cubic feet of buried nuclear waste, and you have one of the most toxic places on the planet. Cleanup operations are underway, but numerous environmental dangers will remain here for decades.

Hanford Reservation occupies 586 square miles and is located about 140 miles southeast of Seattle in south-central Washington, adjacent to the town of Richland. It takes its name from the former town of Hanford, which was evacuated in order to build the facility (see "Unusual Fact" below). Hanford was selected in December 1942, as the location for reactors to make fissionable materials for the Manhattan Project. Construction started in March 1943, and the first reactors were operational and producing plutonium by September 1944. By the end of World War II, 554 buildings had been built inside Hanford.

After World War II, eight production reactors were built at Hanford along with storage facilities for solid and liquid nuclear waste, spent reactor fuel, and several large "retention facilities" where water used to cool the reactors was allowed to cool before being returned to the Columbia River (it was later learned that some radioactive isotopes were released into the river as a result of this process).

As construction of nuclear weapons slowed down in the 1960s and demand for weapons-grade plutonium dropped as a result, several reactors at Hanford were shut down.

By 1971, only one reactor remained operational, and it was converted to produce electricity. Hanford's mission diversified to include research and development into alternative energy technologies. With the collapse of the Soviet Union in 1991, production and processing of nuclear materials ceased at Hanford.

But there was a little problem remaining at Hanford: because it was the first facility for large-scale production of fissionable materials and under military control with little oversight for much of its history, Hanford was one of the most radioactively polluted locations in the world. For example, over 400 billion gallons of radioactive liquids had been directly released to the ground inside Hanford. Many of the containers and storage facilities for nuclear materials were leaking; some of these were located just a few hundred feet from the Columbia River. Over 600 buildings and structures at Hanford were contaminated with dangerously high-levels of nuclear materials. Those are just a few reasons why the major activity at Hanford today is cleanup and remediation of nuclear contamination. More than 11,000 persons are currently employed at Hanford in that effort. The original completion date for the cleanup was 2070, but the Department of Energy now says that, with a little luck, it might be finished by 2035.

What's There: Hanford's operations were divided into three "areas" devoted to specific activities. The 100 Area, located along the Columbia River, is where nuclear reactors were located. These reactors are now being "cocooned" in reinforced concrete and other materials to prevent leakage of radiation; there are also extensive nuclear waste cleanup operations in progress. The 200 Area is in the center of Hanford and is where irradiated nuclear fuel was processed to recover plutonium. This is the most contaminated area of Hanford. The 300 Area is where fuel was fabricated for irradiation of the 100 Area reactors.

Getting a Look Inside: Prior to the September 11 attacks, Hanford conducted driving tours through the facility; tours departed from the Volpentest HAMMER Training and Education Center in downtown Richland. Tours were suspended at the time this book was being written, but may resume in the future.

Unusual Fact: Like the Savannah River Site (see SOUTH CAROLINA), Hanford was built on the site of an existing town—Hanford, WA. Hanford was incorporated in 1907 and came into being as a railroad transportation hub for area farmers. It was home to about 1200 people in February 1943, when the area was selected for use in the Manhattan Project. The population was rapidly evicted and construction of the site began in March 1943. Today the only building remaining from the town of Hanford is the high school building. Unfortunately, it has been used for military and police training exercises with live ammunition, resulting in significant damage to the building. The Hanford town site was included on public tours when they were being conducted.

Getting There: From Richland, get on George Washington Way and continue on it through Richland. Just past the Pacific Northwest national Laboratory building, the road veers left and soon reaches a "T" intersection. Turn right onto Stevens Drive and follow the signs.

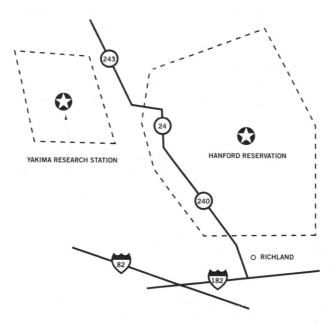

Mpas to Hanford Reservation, Richland and Yakima Research Station, Yakima

Yakima Research Station, Yakima

The only "research" going on here is snooping into traffic carried by communications satellites over the Pacific and North America. If you've made a phone call, sent a fax, or otherwise used a communications satellite covering the Pacific Ocean area recently, odds are it was intercepted here for "intelligence analysis."

The Yakima Research Station is located on the western edge of the U.S. Army's Yakima Firing Range. Its stated mission is to "perform communications research and development in support of the Department of Defense," but this is actually the main listening post used by the National Security Agency to monitor communications from satellites over the Pacific. The Federal Communications Commission has created a "special exclusion zone" at this site and for the surrounding area; the "special exclusion zone" bans all civilian terrestrial use of those radio frequencies on which spy satellite data is received. This facility is located between the Saddle Mountains and Rattlesnake Hills and has an unobstructed view of the western "radio horizon." In addition, this facility is used to monitor communications from satellites over central and eastern North America.

What's There: The most visible structures are nine large dish antennas. One antenna is significantly larger than the others. A few small, windowless white buildings, one or two stories in height, are scattered among the antennas.

Getting a Look Inside: Trespassing is prohibited anywhere on the Yakima Firing Range.

Getting There: The best view of this facility is obtained from Interstate 82 north of Yakima between the eastbound and westbound rest areas; look to the east.

WEST VIRGINIA

1. Continuity of Government Facility, Harper's Ferry 2. Greenbrier Resort, White Sulphur Springs 3. National Security Agency (NSA) Communications Facility, Sugar Grove

Continuity of Government Facility, Harper's Ferry

From the outside, it looks like the National Park Service's National Catalog Clearinghouse. That's because that's exactly what it is. But there seems to be something interesting going on in the basement...

Like other Continuity of Government program fallout shelters (see entries under CALIFORNIA and MARYLAND), the Harper's Ferry facility was intended to house essential government officials and necessary support staff in the aftermath of a nuclear war—in this case, the Secretary of the Interior and staff. Unlike the legendary Mount Weather in Virginia, none of these "secondary" shelters were designed to withstand a direct nuclear hit but instead were meant to provide protection against radioactive fallout.

What's There: Harper's Ferry is home to the National Park Service's Stephen P. Mather Training Center. It resembles a college campus because it is the former Storer College. The COG facility is labeled as "Bomb Shelter" on the official National Park Service map of their Harper's Ferry facility, and is located on Hartzog Drive, off Fillmore Street. It is adjacent to a parking lot and Wirth Hall, the main building for the Center. Aboveground ventilation structures for the facility can be seen from the parking lot. The entrance to the facility is through two metal doors located in a stone retaining wall adjacent to the parking lot.

This interior of this facility is believed to be very similar to the Mount Pony COG facility that was decommissioned in 1992. That would include semi-private bedrooms for high-ranking officials and shared "hot bunks" for the rank and file; the maximum number of people that can be accommodated here is unknown. Food, basic medical supplies, defensive weapons, and communications equipment are also certainly here.

Getting a Look Inside: There is no public admittance to this facility, although the Training Center itself is accessible to the public.

Getting There: From Union Street in Harper's Ferry, turn right on Washington Street to the Appalachian Trail Conference headquarters at the intersection with Storer College Place; turn right. Continue until the intersection with Fillmore Street and Wirth Hall; follow the signs to the parking lot.

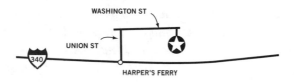

Roads to Continuity of Government Facility, Harper's Ferry

Greenbrier Resort, White Sulphur Springs

From 1961 to 1995, this was the Congressional equivalent of Mount Weather (see VIRGINIA). Under a posh resort in the mountains of West Virginia was a 112,000-square-foot fallout shelter for members of Congress in case of nuclear war. After being decommissioned in 1992, it was turned over to the Greenbrier Resort. Today, you can take tours of this facility and even rent it for private parties!

Virginia's Mount Weather was designed to shelter only the senior Congressional leadership in the event of a nuclear war. What about the other members of Congress and their key aides? They were supposed to travel about 250 miles southwest of Washington, DC, and wait out Armageddon in a bunker under the posh Greenbrier Resort.

The Greenbrier Resort was an unlikely spot for a top secret facility. The main hotel was built in 1913, and quickly became a favored resort of the rich and powerful; Rockefellers, Vanderbilts, and over a dozen U.S. presidents have stayed at the Greenbrier. Recreation includes golf, croquet, and skeet shooting. The resort was a favorite of President Eisenhower because of the golf, and that may be why it was selected in 1959 as the site of Congress's fallout shelter. The shelter was built under a new wing of the hotel, now called the West Virginia Wing, and both the new wing and fallout shelter were paid for by secret government funds. The code name of the project was "Greek Island," and it was completed in mid-1961. It remained a closely guarded secret even among members of Congress; initially, only the Speaker of the House and Senate majority leader were informed of its existence. While senior managers of the Greenbrier knew "something" unusual was going on under their property, they knew nothing about it or its intended purpose. Maintenance of the property was done by a government "front" company known as Forsythe Associates. Managers and employees of the Greenbrier were told the Forsythe employees were there to repair and maintain the resort's telephone, television, and electrical facilities. To avoid detection and suspicion by Greenbrier employees and guests, Forsythe employees entered the facility between 1 to 4 in the morning.

The Greenbrier bunker was built of steel-reinforced concrete and covered by 20 feet of earth; the resort's tennis courts were above it. The doors to the facility weighed 25 tons and could supposedly withstand nearby nuclear explosions.

The Greenbrier facility finally came to the public's attention through a report in the May 31, 1992 *Washington Post*. The report coincided with the collapse of the Soviet Union and a greatly reduced risk of nuclear war, and studies were conducted as to whether the facility was still needed. In July 1995, the bunker was decommissioned and given to the Greenbrier.

What's There: The Greenbrier bunker included two large meeting rooms for each house of Congress and a third, larger room for joint sessions. The living accommodations for most members of Congress were remarkably Spartan, consisting of bunk beds and communal bathrooms; they were only slightly better than an Army barracks (although each bed had a brass nameplate indicating which member of Congress it was for!). The majority and minority leaders of both houses had private quarters resembling rooms at a discount motel. The House Chaplain also had a small office adjacent to the House meeting room. Smaller work areas and offices were also available for Congress members to use. There was also lounging areas with books, magazines, and furniture and an exercise area equipped mainly with stationary bikes. The cafeteria resembled a college dining hall, although to prevent feelings of "entombment" it had numerous paintings depicting pastoral outdoor scenes. Most of the food, however, would have been military "meals ready to eat" rations instead of fresh food.

A decontamination shower area was located immediately after the entrance to the bunker. In case of an actual nuclear attack, the members of Congress were supposed to shower and change into green "jumpsuits" and white sneakers before entering the shelter (this was to prevent nuclear contamination). Three 24,000-gallon water tanks would have supplied fresh water, and there was also water purification and recycling equipment. The bunker had power generating equipment, an infirmary with operating rooms, communications equipment, weapons (mainly small arms like pistols and rifles), and even a complete radio and television studio. The latter included a backdrop of the U.S. Capitol for Congressional representatives to use while making television addresses to their constituents (assuming there were still stations to broadcast such addresses and constituents alive to watch them, of course). And finally there was a "pathological waste incinerator"—a crematorium—for disposing of dead bodies.

Secret Stuff: The infirmary included isolation chambers like those used to house the mentally ill and violent. Apparently the planners of the Greenbrier facility felt some members of Congress might crack under the strain and would have to be isolated from the rest.

Getting a Look Inside: This is a "must" of any tour of Top Secret America! Escorted tours are offered daily (except holidays) and last 90 minutes. Guests of the Greenbrier Resort may tour the resort for free, but non-guests can take paid tours. The adult admission was $25 at the time this book was written; more information can be obtained by calling the Greenbrier Bunker Tour office at (304) 536-1110.

To protect paying Greenbrier guests from the trashy proles who just want to visit the bunker, non-guest visitors meet at a location in downtown While Sulphur Springs and are bused to and from the bunker.

Unusual Fact: The Greenbrier bunker was designed to house only member of Congress and their key aides; spouses and children could not be sheltered there. And that raises the question of exactly how many members of Congress would have gone there in case of a nuclear attack. The 1992 *Washington Post* report that revealed the site's existence quoted former Speaker of the House Thomas "Tip" O'Neill as saying, "I kind of lost interest in it when they told me my wife would not be going with me. I said, 'Jesus, you don't think I'm going to run away and leave my wife? That's the craziest thing I ever heard of.'" According to the *Post*, other former Congressional leaders had expressed similar reservations about leaving their families behind.

Getting There: White Sulphur Springs is located 250 miles southwest of Washington via Interstate 64. Exits for the resort are clearly marked.

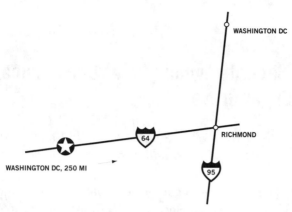

Roads to Greenbrier Resort, White Sulphur Springs

National Security Agency (NSA) Communications Facility, Sugar Grove

Deep in the hills of West Virginia is the main NSA facility for intercepting communications from satellites over the Atlantic Ocean.

Officially known as the Sugar Grove Naval Communications Facility, this is the main National Security Agency listening post for communications and signals intelligence satellites over the Atlantic. While this facility doesn't admit its true purpose (that's why it's officially a "naval communications facility"), the giveaway is the fact that the Federal Communications Commission has created a "special exclusion zone" at this site and for some distance to the east. The frequencies used for downlinking data from spy satellites are also used for civilian industrial and scientific applications in most of the country. A "special exclusion zone" bans all civilian terrestrial use of those frequencies in areas where spy satellite data is received. The FCC has created such a zone with the Sugar Grove facility at the western end and extending 40 kilometers to the east, a pattern consistent with an effort to monitor satellites over the Atlantic.

What's There: Aerial photos show four large satellite dish antennas—one measuring 46 meters in diameter—oriented toward the east. In addition, there are two large support buildings near the antennas and a parking lot. The road from Highway 220 to the facility continues to at least two other large buildings and several smaller buildings are visible; the area has been completely cleared of trees.

Getting a Look Inside: There is no public admittance to this facility and trespassing is prohibited.

Getting There: The facility is located in the woods east of Sugar Grove along Highway 220; the facility is not visible from the road because of trees although a gated, paved road leads north to the site.

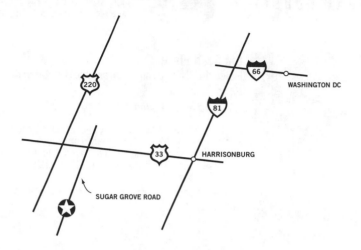

Roads to National Security Agency (NSA) Communications Facility, Sugar Grove

FERAL HOUSE
www.feralhouse.com

Big Dead Place
Inside the Strange and Menacing World of Antarctica
Nicholas Johnson
Foreword by Eirik Sønneland

Is it the pristine but harsh frontier where noble scientific missions are accomplished? Or an insane corporate bureaucracy where hundreds of workers are cooped together in hi-tech communes with all the soul of a suburban office park?

6 x 9 · 276 pages · 16-page color insert · ISBN 0-922915-99-7 · $16.95

process self-reliance series
www.processmediainc.com

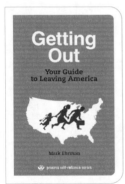

Getting Out
Your Guide to Leaving America
Mark Ehrman

Many people are thinking about it. This book shows how it's done.

Getting Out *walks you through the world of the expat: the reasons, the rules, the resources, the tricks of the trade, along with compelling stories and expertise from expatriate Americans on every continent.*

5 1/2 x 8 1/4 · 360 pages · ISBN 0-9760822-7-6 · $16.95

Preparedness Now!
An Emergency Survival Guide for Civilians and Their Families
Aton Edwards

PREPAREDNESS NOW! *is an essential guide for those who want to be ready and able to handle the new realities of 21st Century life: extreme weather, global warming, bird flu, terrorist attacks, and more.*

5 1/2 x 8 1/4 in · 280 pages · ISBN 0-9760822-5-X · $14.95